The Dawn of Modern Banking

The Dawn of Modern Banking

Center for Medieval and Renaissance Studies
University of California, Los Angeles

NEW HAVEN AND LONDON
YALE UNIVERSITY PRESS
1979

Designed by Thos. Whitridge and set in Baskerville type.
Printed in the United States of America by Vail-Ballou
Press, Binghamton, N.Y.

Published in Great Britain, Europe, Africa, and Asia
(except Japan) by Yale University Press, Ltd., London.
Distributed in Australia and New Zealand by Book
& Film Services, Artarmon N.S.W., Australia; and in
Japan by Harper & Row, Publishers, Tokyo Office.

Library of Congress Cataloging in Publication Data
Main entry under title:

The Dawn of modern banking.

  Selected papers delivered at a conference held at
UCLA Sept. 23–25, 1977.
  Includes bibliographical references and index.
  1. Banks and banking—History—Congresses.
2. Economic history—Medieval, 500–1500—Congresses.
I. California. University. University at Los Angeles.
Center for Medieval and Renaissance Studies.
HG1561.D38   332.1′094   78–14022
ISBN 0–300–02318–9

Contents

Foreword

THE FOLLOWING ESSAYS are selected from those delivered at a conference, the "Dawn of Banking," held at UCLA from 23 to 25 September 1977. Its purpose was to examine various facets, not only of certain medieval and Renaissance practices we now associate with banking, but also of the differing philosophies of credit and its twin, usury, which lay behind them. Not intended as individually exhaustive studies, these essays nevertheless attempt to penetrate beyond the archival records to see fundamental ideological changes in the conceptions of money and wealth, credit and debt, which were then taking place in the European mind and would eventually give birth to modern capitalism. For banking, like most other modern institutions, has a long and complex history as an idea—or rather a series of ideas—sometimes at considerable remove from the economic forces they ultimately served.

Primarily we are indebted to the many scholars who participated in the conference, and to Mr. Martin Mayer, who inaugurated it with effectiveness and verve. Support for the event came from the generosity of the California Council for the Humanities in Public Policy, the Ahmanson Foundation, and the John A. McCarthy Foundation. The directors and administrative officers of these agencies saw the relevance of examining banking's embryology for those engaged in tackling contemporary problems in formulating public policy, and we are as much appreciative of their understanding as we are grateful for their support. We would also like to express our appreciation to the UCLA Graduate School of Management and its distinguished library, to the University Research Library, and to the Center's stoically cheerful staff. Finally, we are pleased to thank the Los Angeles Crocker Bank for supporting the publication of this volume.

Fredi Chiappelli, *Director*
Center for Medieval and Renaissance Studies
University of California, Los Angeles

1 The Dawn of Medieval Banking

ROBERT S. LOPEZ

HISTORY, SAID JACOB BURCKHARDT, "is the one field of study that does not begin at the beginning." Nobody knows when credit was first used as a lubricant of business—probably in prehistory—but banks of a sort existed in ancient Mesopotamia, Greece, and Rome. Although the technical term *bancus* emerged only in the Middle Ages, it was a Latin translation of the ancient Greek word *trapeza*, meaning essentially the same thing: a bench or table where a professional banker displayed his moneys and his records. The medieval dawn of banking was not the earliest, but rather the latest and most decisive. In the early medieval centuries there was an economic collapse, which did not wholly prevent the transmission of older concepts and practices but gave credit and banking a chance to make a fresh start and move gradually from a marginal to a central position in economic development.

Our knowledge of Greco-Roman banking is hazy. No systematic description of the organization and responsibilities of banks, no archives of individual bankers have survived. In a lawsuit, Demosthenes cited as evidence the records of an Athenian *trapezita*; in his correspondence, Cicero mentioned *trapezitai* transferring funds for him. Roman legal enactments and informal papyri often alluded to *nummularii* (literally, "coin dealers"), *argentarii* ("silversmiths"), and *collectarii*

1

("collectors"), variously involved in credit and monetary operations. On the basis of such fragmentary information, it has been argued that altogether these specialists performed more or less the same functions as the late medieval bankers: they were petty usurers or substantial lenders, deposit and transfer bankers, money changers, and inspectors of currency. They also engaged in trade, just as traders also extended credit; then as later, commerce and banking tended to overlap.[1]

It would be incautious to fill this tentative outline with details read back from late medieval sources. There is no proof that the techniques and, above all, the economic and political importance of the Greco-Roman bankers came close to those of their medieval and Renaissance counterparts. Their profession could hardly thrive in what was, all appearances notwithstanding, an underdeveloped society striving for security rather than growth, thoroughly agricultural, and biased against lenders. No doubt there were flurries of commercial activity in the major Hellenic and Hellenistic centers, periods of feverish speculation along the path of Roman expansion, but never enough for a real takeoff. Long before Christian ethics denounced the taking of interest as sinful, Greek philosophy had called it unnatural, for coins are not worn out in the use and do not bear fruit as do trees. Roman law did not forbid reasonable interest charges, but fenced them off from "regular" deposit and ordinary loan as optional riders. While recognizing the usefulness of credit and commerce, the government looked down upon them. Senators were told not to compete with lower people eking out their

1. In spite of its many inaccuracies, the monumental *Wirtschaftsgeschichte des Altertums* by Fritz M. Heichelheim (2 vols. Leiden 1938; English trans. *An Ancient Economic History* [2 vols. Leiden 1958–64]) remains the most useful general work dealing with ancient banking. Later additions to its bulky bibliography can be found in Danielle Giry, *A la recherche des traditions bancaires de l'Occident méditerranéen* (Montreal 1963), and in *The Oxford Classical Dictionary* (2nd ed. Oxford 1970) s.v. "Banks." We still want an analysis of the available evidence carried out with specialized knowledge of banking problems and methods.

living by trade. Successful maritime entrepreneurs were advised to retire as soon as they could and seek status as gentlemen farmers.[2]

In 476 the Roman Empire in the West went down, economically as well as militarily bankrupt. It had bled its subjects white through merciless taxation and discredited its coinage through reckless debasement, but, characteristically, had not thought of borrowing what it needed from bankers against the collateral of its immense assets. There followed centuries of deep economic depression, sharp deflation of prices, and sluggish monetary circulation. Professional banking left no clearly identifiable trace in the desperate poverty of early medieval sources. It is true that in Rome around 600 Pope Gregory the Great still availed himself of the services of an *argentarius*—an early indication of what was to be the Holy See's constantly ambivalent policy of approving banking while reproving "usury" (that is, interest charges). But Rome at that time was less Western than Byzantine, and Byzantium continued to support trapezitai in the ancient style, without blanket condemnation of interest but with the traditional slighting of their business. Moreover, the argentarius of Gregory the Great had no known successors until the eleventh century, when the old terms *trapezita* and *nummularius* suddenly reemerged in the reviving economy and documentation of Western Europe.[3]

What happened to banking and credit between the fall of Rome and the rise of Europe? Though the available evidence is fragmentary and often cryptic, the time has come, I believe, to bring all leads together in a tentative general reconstruc-

2. A less sketchy description of the well-known limitations of ancient economic thought may be read in Robert S. Lopez, *The Commercial Revolution of the Middle Ages, 950–1350* (Englewood Cliffs, N.J. 1971), chap. 1.

3. See especially G. Mickwitz, "Un problème d'influence: Byzance et l'économie de l'Occident médiéval," *Annales d'Histoire Economique et Sociale* 8 (1936) 21–28, a suggestive presentation of ideas which the author did not live to develop into a book.

tion. It is obvious enough that the economic crisis of the barbarian West tended to dry out all channels for banking activity except loansharking, which was not a specialized profession and could be practiced by anyone who had money to spare. Money changing, which might otherwise have benefited by the shift from a single imperial currency to a variety of royal and local coinages, was in fact undercut by the spreading use of payments in kind. As more and more moneyed people hoarded their coins and precious metals or wore them as jewelry, deposit and transfer operations were scarcely in demand. Gregory of Tours's account of King Thierry I's lending his own cash to the bishop of Verdun for distribution to the impoverished merchants of the city seems to imply that commercial loans were no longer available.

On the other hand, one often hears of extortionate consumption loans extended to the needy by profiteers. French, Spanish, and, less frequently, Italian church councils kept hurling ineffective thunderbolts at unnamed usurers; Lombard law strove to shield minors from interest accumulations on their fathers' debts; Carolingian capitularies denounced but did not deter those wealthy ecclesiastic and lay landowners who grabbed the harvests and the land of their defaulting debtors. The latter were not always small people: in the famine year 1096 the Belgian abbot of Gembloux bought at bargain prices the estates of noblemen who had mortgaged them to loansharks at 100% interest. Under these circumstances it is not surprising that a blanket condemnation of moneylending in any form accompanied the first efforts of the reform movement led by Pope Leo IX: "No cleric or layman should be a usurer," stated the Council of Reims in 1049.[4]

Now let us look at the other side of the picture. There is no denying that in the first centuries of the Middle Ages com-

---

4. Hans van Werveke, "Économie–Nature et Économie–Argent," *Annales d'Histoire Économique et Sociale* 3 (1931) 428–40 (with a note of Marc Bloch); Heinrich Fichtenau, *The Carolingian Empire,* trans. Peter Munz (Oxford 1957); *Cambridge Economic History of Europe* 2 (Cambridge 1952) chap. 5, with bibliography.

merce was reduced to a trickle, and money, the lifeblood of banking, to a nonessential role in a thoroughly countrified economy. But neither commerce nor money totally disappeared: they just became rarer, and rarity had a value of its own. A large number of documents, not all of which need be quoted here, strongly suggest that the contracting opportunities for banking were gradually taken over by a more tightly knit organization, that of the moneyers. Two comparatively late statements explicitly say so. In 1037, the count of Anjou reactivated his mint in Saintes by inviting "trapezetas, id est monetarios," who were sworn in, struck coins, and carried out exchange operations. In the early twelfth century, William of Malmesbury translated for his readers what had become an obsolete word: "the *trapezitae*, popularly called *monetarios*"; that the English minters also acted as money changers we know from slightly older Anglo-Saxon laws. Still older Italian texts refer to mint regulations observed in the tenth century and probably originated as early as the seventh: the "mysteries" of sworn monetarii in Pavia, Milan, and other centers had both the exclusive right and the duty of producing coins, changing money, and collecting gold. Lending, deposit, and transfer are not specifically mentioned there, but clues can be found in the eleventh century pamphlets of two proimperial writers who threw back at Hildebrand (the future Gregory VII) his charges of corruption in the church. The self-righteous reformer, they claimed, "has joined the *monetarii* in the money business"; he "has filled his coffers and befriended the son of a baptized Jew, still a practicing *nummularius*, in order to entrust the money to him."

The allusion was so transparent that it can still be seen through today. The maligned supporter of Hildebrand was Leone, son of Benedetto Cristiano (formerly Baruch the Jew) and ancestor of the Pierleoni family, to which another jaundiced writer applied a definition of Ovid: "Queen Money lends to them nobility and beauty: by intermarriage they surround themselves with all the nobles in town." They did more than that: in 1130 Leone's grandson was elected pope by a majority of the cardinals (but not "by the better part" according to St. Bernard, whose questionable judgment demoted him to antipope); in 1144 Giordano Pierleoni got even by becoming the lay leader of the revolutionary Roman commune. The spectacular progress of the Pierleoni family over five generations was not as fast, however, as the personal career of Eloi of Limoges, a seventh century apprentice who had risen to moneyer, adviser of Merovingian kings, bishop of Noyon, and, after death, patron saint of the goldsmiths. The collective climb of the whole profession was perhaps even more stunning. Sweated laborers in the mass-producing mints of the Roman Empire, the moneyers stepped up as soon as money became a rare commodity. Virtually the sole producers, holders, lenders, and spenders of ready cash, they used it as a trump card to acquire land, status, and power. Eventually many of them made their way into the feudal nobility or the urban ruling class—and promptly turned their back on ungentlemanly business. Others continued to strike coins and do some money changing and lending on the side, but played a shrinking role in the Commercial Revolution of the later Middle Ages, which unfroze hoarded metals and made credit the catalyzer of economic growth.[5]

By the time the Pierleoni had completed their social ascent, the new banking was already dawning in Italy under the impulsion of trade. Its ultimate shape has been admirably described by Enrico Besta, Gino Luzzatto, Yves Renouard, Raymond de Roover, Armando Sapori, and Heinrich Sieveking (to mention only a few pathfinders), who used the voluminous documentation available from the last years of the thirteenth century on: account books, private correspondence, personal memoirs, financial records, manuals of business practice. At that time, three classes of credit agents were distinguishable: the pawnbrokers, the money changers and de-

---

5. Robert S. Lopez, "An Aristocracy of Money in the Early Middle Ages," *Speculum* 28 (1953) 1–43, with bibliography, brought up to date in my "Discorso inaugurale," *Artigianato e tecnica nella società dell'alto medioevo occidentale* (Spoleto 1970).

posit bankers, and the merchant bankers. The latter were the new elite of the profession, unprecedented in antiquity and in the early Middle Ages. Wealthy commercial and industrial entrepreneurs, uncrowned governors of their city-states, lenders to monarchs, relatives of popes, they were in no way embarrassed by canonical strictures. At the opposite level of the profession, the pawnbrokers were degraded successors of the early medieval usurers. Indispensable but malodorous, they were deliberate public sinners, likened to prostitutes, and hence tolerated on earth but earmarked for hell unless they repented and made full restitution of their accursed gains. At the middle level, the money changers and deposit bankers, splintered away from the moneyers, formed the core of the profession. They owed their respectability to manual changing, which did not involve credit: they converted on sight one currency into another, and for that service they charged a legitimate fee. No doubt it was an open secret that in long-distance exchange, entailing a delay for transportation, a premium would be worked in by doctoring up the rate of conversion; it was equally obvious that the changer's stock in trade would be largely borrowed and lent at interest rates not openly declared. But these lapses were not public sins, and most changers lightened their guilt by including in their will a token bequest to a charity and calling it restitution of any "ill-gotten" money.[6]

Did this tripartite structure originate in the period of dawn of the new banking or, still farther back, in the earlier development of those Italian cities that awoke before dawn? I think the seeds were planted farther back. What made the new banking different from the old was its shift from an agrarian to a commercial orientation and from an antagonistic to a collaborative attitude of borrowers and lenders. This leads us first

6. Raymond de Roover, "The Organization of Trade," *Cambridge Economic History of Europe* 3 (Cambridge 1963) 42–118, gives the clearest description of the three classes of credit agents—perhaps even too clear, because there never was a sharp, water-tight separation between classes— and offers an excellent guide to further study in his bibliography.

to Venice and Amalfi about 700, then to Pisa and Genoa two or three hundred years later. Here the triangular trade connecting Byzantium and the Islamic countries with the underdeveloped West created a fresh demand for credit to be extended mainly on personal trust, in the hope that higher profits would compensate for higher risks. By the tenth century, trade and the demand for credit on trust also began to expand in several centers of the interior, especially in northern Italy and Tuscany. In overland trade, chances for extraordinary profits were somewhat lower, but so were the risks. Even so, this type of investment would hardly appeal to professional lenders accustomed to secure their loans on mortgages and pawns.

Especially at the start, merchants had to rely chiefly on each other, pooling commodities rather than cash, and often acting in turn as borrowers and lenders. They resorted to ordinary interest-bearing loans whenever they found them convenient, but close mutual acquaintance and the necessity of going literally "in the same boat" (or caravan) inclined them to basic agreements mixing credit with partnership, such as the *commenda* and the *compagnia*. The appearance of these contracts, partly derived from Greco-Roman law but strongly influenced by medieval customs overriding political and religious boundaries, was the first result of the commercial revival and the first chance for banking in a new key. One finds the oldest mentions in Byzantine and Islamic sources around 700; in Western sources the earliest unmistakable allusions go no further back than the tenth century, but there is a probable hint in a document of 829. That memorable document is the will of a Venetian doge, Giustiniano Partecipazio, the first Italian nobleman and landowner known to have staked in commercial ventures at sea a considerable part of his wealth.[7]

7. Examples of the medieval commercial contracts in translation, with introductory critical essays and bibliography, can be found in Robert S. Lopez and Irving W. Raymond, *Medieval Trade in the Mediterranean World* (New York and London 1955); the essays are brought up to date

In the following centuries, as commercial capital grew faster and faster through its own profits and by attracting investments from Italian noblemen and landowners, agrarian credit and consumption loans receded into the back streets of business, not so much because of religious scruples as through economic competition. They still could serve as a start for better things, but only on condition that the lender or his descendants convert either to landowning or to commerce proper as soon as they had the means to do it. The despised class of pawnbrokers was formed by people who had lingered too long in the old tracks, either by choice or, if they were Jewish, because they were forcibly confined to them. Merchants had the best chances to take the lead in banking, but for a long time most of them, especially in the maritime cities, kept the bulk of their capital invested in commodity trade, using credit only or mainly as an accessory to that trade. When, later, some of them, especially in cities of the interior, shifted a substantial part of their investments to moneylending for its own sake, they operated on a larger scale than other lenders, thanks to their commercial resources and connections. These merchant bankers, however, were less attracted to the daily routine of small and medium credit transactions that formed the core of exchange, deposit, and transfer banking. Such transactions, no longer carried out in Italy by moneyers as a subsidiary activity of the mints, had a new spurt as commerce multiplied the occasions for them, and as credit on trust disengaged them from hard cash and solid mortgages. They gave rise to a new class of "money changers" (*cambiatores, campsores,* or *bancherii*), who from generally humble beginnings grew into the largest and most versatile group of late medieval credit agents. Not without reason has the word *banker* become the all-embracing professional term.

---

in Robert S. Lopez, "Les méthodes commerciales des marchands occidentaux en Asie," reprinted in my *Su e giù per la storia di Genova* (Genoa 1975). One of the contracts has recently been discussed in J. H. Pryor, "The Origins of the Commenda Contract," *Speculum* 52 (1977) 5–34.

So far I have kept to generalizations, which had to be hazy because sources prior to the late thirteenth century remain fragmentary and often elusive. The rest of this essay will be devoted to a closer examination of individual bankers and banks as they can be perceived in that light of dawn. Probably the first visible lark is one Paul *cambiator*, showing up in a Roman contract of 1083 whereby he lends money to the church of St. Peter at 20% interest, under a mortgage on real estate. There is nothing new in mortgages, but the moderate interest rate indicates a transition from consumption to commercial loan. In 1120 some unnamed "Romans" lent at the same rate to Genoese ambassadors a sum of money which the ambassadors spent to buy supporters at the papal court in a litigation about the jurisdiction of the Genoese and Pisan archbishops over the Corsican church. The investment was profitable: Pope Calixtus II ruled in favor of Genoa.[8]

Neither Rome nor Genoa became banking leaders in the following medieval centuries, but Genoa happens to preserve the earliest notarial minute books that have survived (from 1154 on), and these books are the first source that contains a fairly large number of documents showing bankers at work. Indeed, nearly all their entries concerned trade and involved credit transactions, but only a minority were drafted by or for bankers, who recorded routine operations in their own books and resorted to notaries only for special contracts. Moreover, Genoa was primarily a city of sea merchants. A large proportion of the bancherii who lived and worked there were of foreign extraction, mostly from two cities of the Italian interior—Asti and Piacenza—with a sprinkling of Provençals. Most or all of them did not personally own their bank but rented it from Genoese capitalists who in turn had bought the

8. L. Schiaparelli, "*Le carte antiche* dell'archivio capitolare di S. Pietro in Vaticano," *Archivio della Società Romana di Storia Patria* 24 (1901) 492–93; Robert S. Lopez, *Storia delle colonie genovesi nel Mediterraneo* (Bologna 1938) 106–09.

permit from their commune and did not choose to practice as bankers.[9]

It appears from the notarial minutes and official records that the tenants of a *banchus, tabula cambii,* or *mensa nummularia* were responsible to the Genoese government for converting domestic and foreign currencies into one another as the market required, ferreting out forged or forbidden coins, and generally watching over the circulation. The government soon required them to keep their cash and records available for inspection, and to obtain guarantors who would be answerable for their outstanding debts up to a certain amount. In return for these restrictions, the government backed the bankers' credibility: it recognized entries in their books as legal proof of transactions carried out through them. Somewhat later, it ordered guardians of minors to deposit the wards' money in a bank. This gave the bancherii an advantage over ordinary merchants in conservative investments and small savings. Most citizens found it convenient to deposit some of their money in a bank account and receive a moderate interest (often camouflaged as an optional bonus) while using the account for receiving and making payments by written transfer in the banker's book. A reliable depositor was often allowed to overdraw his account within certain limits. The banker, in turn, was entitled to invest in his own trade the deposits of his clients.

In the late twelfth century the bankers who resided in Genoa had not yet risen much above mediocrity. Their cash reserve was so modest that some of them took it home in a box every night for safekeeping. Most of their transactions involved small sums, seldom exceeding a hundred pounds at a time.

9. A concise but excellent discussion of banking in Genoa around 1200 can be found in Raymond de Roover, "New Interpretations of the History of Banking," reprinted in *Business, Banking, and Economic Thought in Late Medieval and Early Modern Europe: Selected Studies of Raymond de Roover,* ed. Julius Kirshner (Chicago and London 1974) 200–38, with bibliography. A few additional details, drawn from municipal charters, are quoted in Robert S. Lopez, *La prima crisi della banca di Genova (1250–1259)* (Milan 1956) 23–25.

The margin between the premium they offered to depositors and the interest they charged to borrowers (in one known instance, respectively 10 and 20% annually) was too small to bear comparison with the risky profits of successful merchants (in one known instance, 200% in less than three years). But if around 1200 commerce still was the leading propeller of economic growth, banking already played a significant role at the grass roots, offering a reward to the shyest investor, bringing credit within reach of the petty trader and craftsman, and making mere entries in books of account a flexible substitute for disbursements of cash. In the course of the thirteenth century, the cleavage between bankers and merchants tended to disappear: on the one hand, risks and profits of commercial investments were lowered by better organization and increased competition; on the other hand, risks and profits of banking were heightened as bankers broadened the scope of their operations and relied more on fractional reserves. The ground was prepared for the emergence of the compagnia or partnership of merchant bankers, which combined the methods and the investments of both branches, much as modern corporations tend to diversify their activities in order to balance their risks and get a finger in every pie. The great scholars I have mentioned concentrated their attention on the merchant bankers of the fourteenth and fifteenth centuries; but a study of the dawn of late medieval banking must conclude with a description of one of the earliest partnerships whose main features may be reconstructed from the Genoese records: the Leccacorvo company, which rose and fell in the course of a business cycle between 1244 and 1259.[10]

10. From now on, the documentation of the present paper will be drawn almost entirely from two of my earlier works, La prima crisi, cited in the preceding note, and Settecento anni fa: Il ritorno all'oro nell'Occidente duecentesco (Naples 1955), with the only addition a few documents published or quoted in Franco Guerello, "La crisi bancaria del piacentino Guglielmo Leccacorvo," Rivista Storica Italiana 71 (1959) 292–311, and in Corpus statutorum mercatorum Placentiae, ed. Piero Castignoli and Pierre Racine (Milan 1967), especially in Racine's introduction. It would be pointless to accumulate here references that are

Officially licensed as a *societas banchi* or *tabula nummularia*, the firm was informally called "the bank of William (Guglielmo) Leccacorvo and partners." Under the law, all partners' names had to be registered with the financial department of the Genoese commune; the notarial minutes identify only a few, all of them citizens of Piacenza though resident in Genoa and belonging to distinguished families. Five of Guglielmo's ancestors had been elected consuls (i.e. chief executives) of the Placentine commune for one, two, or three annual terms. William's father was almost certainly a Stefano Leccacorvo, *miles* (i.e. knight; but commoners were often knighted in the Italian communes), who attached himself in 1221 to the service of Cardinal Ugolino of Segni, later Pope Gregory IX. Another Stefano (William's son?) was invited to head the commune of Perugia in 1259, as captain of the people; Uberto Leccacorvo was appointed high justice (*juge mage*) of the commune of Marseille in 1254. Exactly a hundred years earlier, the first known member of the family had been one of the notables who attested that Genoa had paid off a debt contracted with Placentine lenders. His Christian name is unknown; documents just call him Leccacorvo ("lick a raven"), probably a bizarre and possibly an obscene nickname which stuck as the family name of his descendants. A later list of Placentine consuls (he was one of them) dubs him "Viscount Leccacorvi," but this may have been another nickname rather than a vicecomital title.

It was not unusual for a Placentine to move from his landlocked city to Genoa, the nearest and friendliest seaport, but there must have been special reasons for a descendant of five consuls to quit his home forever. As a matter of fact, for over

---

easily available in my earlier books, which in turn have served as references for all later works where the Leccacorvo bank is mentioned; only the tidbits of information that have come to my notice during the last twenty years will henceforth be singled out in notes. No historical essay, however, is definitive, least of all to its author. As I was trying to condense hundreds of pages into less than a dozen, I revised my views and modified some of my comments, so that the new pages are really new.

thirty years an "association of the knights of Piacenza," unwilling to put up with the "popular" government which had seized control of the city, chose to live in exile. Several members of the Leccacorvo were prominent and pugnacious members of the association. William, who apparently had a quieter temperament—he was nicknamed "the Fat"—just settled in Genoa and started a new business: a banker needs no political feuds; anyway, the all-Italian two-party system (Guelphs and Ghibellines), which had been stretched to cover local interests and family quarrels, was breaking down. He did not sever all relations with the Ghibelline government of Piacenza, which availed itself of his bank for some important transactions, but utilized the connections of the Placentine exiles with the Guelph government of Genoa, and with any prominent family in that city. His earliest extant contract is of 5 March 1244; only a few notarial minutes of 1243 have survived. In 1243 the most powerful Guelph family of Genoa (the Fieschi) had seen one of its members elevated to the papal chair; this may have been an additional reason for Leccacorvo's moving, since Innocent IV, his relatives, and his allies were to have intensive if stormy business relations with him and his bank.

Whether by choice or by accident, the timing could not have been better. Genoa, allied with Innocent IV, was gradually beginning to get the upper hand in an uphill struggle against Emperor Frederick II and a number of Genoese exiles. The death of Frederick in 1250 sealed the triumph of the Genoese Guelphs, who felt strong enough to call back the exiles (but an attempt at bringing about a similar reconciliation in Piacenza, with Uberto Leccacorvo as the principal negotiator, failed). Far from stymieing economic development, the war had multiplied opportunities for private gain, most spectacularly in naval construction, simultaneously stimulated by another war, St. Louis's crusade of 1248. By freeing obstructed routes and releasing military budgets, the return to peace added drive and scope to economic growth, with fresh emphasis on expensive consumption goods and long-distance trade, but with considerable progress in humbler local crafts as well. Nor was Genoa alone in riding the tide of the Commercial Revolution, then nearing its peak almost everywhere in Western Europe. Never before had the average standard of living improved so rapidly, or the self-confidence of businessmen been so great. The boom called for an accelerated expansion of credit; as hard commercial credit threatened to fall behind the demand, soft credit through overdrafts or "dry" contracts of exchange became more attractive. By allowing a depositor to overdraw his account, a banker created credit at no greater inconvenience than an additional strain on his fractional reserve. By charging a banker (or, for that matter, another merchant) with supplying foreign exchange in a foreign place, while agreeing overtly or covertly that he would waive repayment abroad in order to receive postponed payment in the currency and place of origin, a merchant (or another banker) created feedback credit. These and other gimmicks uplifted the banks from a subordinate to a leading role in economic development and eventually promoted the transformation of the most powerful among them into "companies of merchant bankers."

The bank of William Leccacorvo and partners was one of the first that presented some of these characteristics. It had fewer employees than the Bardi and Peruzzi banks of the fourteenth century and bore no resemblance to a holding company as did the Medici bank of the fifteenth; in the history of medieval banking, Leccacorvo's time was past dawn but not yet high noon. If we had at least one of his "cartularies" (bank books), to which the notarial books frequently refer, we would probably see that they were not kept in double entry accounting, the first extant, fragmentary examples of which are half a century later; but they must have been in good order, for the Genoese commune was very exacting in that respect. From nearly two hundred randomly preserved minutes concerning the bank, we can, however, get a fairly clear idea of its internal organization, its assets, and its activities. As compared with later companies of merchant bankers, where senior partnership was tightly determined by seniority in a single family tree, while the rank and tasks of all other members were sharply defined by contract, the Leccacorvo bank looks quite unstructured and informal. Nobody by the name of Leccacorvo but William is ever mentioned as attached to the partnership in any way.

Next to him, the most influential partner was Leonardo Rozo, whose pedigree included two former consuls of Piacenza: he countersigned most of the contracts and, after William's death, took over the direction of the already bankrupt company. Only one document also lists Vacario Rozo (Leonardo's brother or cousin?), Alberto Diano, "and other partners." It is impossible to tell whether Rozo Rozi, Guglielmo Rozi (Vacario's son), Giacomo Diano, Bulgarino Pegoraria, and Stabile Mussadibove, who at different times were given unlimited proxies, were partners or salaried employees. Curiously, Leonardo Rozo himself could not make up his mind in a contract as to whether Iacobino Pegoraria should be called a "partner or agent" of his. The bank does not seem to have established any permanent branch outside Genoa, although it occasionally appointed temporary agents to look after its extensive interests in one or another foreign place. Leccacorvo himself did not hesitate to do business on his own, independently of his bank, especially on behalf of a commercial association formed by three close relatives of Innocent IV—Obizzo, Nicola, and Tedisio Fieschi—for a value of 1,400 pounds in 1253. By the early fourteenth century such a separate action would have been regarded as a conflict of interests.

The organization was loose, almost rudimentary, but its business was not. There is no question that the basic activities of the Leccacorvo company were in the field of exchange and deposit banking. Long-distance contracts of exchange are the most frequent item in the series of notarial minutes concerning that company. The majority provided for "dry" exchange, with the fairs of Champagne as the first and fictitious destination and the option of postponed reimbursement in Genoa, but a few embodied a bona fide transfer of funds needed abroad; one of them, a notarized letter, looks like the missing link between contracts and bills of exchange. Transfers through entries in the bank books, mostly entailing overdrafts, are mentioned almost as often—just mentioned, because a notarial certification of an entry in a banker's book was hardly ever needed. Notarial contracts usually were instruments of credit for people of means: the Leccacorvo bank did most of its business with established merchants, bankers, and government officials, including the communes of Genoa and Piacenza, Louis IX of France, and the pope. With craftsmen and other small fry, it used the traditional "free and loving loan" (*mutuum gratis et amore*)—that is, actually, a loan with concealed interest built in. The rate did not have to be exorbitant: prosperity was around the corner, and an enterprising woolmaker could be a good risk.

The notarial minutes also show that the bank was steadily expanding its investments in the direction of trade. Some of them may look whimsical: at least once in his life, William Leccacorvo, the "fat" banker from the flat city of Piacenza, decided to get a taste of the life of the sea captains and merchants who surrounded him in Genoa. He embarked for Sicily as the traveling party of a commenda (a popular contract mixing loan with partnership), carrying along a batch of cheap German and Lombard cloth borrowed from a Placentine fellow-banker. Another time he bought a flock of goats, for what purpose we cannot guess. The other known investments were of the usual kind: fine French cloth, Oriental silk, spices, furs, cotton goods, wool for the growing local industry, salt for universal consumption—all this through the usual commercial contracts of sea loan or commenda. The destinations, too, were not unusual—Genoa, other Italian cities, France, the Levant, the African ports of the Mediterranean—except one. In 1253 Leccacorvo invested some Fieschi money in a commenda for Safi, a Moroccan port on the Atlantic coast and a terminus for caravans bringing gold dust from the interior. Preceding by a few days another commenda by another investor for the same destination, this is the earliest extant evidence that the Genoese were pushing that far south along the route that would eventually take Vasco da Gama to India. It also is one of several pieces of circumstantial evidence suggesting that the Leccacorvo company may have been involved in a decision of great and durable historical importance: the return of Western Europe to gold coinage as the best remedy against money shortage and rampant inflation.[11]

The long and intricate story of the transition from the age of the silver denier to that of the gold genoin, florin, and ducat can only be summarized here. For half a millenium, nearly everywhere in Western Europe, deniers had been virtually the only coins struck by the mints; if gold coins were desired, they had to be imported from the Byzantine and Muslim world. As time went by, the growth of the population, the increase in monetary transactions, and the price inflation that often goes along with economic expansion caused the supply of deniers to be chronically inadequate. No matter how much the mines and the mints accelerated their production, there was always too little cash at hand. This encouraged the ever-present temptation for governments to multiply the currency by adding copper to the alloy and eroding the weight of their deniers; to little avail, for debasement was easily recognizable, and the purchasing power of a denier was not determined by its nominal value but by its actual silver content. Credit, for those who could get it, rose to every emergency to fill the gap; still, hard cash was indispensable at some point, and the lack of a stable monetary unit greatly

11. My interpretation of the monetary reform of 1252, assigning to the gold genoin a slight priority over the gold florin, was further elaborated in two papers of mine, "Back to Gold, 1252," *Economic History Review* 2nd ser. 9 (1956) 219–40, and "Prima del ritorno all'oro nell'Occidente duecentesco," reprinted in my *Su e giù* (n. 7 above) 305–12. I do not know whether they have convinced Philip Grierson, who had expressed some skepticism in a review of *Il ritorno all'oro* (n. 10 above); otherwise my thesis seems to have been generally accepted, except in Genoa (*nemo propheta in patria!*). A number of Genoese scholars still hold to the thesis that the gold genoin was first struck in the early thirteenth century; see lastly Giovanni Pesce and Giuseppe Felloni, *Le monete genovesi* (Genoa 1975). Their interpretation, which has found no support outside of Genoa (Grierson's doubts concerned a possible priority of the gold florin), leaves me unconvinced; but this is not the proper place for a detailed discussion.

embarrassed all people—bankers and bookkeepers more than anybody else. Responding to pressure at long last, one government after another introduced at the side of the debased coins a "strong" or "groat" denier with a better weight and alloy. This, however, provided only a partial solution, for the gap between supply and demand began in the mines. The groat was dragged into the same pattern of debasement as the "petty" denier, which had been degraded to the role of fractional currency.

By the mid-thirteenth century the monetary confusion had reached nightmarish proportions. Each Italian commune and foreign state used its own system of weights and alloys; each of them kept going two series of differently debased deniers, old deniers circulated simultaneously with younger ones of a worse kind. Bookkeepers had to reckon with innumerable systems of account, pegged to deniers of different quality; businessmen had to juggle with coins of unpredictable quality; mints had to do the best they could with whatever silver they received. In a contract of 1253 the Leccacorvo bank defined a cash payment in the following terms: "£2,053 10s. 8d. Genoese . . . for which we promise to give . . . as much silver in old Genoese or Venetian groats, at the rate of £5 8s. 8d. per pound of silver, as will make up that sum." Bankers who found it difficult to get hold of exactly the number and type of groat they needed tried to acquire control of a mint. In 1253, the Leccacorvo bank tried to activate a mint near Genoa and strike groats of the best Genoese standard, through a partnership with Giacomo Fieschi and the Bonsignori bank of Siena, but the plan apparently failed to obtain the required authorization of the Genoese commune. Undeterred, in 1258 the bank bought its way into the mint of Cuneo, which produced "strong" deniers.

By that time, however, the importance of the groat had been reduced by the success of a more radical reform. The gold genoin, issued in 1252, a few months before Florence followed suit by issuing the gold florin, had placed at the disposal of business the stable coin it needed; gold had been mobilized to supplement the output of silver. The official

Genoese annals recorded the event tersely, without fanfare and with no mention of the people behind the reform; the plain, unassuming appearance of the genoin indicates that it was not meant to be a political symbol or an artistic feat but primarily an economic tool. Who were the promoters? The coin was launched precisely at the moment when the gold-silver ratio hit its lowest point in many centuries; as soon as gold became a metal for minting, its price in terms of silver jumped. Only a shrewd handler of money could have thought of that and turned it to his profit. The fact that Leccacorvo responded to the reform by trying to strike silver and to get close to African gold dust would be no proof that he was one of its authors. That he invested Fieschi money in both operations at a time when the Fieschi were all-powerful in Genoa may also be irrelevant. There is, however, stronger if circumstantial evidence: Perugia, after Genoa and Florence the third city to plan the adoption of gold coinage, in 1259, was then governed by Stefano Leccacorvo.

The year 1259, however, was ill-starred for the Leccacorvo family. Perugia did not succeed in carrying out the monetary reform. In Genoa the Leccacorvo bank suddenly crashed. Shortly after (some time between 28 July and 4 August), Guglielmo Leccacorvo died. A writer of historical fiction might suggest that a prolonged illness of Guglielmo caused panic among his creditors and deprived Stefano, his son(?), of backing for the minting of gold. But an economic historian cannot indulge in such guesses and does not actually need them. The failure of the bank is not surprising in view of the dramatic economic and political changes in Genoa from 1254 on. The postwar boom had spent its impetus. Shipbuilding, banking, and the crafts had overexpanded. Military successes against Pisa had been offset by serious reverses in Sicily and the Levant. With the arrogance of power, the dominant Guelph families had appropriated the spoils of war, turned the financial difficulties of the commune to their personal gain, antagonized the lower classes, and yielded to papal pressure against religious dissenters. In 1255 and 1256 several woolmakers and at least two banks failed, while governmental corruption was becoming an open scandal. In 1257 a popular revolution with support from prominent Ghibelline families delivered full powers to a wealthy bourgeois, Guglielmo Boccanegra, who began putting public finances in order, assisting the unemployed with a program of public works, and aiding tottering businessmen as best he could. Under his stern, careful administration the economy gradually improved, but the lingering slackness of the market caused a number of additional failures. A favorable treaty with the Byzantine Empire in 1261 brought prosperity back, but its commercial and political dividends came home only the following year—too late for Boccanegra, who was ousted by a Guelph counterrevolution. Seven years up, seven years down between 1248 and 1261: that, according to extant sources, was the span of the business cycle.

Why did the mighty Leccacorvo bank succumb to a conjuncture which, unfavorable as it was, spared many of its smaller rivals? No doubt because its persistent fortune lured it into overexpansion. In an interesting paper, published on the seven-hundredth anniversary of the crash, Franco Guerello pointed out that the company had an earlier close call in February 1250, but escaped bankruptcy because its guarantors and friends pledged to raise at short notice £13,500 in Genoa and £5,500 in Piacenza, a very considerable sum for that period.[12] That prowess could not be duplicated nine years later, when Leccacorvo and his partners came again to grief after spreading their commitments steadily through boom and bust. In 1258 they were still reaching for control of the mint of Cuneo; by January 1259 they had already been pronounced bankrupt, with more than a hundred creditors, including a cross-section of the Genoese upper class (both Guelph and Ghibelline) and many foreign merchants living in Genoa. All that their guarantors could do in their behalf was to agree with the creditors on a 10% rebate on the debts, and to have them honorably confined under guard in a counting house instead of the debtors' jail, significantly dubbed Malapaga

12. See n. 10 above.

("bad payment"). Even the latter concession, which made it easier for the disgraced bankers to trace and reclaim their outstanding credits, was begrudged by that Giacomo Fieschi who not long before had joined Leccacorvo in a plan for striking silver groats: apparently he had not objected as long as his former partner was alive, but shortly after Guglielmo's death he demanded that the survivors be locked up in a more secure place. Indeed, the Fieschi were impatient creditors: in 1253, when the bank was in its prime, Pope Innocent IV, Giacomo's uncle, had threatened Guglielmo with excommunication unless he completed at once the payment of a sum due to the pontiff.[13]

The story of the Leccacorvo company largely anticipates that of the better-known banks that rose and fell after it— Bonsignori of Siena, Bardi and Peruzzi of Florence, Fugger of Augsburg, and many others. Only one comment seems necessary here. Without minimizing the psychological and practical impact of doctrinal condemnations of interest, I would stress that they never were a major hindrance to the growth of credit institutions. Deep in their hearts, people realized that there was a difference between consumption and business loans; Innocent IV would not have excommunicated Leccacorvo as a usurer but only as a dilatory payer. Men will sin; casuists and traders will find ways to turn obstacles; losing patience with cavils, the Genoese government eventually decreed a stiff penalty for debtors who would invoke canon law to get out of their obligations. The ingrained conviction that credit on trust should always entail punishment on default was a far more serious impediment; prisons for debtors still existed in

13. Guerello's comments on the documents of 1250 which he found and published convince me in all but one respect: I do not believe, as he does, that the loss of support from the Fieschi family had a crucial importance in the failure of 1259. The only ascertainable support they had given in 1250 amounted to one hundred pounds pledged by Giacomo Fieschi; in 1259 he had lost his influence on the government, and his request for a stricter custody of the bankers received a curt answer from the guarantors of the bank, who obviously had no intention of taking action.

the nineteenth century. In the Middle Ages, when the recovery of credits was infinitely slower than now, kings like St. Louis being among the worst payers, every bank that soared was sooner or later destroyed by an often unjustified rush of its creditors. There is no indication in the sources that the Leccacorvo company ever tried to evade its responsibilities; though its failure had serious and lasting repercussions, twenty years after the crash another Placentine bank had hired one Gianone Leccacorvo as its agent in the Levant. It did not matter: in 1259 Guglielmo Leccacorvo could not pay all creditors at once, and a bank which really was not incurable had to fail.

2 The Usurer and Purgatory

JACQUES LE GOFF

THE CHURCH'S CONDEMNATION OF USURY did not stop usurers from existing or practicing their trade, and it did nothing to shackle the development of capitalism. From at least the beginning of the thirteenth century, theologians and canonists distinguished usury or profit on a loan (*mutuum*) from such everyday medieval transactions as contracts of association (*societas*), of location (*locatio, conductio*), and of sale (*emptio, venditio*). Nor did the growth of modern business methods arise from the drive to circumvent the condemnation of usury.[1] Hence, historians studying medieval usury have viewed it less as an episode in economic history than as a chapter in the history of ideas.[2] As John T. Noonan said, "Even when it [the prohibition of usury] did not affect commercial practice, it did affect the spiritual state of businessmen, and who will

1. William J. Ashley, *An Introduction to English Economic History and Theory* (2 vols. London 1888) first pointed out the terminological distinctions, according to Benjamin N. Nelson, "The Usurer and the Merchant Prince: Italian Businessmen and the Ecclesiastical Law of Restitution," *Journal of Economic History* Supplement 7 (1947) 104.
2. John T. Noonan, Jr., *The Scholastic Analysis of Usury* (Cambridge, Mass. 1957) 5: "This is a history of thought. . . ."

say that there is no meaning to the salvation or damnation of a man?"[3] Benjamin Nelson points out that from the thirteenth to the fifteenth century there was a "divorce between the usurer-pawnbroker and the merchant prince," adding, "The near exemption of the merchant and financier from the stigma of usury . . . was a prerequisite to the expansion of Europe along capitalist lines."[4] Nevertheless, it took a long time to distinguish between the merchant and the usurer. And with good reason: if the merchant practiced methods tolerated by the church, he usually practiced others too which it branded and condemned as usury.

But too many studies have been devoted to the abstraction "usury" without taking sufficient account of the historical reality, the usurer. Though Henri Pirenne took too literally the medieval topos of the merchant's condemnation, *homo mercator vix aut nunquam potest Deo placere* ("Seldom or never can a man who is a merchant be pleasing to God"), he realized that the problem of the merchant's salvation was central to the questions surrounding the birth of commercial capitalism in the Middle Ages.[5] But the topos applied even more to the usurer, and rightly so, since the merchant and the usurer were often one; or rather, the usurer was the shadowy half of this Dr. Jekyll and Mr. Hyde, the medieval merchant. One example well illustrates his ambiguity and the problems he posed for contemporary society. John W. Baldwin cites a revealing passage from the *Summa* of Peter the Chanter (last decade of the twelfth century) in which the Parisian master professed himself confused by the case put to him by a notary, the accomplice and scribe of a merchant doing business at fairs: "I was recently perplexed by a question a certain God-fearing man put to me; he had for a long while been working for a merchant at the fairs, recording his

3. Ibid. 36.
4. Nelson (n. 1 above) 121.
5. Henri Pirenne, *Histoire économique et sociale du Moyen Age*, rev. ed. Hans van Werveke (Paris 1969) 12.

usurious debts, his exchange transactions, and other legal and illegal business."[6]

The concern of this paper will be the usurer, the merchant's satanic alter ego. I shall concentrate on the problem of his salvation and on society's changing attitudes toward it.[7] But first a methodological note. Whereas Marxism sees economic activity as an infrastructure and ideological debate into which it enters as superstructure, idealism makes religious debate the driving force behind economic history. The theses of Max Weber and of Tawney (which, by the way, I do not compare to these summary conceptions) seem to me, however, to separate the *homo oeconomicus* and the *homo religiosus* in a way that impoverishes and distorts historical reality.

Where, then, is one to look for documentary evidence on the medieval usurer's salvation, evidence that adequately comprehends both material and spiritual factors? If one is too interested in usury and not interested enough in the usurer, then one is tempted to concentrate too exclusively on theological and legal sources which reduce to abstractions the concrete details of life. In the course of the long but divided thirteenth century (ca. 1180 to ca. 1280 being the calm before the gathering storm), when the monetary economy was undergoing its great expansion, the eternal—and therefore terrestrial—fate of the usurer was decided by the fulminatory condemnations of the general councils: Lateran III in 1179, Lyon II in 1274, Vienne in 1311. In the struggle against usury the

6. John W. Baldwin, *Masters, Princes and Merchants: The Social Views of Peter the Chanter and His Circle* (2 vols. Princeton 1970) 1.306–07, 2.209 n. 75: "Unde titubavi nuper quidam timoratam habens conscientiam quesivit a me de hoc quod cum ad nundinas diu servavit mercatori in scribendo debita usurarum suarum et cambiaciones et cetera licita cum illicitis. . . ."

7. Nelson (n. 1 above) poses the question thus: "The insights of Ashley and some recent writers into the technical refinements of the analysis of usury do not by themselves provide us with answers to the varied questions connected with estimating ecclesiastical and culture factors in economic growth" (105).

Lyon and Vienne councils only completed—on important points, true—the interdictions of the last third of the twelfth century.

The Second Lateran Council (1139) had condemned usury as "ignominious." Lateran III went further: canon 25, *Quia in omnibus*, enacted three capital decisions: (1) excommunication for open usurers (the church's categorization of the usurer during this period thus excluded him from the Christian community); (2) refusal of inhumation in Christian ground (situating the drama of the usurer in the great liturgy of death here on earth and in the "other world"); (3) interdiction of usurers' offerings (thus excluding them from the essential practice of medieval public beneficence).

The canon *Quia in omnibus* should be compared to three other texts with which it forms a whole: the collection of texts against usury gathered by Gratian in his *Decretum* (*Concordia discordantium canonum*, Bologna, 1140); the decretal letter *In civitate* from Alexander III (1159–81) to the archbishop of Genoa condemning the practices of the Genoese usurers (those great precursors of capitalism) and the decretal *Consuluit* of Urban III (1185–87) to a priest of Brescia, which took up the scriptural texts against usury brought together by Lateran II and Lateran III and highlighted the text which would henceforth be the great antiusury injunction: *mutuum dantes et nihil inde sperantes*, "lend freely, hoping for nothing thereby" (Luke 6:35). *In civitate* and *Consuluit* were taken up again in the *compilatio prima of* Bernard Balbi of Pavia (d. 1213) and finally joined to the canon *Quia in omnibus* of Lateran III in the *Decretales* of Gregory IX (1234).

The canon *Usurarum* of Lyon II (1274), in the authorized interpretation of William Durandus in his *Commentarius*, written soon after the council, while not extending the preceding condemnations to secret usurers, did extend them to foreign open usurers such as the Sienese and Florentines in England, and those called *prestatores* in Italy, *Cahorsini* in France, and *renovatores* in Provence. Foreigners were being confined to the ghetto of usury.

The isolation of the usurers was completed by canon 15 of

the Council of Vienne (1311), which extended excommunication to those who authorized usury or protected usurers: legislators authorizing a minimum usury rate and public authorities who utilized it, princes and public powers protecting usurers, and—particularly important from my point of view—confessors giving absolution to unrepentant usurers. These dispositions were integrated into the *Corpus juris canonici: Clementines* V, 5 (*De usuris*) and *Sextus* V, 5 (*De usuris*).

These are the essentials of the judicial framework, which certainly must not be ignored. But canonists and theologians had less impact on common practice and opinion than what the pastors—in touch with the beliefs, behavior, and attitudes of everyday life—did with their texts. Since usury presented itself to the age in terms of whether this living person the usurer could be saved, it may be interesting to consult the thirteenth and fourteenth centuries' principal source concretely concerned with the salvation of men according to their character or socioprofessional definition, their trade or activity: the exempla. These were short but striking lessons or edifying anecdotes designed for inclusion in sermons to be heard *by all the faithful.* Battaglia has rightly called them "la bibbia della vita quotidiana," the Bible of everyday life.[8]

Two great socioideological phenomena upset Christianity in the thirteenth century: the generalization of confession and the renewal of preaching. The canon *Omnis utriusque sexus* of the Fourth Lateran Council (1215) prescribed for every Christian auricular confession at least once a year. The disorder of religious practice which followed resulted in a document of exceptional interest: the manual for confessors.[9] But

---

8. Salvatore Battaglia, *La coscienza letteraria del Medioevo* (Naples 1965) 474. On the importance of the short narrative in medieval literature, see Nora Scott, *Contes pour rire? Fabliaux des XIIIe et XIVe siècles* (Paris 1977) 7ff.

9. Nelson (n. 1 above) has shown, concerning the notion of the open usurer and the distinction between *certa usura* and *incerta usura*, the role of the *forum internum*, that is, confession, in the evolution of medieval attitudes to usury and the usurer. It is the impact occasioned

it very quickly came under the thumb of scholasticism, itself overrun by legalism. Canon law swamped theology and pastoral care. The living word resisted better, and particularly the exemplum: widely and successfully employed as a preaching tool by the new mendicant orders, it leaves us concrete, normative testimony.[10]

What can we learn from the exempla about the image of the usurer at the beginning of the thirteenth century? This is the moment of what John W. Baldwin called "the campaign against usury," which he placed in the years 1195–1215 (but extending it, following the work of John H. Mundy, to include the antiusury measures of the bishop of Toulouse, Foulques of Marseille (1206–31).[11] The question has not escaped several historians interested in usury. Nelson, having based his study of restitution for usury primarily upon wills, declares: "If one be loath to rely solely upon wills and testaments, one has only to turn to literature to find confirmation. One need only recall the biographies of St. Godric, Peter Waldo, St. Francis, Blanquerna (Raymond Lull's hero), *not to mention the tales of the gruesome fates of usurers in the exempla.*"[12] Better yet, Baldwin recognized the importance of the exemplum for the history of usury and usurers: "But perhaps the masters' most valuable contribution to the preachers' effectiveness was their use of the *exemplum*, the brief story drawn from saints' lives and other tales, to portray most vividly the dire consequences to those who practiced usury. . . . Among the various themes embodied in the *exempla*, the most popular depicted the wretched death of usurers."[13]

---

by the changes in confession and the appearance of the psychology of intention in the twelfth and thirteenth centuries which I attempted to stress in "Métier et profession d'après les manuels de confesseurs du Moyen Age," *Miscellanea Mediaevalia* 3, Beiträge zum Berufsbewusstsein des mittelalterlichen Menschen (Berlin 1964) 44–60.

10. See my forthcoming study with Jean-Claude Schmitt, *Les Exempla*, in the series Typologie des sources du Moyen Age occidental.

11. Baldwin (n. 6 above) 1.296–311 and 2.191–203.

12. Nelson (n. 1 above) 122 (my italics).

13. Baldwin (n. 6 above) 1.302.

The principal contributing texts are: (1) Peter the Chanter's *Summa* and especially the *Verbum abbreviatum* ("his popular manual on ethics," in Baldwin's words, crammed full of exempla), both composed at the end of the Parisian canon's life (d. 1197); (2) the exempla drawn by Thomas F. Crane from the *Sermones vulgares* of Cardinal Jacques de Vitry (ca. 1180–1240), student at the University of Paris in the reign of Philip Augustus; (3) the treatise *De usura* taken from the *Penitentiale* (ca. 1204) of Robert of Courson, disciple of Peter the Chanter, master at Paris in the first decade of the thirteenth century, cardinal legate of the pope in France from 1213 to 1215; (4) the *Summa confessorum* (ca. 1215) of the Englishman Thomas of Chobham (or Chabham), student at Paris, also rich in exempla, often borrowed from Peter the Chanter;[14] and (5) the *Dialogus miraculorum*, composed between 1214 and 1223 by the German Cistercian Caesarius of Heisterbach—an orderly collection of little edifying stories in which the traditional brief narrative of the *miraculum* is transformed into an exemplum; this last collection played a decisive role in establishing the exemplum as a successful "genre" or literary "form."[15] And the occasional later testimony may help us understand the long battle of the merchant banker–usurer to escape from hell.

At first sight, the outlook is very black. Against the usurer were aligned three of the principal ideological concerns of the moment: those with work, with time, and with occupations.

Work was emerging from a long malediction bequeathed by archaic societies and sanctioned by Genesis, where work was man's punishment for Original Sin: work was the penitence of the *laboratores*, atoning for the whole society; work was the voluntary labor of monks ransoming man from his sins. Around the middle of the twelfth century, work became a positive virtue and a touchstone of the socioreligious value

14. Baldwin (n. 6 above) says correctly: "As a practical handbook, Thomas' treatise lacks an academic style and apparatus, yet it probes the varieties of human conduct more deeply and broadly than any previous penitential" (1.36).

15. Le Goff and Schmitt (n. 10 above).

system.[16] As John W. Baldwin saw so well, "since the middle of the twelfth century the two factors of *labores* and *expensae* were of crucial importance in the Canonists' justification of all kinds of economic increment and profit."[17]

From this new image of work two new types of professionals benefited, especially at the turn of the century: the university professor, the intellectual worker, and the merchant, the economic worker.[18] The first circumvents the accusation that he is selling knowledge which belongs only to God and hence cannot be sold, by arguing that he is working and therefore merits a salary. The second deflects the double accusation that he is selling time (which also belongs only to God) and making money (which is unproductive) grow, by arguing that he too is a worker, worthy of a just profit if he respects the just price.

But the usurer is the merchant banker, who receives the most shameful profits of all, since lending at interest brings him money without his having worked. Peter the Chanter emphasizes that even during sleep the usurer is making a profit.[19] Thomas of Chobham insists that "the usurer wants to make a profit without any work at all and even while sleeping, which is against the teaching of the Lord: 'You will earn your bread by the sweat of your brow.'"[20] The *Tabula*

16. As I have already tried to show in "Travail, techniques et artisans dans les systèmes de valeur du haut Moyen Age (Ve-Xe siècles)," *Artigianato e Tecnica della società dell'alto Medioevo occidentale*, Settimane di studio del Centro italiano di studi sull'alto medioevo 18 (Spoleto 1971) 239–66, and in the article cited in n. 9 above, the beginnings of research in progress on *Les images du travail du Moyen Age*.

17. John W. Baldwin, *The Medieval Theories of the Just Price: Romanists, Canonists, and Theologians in the Twelfth and Thirteenth Centuries*, Transactions of the American Philosophical Society ser. 2 vol. 49 part 4 (Philadelphia 1959) 49.

18. See Jacques Le Goff, *Marchands et banquiers du Moyen Age* (Paris 1956) and *Les intellectuels au Moyen Age* (Paris 1957; rpt. 1976).

19. Baldwin (n. 6 above) 2.191 n. 13: "Numquam enim dormit fenerator quin lucretur. . . ."

20. Thomas of Chobham, *Summa confessorum*, ed. F. Broomfield, *Analecta mediaevalia Namurcensia* 25 (1968) 505: "Praeterea, fenerator

exemplorum goes one better: not only does the usurer not work but he makes his money work for him;[21] furthermore, while the peasant lets his cattle rest on Sundays and feastdays, the usurer does not even let his money, which is his cattle, respect the day of rest.[22]

Here, then, the usurer is disdaining the appropriate time for work. Even worse, he is selling something that does not belong to him but belongs rather to God—time itself. In the passage where he stigmatizes the usurer who profits while he sleeps, Peter the Chanter adds, "et ita vendit tempora dei"— and so he sells God's time.[23] There is the same stigma in the work of Thomas of Chobham: "fenerator nihil vendit debitori quod suum est sed tantum tempus quod dei est," the usurer sells nothing which actually belongs to him, but he sells only time, which belongs to God.[24] An exemplum of rubric 304 in the *Tabula exemplorum* says that usurers act against the universal law, because they sell time which is a common good of all creatures, and they sell light and repose, the light of day and the repose of night.[25]

In the fifteenth century, in the framework of a new, rigorous condemnation of usury, the great reactionary who preached

---

vult consequi lucrum sine omni labore etiam dormiendo, quod est contra preceptum domini qui ait: *in labore et sudore vultus tui vesceris pane tuo"* (Gen. 3:19).

21. Partecipazio, doge of Venice, had already spoken of *solidi laboratorii* in his testament of 829: Latin text ed. Andrea Gloria, *Codice diplomatico padovano dal secolo sesto a tutto l'undecimo* (Venice 1877) 12–16; English translation by Robert S. Lopez and Irving W. Raymond, *Medieval Trade in the Mediterranean World* (New York 1955) 39.

22. *Tabula exemplorum secundum ordinem alphabeti*, ed. Jean T. Welter (Paris and Toulouse 1926) 83: "Quilibet homo cessat in diebus festivis ab opere suo, boves autem usurarii i.e. denarii semper laborant ut Deum et omnes sanctos offendat. . . ."

23. Baldwin (n. 6 above) 2.191 n. 13.

24. Thomas of Chobham (n. 20 above) 505.

25. *Tabula exemplorum* (n. 22 above) 82: "Item faciunt contra legem universalem, quia vendunt tempus, quod est commune omnium creaturarum. . . . Item usurarii vendunt lucem et requiem, lucem diei et requiem noctis. . . ."

to the masses, the Franciscan Bernard of Siena, took up and
developed the old concept that it was Jesus Christ himself
who declared that God alone knew time and the hour and that
it was not for man to know time, much less to sell it. On
Judgment Day the usurer will be reproached with having sold
time which is common to all creatures, and thus with having
offended all creatures.[26] Finally, the usurer did not benefit
from the gradual curtailment of the list of occupations that
the church and public opinion, which it fashioned, considered
illicit or ignominious.[27]

Instead, the usurer found himself linked with the worst
evildoers, the worst occupations, the worst sins, and the worst
vices. For he was an evildoer of the highest degree, a pillager
and robber. When Gregory the Great, the great designer of
topoi for medieval man, made the influential statement that
it is difficult for the merchant (soon to be the usurer) to
please God, he gave him a companion in sin, the soldier: to
one *furtum*, robbery, to the other *rapina*, pillaging.[28] The
church, in spite of its compromise with the military aristocracy,
would always be suspicious of the soldier, the man of blood
and violence. It would play on the semantic confusion between the classical Latin meaning for *miles*, a soldier, and its
specialized medieval meaning "knight," the low or middle
nobility. But little by little the knight escaped malediction.
When Peter the Chanter recalled Gregory the Great's dictum
he changed "knight" to "mercenary knight."[29]

But the usurer was, above all, a robber: a robber of time, a
divine possession, a common possession. He was at once a *fur*,

26. Sermons 43 and 45; cf. Noonan (n. 2 above) 76.
27. See Jacques Le Goff, "Métiers licites et illicites dans l'Occident
médiéval," *Etudes historiques. Annales de l'Ecole des Hautes Etudes de
Gand* 5 (1963) 41–57.
28. Gregory the Great, *Homilia XXIV in Evangelio*, I, Patrologia
latina 76.1184, taken up by Gratian (*Decretum, De poenitentia*, D.5. c.6)
and by the bishop of Paris Peter Lombard (d. 1160) in his celebrated
commentary of sentences (*Sententiarum libri quatuor*, IV 16, 2, Patrologia
latina 192.878–79).
29. Baldwin (n. 6 above) 2.44 n. 100.

the detested robber of common law,[30] and a *latro*, the high-wayman, the outlaw, the medieval gangster. Thomas of Chob-ham explains that secular law did not punish usurers by hang-ing them, as it did *fures* and *latrones*, because usurers did not disturb the public order and sometimes were even useful to the public; but he reminds us that the church pursued them like all other robbers (fures) because they lived off their usury.[31] Robert of Courson equated usurers' helpers with ravagers whom the church must bring back to the right path.[32] In his *Verbum abbreviatum*, Peter the Chanter had lumped together under one heading his discussions "de furto, rapina, usura et huiusmodi."[33] The *Tabula exemplorum* stated again that usurers were bandits (latrones) because they sold time, which did not belong to them.

The second ignominious occupation often mentioned in relation to usury was prostitution. The open usurer, like the prostitute, practiced a public occupation that was both well known and shameful, said Peter the Chanter in his *Summa*, followed by Robert of Courson and Thomas of Chobham.[34] Still, with prostitutes there were extenuating circumstances; for, as Thomas of Chobham remarked, they work even if their work is ignominious, and also, as canonists like Huguccio and

30. Bronislaw Geremek, *Les marginaux parisiens aux XIVe et XVe siècles* (Paris 1976) has brought together a rich collection of evidence for the great seriousness with which the medieval robber was viewed.

31. Thomas of Chobham (n. 20 above) 509: "Tamen licet raptor sit vel fur, quia est benignus fur nec turbat rem publicam sed quandoque prodest, ideo non suspenditur sicut alii fures et latrones per leges secu-lares. Et tamen ecclesia persequitur feneratores sicut alios fures quia assument sibi officium fenerandi publicum ut inde vivant. . . ."

32. Robert of Courson, *Summa*, X, 9, cited by Baldwin (n. 6 above) 2.209 n. 72 ("de servientibus feneratorum et raptorum qui incorrigibiles sunt").

33. Baldwin (n. 6 above) 2.206 n. 52.

34. Peter the Chanter, *Summa*, par. 147, II, 351; cf. Baldwin (n. 6 above) 1.300. Robert of Courson, *Summa*, XX, 10–11; cf. Baldwin (n. 6 above) 2.44 n. 99. Thomas of Chobham (n. 20 above) 509: "ecclesia persequitur fenatores . . . sicut meretrices ideo persequitur ecclesia quia in contumeliam dei habent meretricium suum quasi officium de quo vivant."

Robert of Courson said, ownership of the money actually passed from the client to the prostitute, and this is not the case with the usurer's loan to the debtor.[35]

The bishop of Toulouse, Foulques of Marseille, whose preaching and antiusury measures ruined, for example, a great merchant-usurer, Raymond Durand, waged a triple-pronged attack against usury, prostitution, and heresy. For in the end the usurer was grouped with the great religious sinners: simoniacs and heretics.[36] Thomas of Chobham, for example, began his *questio de usura* with the affirmation, "There are two detestable kinds of avarice that are subject to trial and punishment: usury and simony."[37] The cardinal sin of which usury was one of the most pernicious examples was *avaritia*, cupidity. Lester K. Little has shown that, around 1200, avaritia was rising to the top of the fatal pleiad of capital sins, dethroning *superbia*, pride. The sin of the bourgeois was surpassing the sin of the nobles.[38]

Two principal types of socioreligious classification divided the conceptions of society in the thirteenth century: a classification by sins and vices, and a classification by social rank and occupation. The usurer is the great loser in both lists. When Caesarius of Heisterbach announced the series of exempla that were to illustrate the horrible death of the great sinners, here was his list: usurers, the covetous, the avaricious, knaves, the prideful, brigands, murderers, quarrelers, the lustful, and all those subject to similar vices, called by St.

35. See Baldwin (n. 6 above) 1.303 and 2.2, 93, and 106. Stephen Langton in his *Quaestiones* says succinctly, ". . . turpiter facit meretrix, sed non turpiter acquirit" (Baldwin [n. 6 above] 2.92 n. 124).
36. The comparison of usurers to Jews poses a complex problem that will not be touched on here. I only note that according to Baldwin (n. 6 above) 1.298, "the terms 'Jew' and 'usurer' became synonymous around the end of the twelfth century."
37. Thomas of Chobham (n. 20 above) 504: "Sunt autem duo detestabilia genera avaritie que puniuntur in iudicio per sententiam, scilicet usura et simonia."
38. Lester K. Little, "Pride Goes before Avarice: Social Change and the Vices in Latin Christendom," *American Historical Review* 76 (1971) 16–49.

Paul "works of the flesh." The usurer opened the dance of the damned.[39]

When Jacques de Vitry listed in an exemplum the occupations which rose to a preacher's call to absolution, blacksmiths were called first and rose, then the furriers, then all the other professions. Finally the preacher called out, "Let the usurers rise to receive absolution." Though the usurers were more numerous than the rest of the audience, not one dared to rise, from shame. They hid, and all the other occupations began to laugh and taunt those who did not dare to admit their profession; the usurers, embarrassed, fled.[40] In this urban world of triumphant occupations, only the usurers dared not speak their name. Where, here, is the canonical difference between the open usurer and the hidden usurer? There are only shameful usurers.

The usurer appeared as a diabolic, infernal person in three recrudescent obsessions of this unstable time—money, the body, and animals.

Money was diabolic. Francis of Assisi entreated his brethren to think no more of a coin than of a stone, if they would ward off evil. Now in the hands of the usurer money comes to life and becomes a devouring monster. In an exemplum of the *Dialogus miraculorum* of Caesarius of Heisterbach, a usurer deposits his money in a Cistercian monastery. The keeper puts it in the monastery coffer. When the usurer wants to take it out the keeper finds the coffer empty. The lock has not been broken, the seals on the sacks of money are intact. Robbery, therefore, is excluded. There is only one hypothesis—the

39. Caesarius of Heisterbach, *Dialogus miraculorum*, ed. Joseph Strange (2 vols. Cologne 1851) 2.300, *Distinctio undecima: De morientibus:* "Quam misere, quam horribiliter moriantur usurarii, avari, pecuniosi, dolosi, superbi, praedones, homicidae, contentiosi, luxuriosi, viciisque similibus subiecti, quae Apostolus appellat opera carnis, quibusdam tibi pandam exemplis."

40. Thomas F. Crane, ed., *The exempla or Illustrative Stories from the sermones vulgares of Jacques de Vitry*, Publications of the Folklore Society 26 (1890; rpt. Nendeln, Lichtenstein 1967) 76.

usurer's money has devoured the money of the monastery: "cognovit, quod pecunia usurarii devorasset pecuniam monasterii."[41]

The body is the receptacle, the instrument, the sign of sin— especially the female body, whose sex itself is diabolic.[42] Possession, leprosy, and bodily infirmities mark some of the worst outcasts of medieval society. Caesarius of Heisterbach describes the behavior of the corpse of a female usurer, one Jutta of Frechen, near Cologne. She dies without repenting and her body is placed on the ground for burial—the fatal moment of decision when she must pass to eternal life or eternal death. The devil, taking hold of the inert body, makes the arms and hands move as if they were counting money, "et ecce diabolus manus eius et brachia movit, ad instar numerantis pecuniam." Gerlach, the parish priest, comes to exorcise the corpse. The body becomes inert. But when he stops the exorcism, the cadaver begins to move again, this time the legs and the hands. The priest takes a piece of straw, soaks it in holy water and puts it into the mouth of the corpse. Avidly the corpse begins to chew the straw. Gerlach has to knot his stole around the dead usurer's neck before she becomes inert for good.[43]

Finally, at a time when theologians reminded man that he was made *ad imaginem Dei*, when carnival animal disguises were condemned as blasphemous, and when the diatribes of St. Bernard against representations of monsters in Roman art

41. Caesarius of Heisterbach (n. 39 above) 1.108, *Distinctio secunda: De contritione*, cap. XXXIV.

42. An exemplum of the *Tabula exemplorum* (n. 22 above), a Parisian text of the thirteenth century, punished a usurer's infidel legatees for hoarding his accursed money, instead of restoring it to the victims, by inflicting on them the evils they had professed to dread the most: poverty, leprosy, and St. Anthony's fire. If leprosy and the fire refer to diabolical links between the sin of usury and bodily corruption, the presence of poverty in this trilogy reminds us that poverty is not to be numbered among the highest values of medieval Christianity without qualification.

43. Caesarius of Heisterbach (n. 39 above) 2.300-01, *Distinctio undecima: De morientibus*, cap. XL.

still resounded, men saw the usurer surrounded by a diabolic cohort of evil beasts. In Peter the Chanter's famous exemplum on the burial of the usurer, there are leeches, flies, and spiders. Caesarius of Heisterbach mentions two toads in the grave of the usurer of Metz. A dying female usurer of Bachein, in a nightmarish vision, sees a cloud of crows come to take possession of her soul while, by night, demons come to snatch her body from its coffin. But they drop it on the doorstep, and the men who find it the next morning throw it into an animal's grave. One of Jacques de Vitry's exempla plays on the association of usurers with foxes and monkeys. And the *Tabula exemplorum* compares usurers to the lion who gets up early and does not rest until he has found prey to feed his young.[44]

There is nothing astonishing in all this if the usurer's habitual companions in the exempla are Satan and the demons. What Welter wrote of the author of the *Tabula exemplorum* agrees with the usual image of the usurer in the thirteenth century: "For him, the usurer is a being damned in advance because he sells light and repose, the day and the night. He seems while living to be under the special protection of the devil whose victim he finally becomes. He dies impenitent and is eternally chastised in the other world."[45] Even in death the usurer carries with him his purse full of damned money—one sees him in sculptures and frescoes—and the purse drags him toward the infernal depths like a millstone. (At a time when Christianity assigned certain exterior signs to the damned and outcast that good Christians might avoid them—the wheel for Jews, the rattle for lepers—Peter

44. See Baldwin (n. 6 above) 2.260; Caesarius of Heisterbach (n. 39 above) 2.300, *Distinctio undecima: De morientibus,* cap. XXXIX; ibid. 2.301: "Haec cum moritura esset, campum totum corvis ac cornicibus vidit repletum. Et clamavit fortiter: 'Ecce modo appropinquant ad me.' Et adiecit; 'Owi, owi; modo sunt in tecto, modo in domo, modo pectus meum laniant, modo animam meam extrahunt' "; and finally: "Quod [corpus homines] bestiali sepulturae tradiderunt." Jacques de Vitry (n. 40 above) 76, no. 179. *Tabula exemplorum* (n. 22 above) 82.

45. Ibid. xxxxiv.

the Chanter claimed that the usurer should wear a purse on
the end of a stick.) [46]

Death is the crucial moment for the usurer. Because his fate
is to die impenitent, his is the atrocious death of the great
sinners before whom gapes the mouth of hell. Devils are at
the head of his bed and lie in wait for him. Then comes the
problem of the burial place. The interment of the usurer is
tragic. Normally he is refused a Christian grave, in compliance with the prescriptions of the Third Lateran Council.
But if by aberration or ignorance there are churchmen who
give him a Christian funeral, either his interment is disturbed
by diabolic incidents, as in the case of the female usurer of
Frechen, or it is only a simulacrum of the corpse which is
interred, the true burial place of the usurer being hell.

Let us follow the usurer from his deathbed to the infernal
grave, in the works of Caesarius of Heisterbach and Jacques
de Vitry, and in the *Tabula exemplorum*.

First, here are four usurers from the chapter *De morientibus*,
"Of the dying," in Caesarius of Heisterbach's work. The
usurer of Metz, on his deathbed, begs his wife to place a purse
full of money near him in his grave. When the grave is
opened, a toad escapes from the purse. Another toad is on the
dead usurer's chest. The first toad takes the pieces of silver
from the purse and the second sticks them in the heart of the
cadaver. Caesarius's conclusion: If something so horrible happens to the usurer's body, what must his soul suffer from the
immortal serpents in hell?[47]

Next is the case of the gesticulating corpse of the female
usurer of Frechen. Then comes the female usurer of Bachein
who sees crows coming to seize her soul just before her body

46. "Qui publice fatentur se esse usurarios vel aliquo noto signo hoc
indicant, ut quasi capistra venalia in summitate haste vel virge feneran-
dum pecuniam circumferent," says he in the *Verbum abbreviatum*, and
in the *Summa*: ". . . nisi suspenso marsupio ad hastam, omnibus se
exponat" (Baldwin [n. 6 above] 2.205 n. 31).

47. Caesarius of Heisterbach (n. 39 above) 2.300, *Distinctio undecima:
De morientibus*, cap. XXXIX.

is thrown by demons on a doorstep, to be buried in an animal's grave.[48] Finally, there is the death of Thierry, the usurer of Würm in the diocese of Cologne. He is sick and, matter having risen to his brain, he becomes mad. His mouth and teeth move incessantly. "What are you eating, Sire?" they ask him. "My money," he answers, and indeed certain people see demons putting silver pieces in his mouth. He has himself taken to the monastery at Klosterrode in the hope of being delivered from the devils. In vain. There, the demons are more numerous than in his own house. Brought back home, he dies, pursued by hellhounds amidst a thousand torments.[49]

Jacques de Vitry devoted thirteen exempla to usurers (numbers 167 through 179 in Crane's text). In ten of them he shows their death throes, actual death, or grave. In exemplum 167 a usurer puts aside his profits in the hypocritical and vain intent of restoring them before he dies. But many usurers at the moment of death lose the power of speech and can neither confess nor express their last wishes. Another becomes crazy at the moment of death.[50]

One usurer, on his deathbed, divides his money into three parts, one for his wife to remarry, another for his children, and the third to be put in a sack attached to his neck and buried with him. This last amount is considerable and the usurer's family, wishing to recover it, opens his grave during the night. They see demons stuffing burning pieces of silver in the usurer's mouth and flee in terror.[51]

In another exemplum, the usurer, having tried in vain to bribe his soul not to leave him, commends it to the demons of hell. In effect he delivers it into their hands, and is buried in hell, *sepultus est in inferno.* The same expression is used of a usurer who had reduced a knight to poverty and ruin.[52]

---

48. Ibid. 300–01, cap. XL; 301, cap. XLI; see n. 44 above.

49. The Cistercian Caesarius takes advantage of this situation to land a blow against the house of regular canons. Caesarius of Heisterbach (n. 39 above) 2.301–02, *Distinctio undecima: De morientibus,* cap. XLII.

50. Jacques de Vitry (n. 40 above) 71–72; 72, no. 169.

51. Ibid. no. 168.

52. Ibid. 72–73, no. 170; 73–74, no. 176.

Exemplum 175 depicts a knight in debt to a usurer. The knight is shocked to come upon monks burying the condemned usurer. This is the exemplum of the usurer's burial, already cited in the work of Peter the Chanter, where the usurer is compared to a spider who eviscerates herself to catch flies and delivers herself as well as her children to the demons.[53]

In the following exemplum a usurer, interred by monks in their church, comes out of his grave at night and, while the monks sing their matins, rushes at them like a crazy man, holding a candelabrum. He wounds several of them, shouting, "these traitors accepted my money and promised me salvation but they cheated me, for I have found eternal death."[54]

Exemplum 177 praises a parish priest who refuses to bury a usurer because such pestiferous men as they should not have a Christian burial place and deserve only an ass's grave. The friends of the dead usurer insist and the priest consents to say a prayer; but afterward he loads the corpse onto an ass and takes him out of the churchyard directly to the gibbet and thence to a dung hill where he abandons him with the robbers.[55]

For the author of the *Tabula exemplorum*, death plays with usurers like a conjurer who seems to have put many objects under a hat, but when it is lifted either nothing is there or something else—for example, a stone instead of an egg. Thus, the usurer makes the rope with which he will be hanged on the gallows of hell. Furthermore, the *Requiem* is said in vain for the usurer, because neither night nor feastdays—since usury never stops—has he allowed his money *requiem*, repose.[56]

Only one demon watches over a borough where a number

53. Ibid. 74; and cf. Baldwin (n. 6 above) 2.260.
54. Jacques de Vitry (n. 40 above) 74–75, no. 176.
55. Ibid. 75.
56. *Tabula exemplorum* (n. 22 above) 5: "Sic avarus facit funiculum, quo ad patibulum inferni suspenditur. . . . Item nota quod in vanum dicitur *Requiem* pro usurario, quia neque nocte neque aliquo festo dedit requiem quin semper usura curreret."

of usurers live, while a crowd of demons guards an abbey. Satan is so sure of having the souls of that particular borough that he needs only one bailiff to watch them.[57]

Another exemplum tells the paradoxical story of a usurer's field which remains intact while his neighbors' are laid waste. The reason: the usurer's numerous friends among the demons have protected his field.[58]

The same collection tells the story, according to the bishop of Paris, Eudes de Sully (1196–1208), of a usurer in France whose valet is named Hell and whose servant is named Death. He dies a sudden death (the worst possible death, since it prevents him from contrition and confession) and only his valet and servant bury him. The bishop's prescription—that only hell and death could bury a usurer—was thus duly respected.[59]

Finally, in the fifteenth century, Bernard of Siena orchestrates his version of the usurer's infernal grave theme with the rhetoric of repetition. Since the usurer breaks Christ's law on time by selling that which is common to all creatures, when he dies and Judgment Day comes, "all the saints and all the angels of paradise then cry out against him, saying, 'To hell, to hell, to hell.' Also the heavens with their stars cry out, saying, 'To the fire, to the fire, to the fire.' The planets also clamor, 'To the depths, to the depths, to the depths.' "[60]

In terms of eternal salvation, which was, let me repeat, the essential concern for the great majority of people in the thirteenth century (including usurers), the situation seems dramatic. Only the complicated mechanism of restitution could save some of them; this was technically difficult, however, and presupposed that the usurer had not died intestate. But the choice was not just between heaven (unthinkable for the majority of usurers) and hell. A third path to eternity

57. Ibid. 19.
58. Ibid. 22–23.
59. Ibid. 83 and 139 n. 307.
60. Sermon 45, 3, 3 (Noonan [n. 2 above] 77).

opened up at the end of the twelfth century: purgatory, excised from hell to become an antechamber of heaven.

Of course, from early Christian times the belief existed that one could be saved *post mortem* and that certain actions of the living (alms, prayers, masses) could aid in this posthumous salvation, and especially, could shorten the testing time of purgatorial suffering in the purgatorial fire. But no one knew exactly *where* in the other world this suffering took place. There was no distinction between hell and what was to become purgatory; the mechanics of entering and leaving purgatory were poorly defined. The noun "purgatory," *purgatorium*, did not exist; only the adjective "purgative," used in two expressions, *ignis purgatorius* and *poena(e) purgatoria(e)*. Christians of the High Middle Ages were Manichean in their actual beliefs if not in their official faith. There was no more room for a true "in-between" in the other world than there was room for an intermediate position between powerful and poor, clerics and laity. Around 1140 the Paris theologian Hugh of St. Victor still affirmed that no one knew where purgative punishment took place; and postmortem redemption played only an insignificant role in religious and social life.

The landscape of the other world changed profoundly in the second half of the twelfth century, when "purgatory," the place and the word, appeared. The first person to benefit from it was probably a knight who, protected by St. Patrick, took a trip during his life to purgatory, descending by way of a cave on a lacustrine island in Ireland. King Arthur, too, in the adaptation of his legend in Italy, came to Etna to be purged.[61] Between about 1180 and 1230 the geography of the other world was revolutionized. A new triple abode for those awaiting the Last Judgment replaced the traditional double house of eternity. There had been only hell and heaven before; and for innocent, just but unbaptized souls no better receptacle had been found than Abraham's bosom. Now there were hell, purgatory, heaven, and—separate yet connected—limbo too.

61. Arturo Graf, "Artù nell'Etna," in *Miti, leggendi e superstizioni del Medio Evo* (2 vols. Turin 1892–93; rpt. New York 1971) 2.303–59.

This was a fundamental change, in that the horizon of salvation was everyone's essential preoccupation. The relationship between the living and the dead was remodeled. Helping your suffering loved ones in purgatory became a primary concern of the living. The new goal of a growing number of Christians was, during terrestrial life, if not to open the doors of heaven directly (reserved for a chosen few), at least to escape hell and, by as short a sojourn as possible, to prepare oneself for heaven. Just as threefold division was now recognized in terrestrial society—the *mediocres* appearing between the *maiores* and the *minores* (or the *potentes* and the *pauperes*), and the *laboratores* being added to the *oratores* and the *bellatores*—so three classes of people made up the society of the other world awaiting the Last Day: the triumphant in heaven, the suffering and militant in purgatory, and the outcasts in hell.[62]

In this saving by means of purgatory of many of the personally or professionally damned, the exemplum plays an important role. For with the renewal of preaching, it was through exempla in sermons, through the concrete presentation of sinners succeeding or failing to enter purgatory, that the new belief was popularized and clarified. At length the church recognized it officially, first in a letter of Pope Innocent IV in 1254 and then in the deliberations of the Second Council of Lyon in 1274. Throughout the thirteenth century the new conception of the other world was enriched and sophisticated by the introduction into the spiritual domain of the doctrine of economic accountability, and by the science of casuistry developing in scholastic theology and canon law.

While Dante was still completing his three-part other world in the *Divina commedia*, it was the Cistercian Caesarius of Heisterbach, around 1220, who was the first, to my knowledge, to articulate clearly and systematically the new conception of the "in-between" separating the individual judgment from the Last Judgment. In the preamble to the twelfth and last part

62. On the history, meaning, and implications of this important phenomenon, see my *Naissance du Purgatoire (XII–XIII s.)*, forthcoming.

of the *Dialogus miraculorum*, devoted to the fate of the dead in the other world (*De praemio mortuorum*), he declared:

There are two places prepared by God for all eternity,
in which a man is recompensed for his toil on earth:
heaven and hell. In heaven the just are recompensed, in
hell the damned. . . . But there is also a third place
prepared for certain chosen ones after death, that they
may be purged; and for this reason it is called purgatory.
This purgatory is temporary and lasts only until
Judgment Day. It will be the glory of the good, the
chastisement of the wicked, and by its help those who are
in purgatorial suffering may be aided. I am going to
teach you the essentials with the aid of the following
exempla.

The novice answers: "First show me the tortures of the damned, then the purgatorial sufferings of the good, and finally the glory and joy of the just."[63] In this trilogy of the just, the good, and the damned, the suffering sinners of purgatory are already aligned with the good, the chosen, the saved.

But what is the importance to the usurer of this opening up of purgatory, the antechamber of heaven? He is hell's prey, how could he force heaven's doors without making restitution?

Let us return to this last book of the *Dialogus miraculorum* of Caesarius of Heisterbach, *De praemio mortuorum*. It contains eighteen exempla on hell, seventeen on purgatory, sixteen on heaven. The usurer appears neither in hell nor, obviously, in heaven. The first exemplum concerning purgatory is devoted to him, entitled "Of the Purgatory of a Usurer of Liège":

There was at Liège in our own time a usurer who died,
and the bishop refused to admit him to the cemetery.
His wife went to the Apostolic See and pleaded that he be

63. Caesarius of Heisterbach (n. 39 above) 2.315–16.

accorded the right of burial in the cemetery. The pope refused. So she pleaded: "They tell me, My Lord, that husband and wife should be one, and that St. Paul says the unfaithful husband can be saved by the faithful wife. For everything that my husband did, down to the smallest action, I who am a part of his body will gladly make amends. I am ready to become a recluse and render satisfaction to God for my husband's sins." The cardinals took her side and beseeched the pope to give him the right to be buried in the cemetery. She chose her domicile near her husband's grave and became a recluse, trying day and night by alms, fasts, prayers, and masses to appease God to favor his soul. At the end of seven years her husband appeared to her in black attire and thanked her: "May God repay you for what you have done: for thanks to your ordeal I have been snatched from the depths of hell and from the most terrible chastisements. If for the next seven years I can benefit from similar good works on your part, I will be completely freed." This she did. At the end of that time he reappeared, this time in white garments and with a happy air. He told her: "Thanks to God and to you, just today I have been freed."

The novice who listened to this story was amazed: "How can he have said he was freed from the depths of hell when there can be no redemption in hell?" The monk, that is Caesarius, answered: "The depths of hell here means the bitterness of purgatory. Likewise, the church says in its prayers for the dead, 'Lord Jesus Christ, King of glory, liberate the souls of all the faithful departed from the hands of hell and from the depths of the pit,' etc. . . . It does not pray for the damned, but for the salvageable souls, and 'the hands of hell,' 'the depths of the pit,' or 'the mouth of the lion' all mean the bitterness of purgatory. But the usurer of Liège would not have been delivered from his sufferings if he had not been contrite at the point of death. And I am now going to tell you how God punishes his chosen ones in purgatory for the vice of cupidity."[64]

Without entering into a detailed commentary on this surprising text, let me make three remarks.

1. A pope's decision was necessary to have the usurer interred in Christian ground, and the terms describing purgatory are still borrowed from hell; this shows that the belief in purgatory is relatively new and has not yet passed into common attitudes and practices. The saving of the usurer represents, that is, an exceptional case.

2. The salvation of the usurer is due to the fidelity and devotion of his wife. The fate of the usurer's wife greatly occupied the canonists of the time,[65] but here the situation is completely different and it is simply a question of the fate of the usurer himself.

3. Finally, Caesarius takes the precaution at the end of saying that if the usurer was saved it was certainly because he had repented before dying. But this repentance, of which there is no other proof, comes not even from the *forum internum* of confession but from the *forum internum* of conscience. The door is opened to every kind of supposition, every laxity.

If one looks, then, at the chapters that the *Dialogus*

---

64. Ibid. 335–36. "Septem vero annis expletis, ille ei apparens in veste pulla, gratias egit dicens: Reddat tibi Dominus, quia propter tuos labores erutus sum de profundo inferni, et de poenis maximis. Quod si adhuc aliis septem annis similia beneficia mihi impenderis, omnino liberabor. Quod cum illa fecisset, iterum ei in veste alba et facie iocunda apparens, ait: Gratias Deo et tibi, quia hodie liberatus sum. *Novicius:* Quomodo dixit se liberatum de profundo inferni, cum nulla in eo sit redemptio? *Monachus:* Profundum inferni, acredinem vocat purgatorii. Simile est illud quod Ecclesia orat pro defunctis: Domine Jesu Christe Rex gloriae libera animas omnium fidelium defunctorum de manu inferni et de profundo laci, et cetera. Non orat pro damnatis, sed pro salvandis; et accipitur ibi manus inferni, profundum laci sive os leonis, pro acredine purgatorii. Nequaquam praedictus usurarius fuisset a poenis liberatus, si non habuisset finalem contritionem."

65. See especially Thomas of Chobham (n. 20 above) 506–07, *De uxore feneratoris;* and Baldwin (n. 6 above) 1.305–06.

miraculorum devotes to contrition and to confession, one sees the last chapter confirming a hope that the usurer may be saved.

In the chapter on contrition an exemplum describes the fate of a very rich usurer who, laid out on his deathbed, maintains that he can restore nothing since the main part of his fortune is made up of church treasures which he holds on pledge. A Benedictine abbot, therefore, has him interred in his monastery of black monks and dispenses large amounts of alms for the salvation of his soul. But at night, while the monks are singing psalms around the usurer's casket, four demons spring up on the left. Four angels then appear on the right and a verbal battle of scriptural quotations ensues between them. The angels win and the conquered demons retreat. A novice asks Caesarius if the usurer was saved by his own contrition or by the alms of the monastery. Caesarius replies that without a doubt had the usurer not repented, the alms would have been of little help.[66]

In the chapter on confession, an exemplum tells of a parish priest of St. Martin of Cologne urging a usurer and a murderer, who are chatting together in a corner of his church, to confess. The usurer decides to go first. The priest says, "Friend, you and I are really going to fool the devil today. I ask you only to confess your sins well, to renounce the will to sin, and to follow my advice, and I shall promise you eternal life." The usurer lets himself be convinced, and when he shows his satisfaction after confession the murderer follows his example. No question here of restitution.[67]

If the new belief in purgatory and the new practices resulting from it held so much of interest—so to speak—and importance for the usurer, it is because they defined spiritual perspectives perfectly adapted to his case. Ashley and other historians of the economy and law of the Middle Ages were correct in showing that the church had known from the beginning of the

---

66. Caesarius of Heisterbach (n. 39 above) 1.103–05.
67. Ibid. 169.

thirteenth century how to distinguish illicit usury from licit
commercial practices. But in reality the same man most often
engaged in both, since in general the usurer, the merchant,
and the banker were one and the same man.

Several texts offer enlightening testimony on the com-
plexity of the usurer's business affairs and on the ambiguity
of his social and moral position. From the psychological
perspective of intention, where does licit commerce end and
usury begin? St. Augustine understood the problem; Gratian
summarized it; and Pope Urban III, in the decretal *Consuluit*, adapted it to late twelfth century reality: in the *forum
internum* of confession his admitted desire for usury turned
many a merchant into a usurer.[68] In Peter the Chanter we
have already seen reflected a real situation, the usurer's notary
unable to make the distinction between the *licita* and the
illicita in the proceedings he has handled (see p. 26 above).

Another story is, it must be said, exemplary. It is an
exemplum in the *Dialogus miraculorum* of Caesarius of Heisterbach which mentions Peter the Chanter. Thibaut, a fab-
ulously rich Paris usurer, wished to make restitution by
donating most of his profits to a pious work. Bishop Maurice
de Sully invites him to make a contribution to the rebuilding
of the cathedral of Notre Dame de Paris. But Peter the
Chanter says he must first restore their money to all his victims. Thibaut makes it known in Paris that he is ready to
make restitution. When he has compensated his debtors, he
still has quite a considerable fortune to make a large contribution to the building of the new cathedral.[69] From the end of
the twelfth century, then, usury per se was only part of the
activity of businessmen in economically vigorous cities and
regions.

Finally, an exemplum from the *Tabula exemplorum* tells
the story of a pilgrim usurer whose purse is stolen by a monkey

68. See Baldwin (n. 6 above) 1.273 and 2.193 n. 33. See also n. 9 above.
69. Caesarius of Heisterbach (n. 39 above) 1.107 and Baldwin (n. 6
above) 1.309.

on the boat taking him, no doubt, to the Holy Land. This preternaturally discerning monkey climbs to the top of the mast, opens the purse, and throws out the pieces of silver gained by usury and returns the purse with the legitimately acquired money to the pilgrim.[70]

Only a belief in purgatory and the practices to which it gave rise could permit the exigencies of religion to be thus adapted, by the devices of reparation and the reduction of suffering, to the complexities of a new reality. Certainly not everything is won for the usurer at the beginning of the thirteenth century. Caesarius of Heisterbach, himself a liberal and enlightened mind, still sent most usurers to hell. And the *Tabula exemplorum*, no doubt typical in its attitudes, did not open the doors of heaven to the usurer. The great "reactionaries" of the late Middle Ages—the Dantes, the St. Bernards of Siena— always refused to indulge the usurer. In the *Divina commedia* there are no usurers in purgatory: they are all in hell, at the end of the seventh circle in the rain of fire. They are the sad people ("la gente tresta"), each with a purse hanging perpetually from his neck. On these purses Dante recognized the colors and coats of arms of several noble Italian banking families who were in fact nothing but usurers: Catello Gianfigliazzi, a Florentine who became a banker in France; the Ubriacchi and the Becchi, also Florentines; and a Paduan, Reginaldo Scrovegni, of the family who ordered from Giotto the famous frescoes for the family chapel at Padua.[71]

But with the beginning of the thirteenth century new ideological possibilities emerged. As Caesarius of Heisterbach says so well, in an exemplum depicting not a usurer but—just as serious—a cloistered nun who loses her virginity to a monk: henceforth, purgatory gives us hope;[72] and the hope of salvation opens up for the usurer.

70. *Tabula exemplorum* (n. 22 above) 83.

71. Dante, *Divina commedia*, Inferno XVII. 43–78.

72. Caesarius of Heisterbach (n. 39 above) 2.338: "Cuius hortatu parentes *spe concepta,* coeperunt ei beneficia impendere."

In sum, my claim is neither that a religious or ideological event created the conditions for the economic evolution of the late Middle Ages, nor inversely that the pressure of a new economic situation gave birth to new spiritual superstructures; but rather that, along with the practice of restitution and the evolution of what Benjamin N. Nelson saw as the distinction between the modern usurer (the pawnbroker) and the merchant prince, a third factor, that of salvation through purgatory, played its part in the development of capitalism. The birth of purgatory is also the dawn of banking.

3 The Dawn of Banking in an Italian Commune: Thirteenth Century Lucca

Thomas W. Blomquist

THE TUSCAN CITY OF LUCCA, although overshadowed by her neighbor Florence in the later Middle Ages, was in the thirteenth century the chief center of the silk industry in the West and the hub of a network of mercantile banking partnerships which by 1300 extended to every major European financial and commercial center.[1] Locally, her money changers,

The archival research upon which this study is based was made possible by fellowship support from the American Council of Learned Societies and grants from the Penrose Fund, the American Philosophical Society, and The Dean's Fund, Northern Illinois University. To each I am deeply grateful.

1. Two excellent surveys of medieval Italian commercial and business history are Robert S. Lopez, "The Trade of Medieval Europe: The South," *Cambridge Economic History of Europe*, ed. Michael M. Postan et al. 2 (Cambridge 1952) 257–534, and Raymond de Roover, "The Organization of Trade," ibid. 3 (Cambridge 1963) 42–104. Robert S. Lopez, *The Commercial Revolution of the Middle Ages, 950–1350* (Englewood Cliffs, N.J. 1971) presents an analytical survey of the European economy in the High Middle Ages, while John K. Hyde, *Society and Politics in Medieval Italy: The Evolution of the Civil Life 1000–1350*

at first catering primarily to foreign visitors—pilgrims flocking along the Via Francigena to Rome and those pausing to venerate the local icon, *Il Volto Santo,* or merchants needing to exchange foreign currency brought from abroad—had moved beyond manual exchange and dealings in bullion into the area of deposit and transfer banking.[2] Both abroad and at home, men of Lucca were in the forefront of the Commercial Revolution of the thirteenth century as essential protagonists in the early history of European banking and credit.[3]

Fortunately, the state archive and the archiepiscopal and capitular archives of Lucca preserve a mass of notarial materials in which the development of banking techniques as well as the organization of the local capital market can be traced.[4] This essay summarizes my findings after extensive work with these documents; it will be followed by a more comprehensive account later.

In thirteenth century Lucca two groups of professional

(New York 1973), provides a recent synthesis of Italian urban history in the communal period. For Lucca, Thomas W. Blomquist, "Commercial Association in Thirteenth Century Lucca," *Business History Review* 45 (1971) 157–78.

2. Thomas W. Blomquist, "The Castracani Family of Thirteenth-Century Lucca," *Speculum* 46 (1971) 459–76, examines the history of a family of Lucchese changers.

3. On the concept of a "commercial revolution of the thirteenth century," see Raymond de Roover, "The Commercial Revolution of the Thirteenth Century," *Bulletin of the Business Historical Society* 16 (1942) 34–39.

4. For a description of the Lucchese notarial archives housed in the *Archivio di Stato di Lucca* (hereafter *ASL*) see Robert S. Lopez, "The Unexplored Wealth of the Notarial Archives of Pisa and Lucca," *Mélanges d'histoire du Moyen Age dédiés à la mémoire de Louis Halphen* (Paris 1951) 417–32. Eugenio Lazzareschi, "L'Archivio dei Notari della Repubblica lucchese," *Gli archivi italiani* 2 (1915) 175–210, catalogues the cartularies. On the archiepiscopal and chapter archives, see Sac. Giuseppe Ghilarducci, *Le biblioteche e gli archivi arcivescovili e capitolari della Diocesi di Lucca* (Lucca 1969) and Duane J. Osheim, "The Episcopal Archive of Lucca in the Middle Ages," *Manuscripta* 17 (1973) 131–46. The information regarding the money changers is derived primarily from the LL series in the chapter archive (hereafter LL).

bankers may be distinguished. The first, the money changers, had already flourished a long time before our sources allow anything like a detailed analysis of their business. The second, merchants engaged in long-range commerce, were perfecting the financial techniques and business organization upon which thirteenth century international commerce and finance were to rest. Although the process was by no means complete, the money changers were evolving into deposit and transfer bankers at the same time the international merchants increasingly generated commercial credit by routine dealings in foreign exchange. For Lucca, this was a formative period in which deposit and transfer banking was maturing side by side with international exchange banking.

The art of money changing was a venerable one in Lucca. In 1111 the oath required of all money changers (*campsores*) or spice dealers (*speciarii*) wishing to set up shop in the cathedral square was inscribed upon the façade of the cathedral of San Martino, where it can still be seen today.[5] The oath, in which the changers and dealers in spices swore to commit "no theft, nor trick nor falsification," was also visible to their customers, who thronged the cathedral square to change money or to buy exotic herbs and medicines at the portable tables and stalls set up there. No other twelfth century reference to money changers is to be found in the Lucchese sources; however, one can infer that the primary activity of campsores in this earlier period was manual exchange, which by its nature did not involve a contract and hence the intervention of a notary. Although manual exchange certainly continued as an essential service of the money changers, by the thirteenth century they were adding other functions to their repertory.

The cathedral square remained the center of the changers' activities throughout the Middle Ages. Outdoor business was

5. Eugenio Lazzareschi, "Fonti d'archivio per lo studio delle corporazioni artigiane di Lucca," *Bollettino storico lucchese* 9 (1937) 78. The inscription is translated in Robert S. Lopez and Irving W. Raymond, *Medieval Trade in the Mediterranean World* (New York and London 1955) 418–19.

conducted from a seat behind a portable table (*tavola* or
mensula), probably covered by a canopy. The ground upon
which the table stood was either owned or leased by the
changer.[6] Whether all money changers maintained outdoor
tables is problematical; I tend to doubt it. Much of the
changers' business was conducted from shops, *apothece*,
ranged in houses fronting upon the Court of San Martino,
which also served as offices and supply depots for the various
campsores and their associates.[7] Considerable business was conducted in a tower, also fronting on the square, which belonged
to the Passavanti, a patrician family long associated with the
money changers' profession.[8] In fact, the tower seems to have
been an informal gathering place for the changers, and it was
here in the *turre (Passavantis)*, as it was familiarly styled in
the contracts, that the money changers guild held its meetings.[9]

Precisely when the changers organized themselves into a
corporate body is not known. The oath of 1111 makes no men-

6. See *Archivio capitolare*, LL 5, fol. 81v, 14 Oct. 1230 for the one-
year rental of a *locum campsorum* to Bonconsilius Genovensis at an
annual rent of 40s. Lucchese; LL 23, fol. 73v, 23 April 1249 for the
cathedral chapter's formal possession of the table bequeathed to it by
Quiricus Sciagri, which was under the porch of the cathedral and in
front of the table belonging to Rogerius Castracanis; LL 28, fol. 150v,
24 Oct. 1254 for Gerardus Arzuri's rental of a table, formerly belonging
to Genovese Anticus, which was next to the door of the cathedral and
"against the ground and table of the late Pilius Castracanis" ("qui est
contra locum et tabulam quondam Pilii Castracanis iuxta portam S.
Martini"). See also Blomquist, "Castracani" (n. 2 above) 463–64 for the
purchase of a table and ground in 1252 by Rogerius and Luccerius
Castracanis for £15 from Bonifatius Ubertelli Baiori.

7. LL 20, fol. 43v, 8 April 1245: "Actum Luce in apotheca ubi Vethus
moratur ad cambium"; LL 36, fol. 33, 7 June 1271: "Actum Luce in
apotheca cambii ipsius Castracanis."

8. Rolandus Passavantis owned ground and a table in 1172: LL 27,
fol. 18v, 10 Nov. 1252. In 1245 the changer Albertinus Malagallie married the daughter of Orlandus Passavantis: LL 20, fol. 7v, 13 Jan. On
10 March 1251, Orlandus and his brother, Genovese, elected their third
brother "captain or consul" of their clan (*domus*): LL 26, fol. 82.

9. Elections of the consuls of the changers guild were held in the
tower: LL 11, fol. 4, 7 Feb. 1236, . . . *in turre Passavantis;* fol. 69v, 20
Jan. 1237, . . . *in turre;* fol. 160, 30 Jan. 1238, . . . *in turre Passavantis.*

tion of a corporate organization. A document dated 7 February 1236 refers to the assumption of office by Bonconsilius Genovensis and Ubertus Rodolosi, "the new consuls of the money changers of the Court of Saint Martin" (*novi consules campsorum curie Sancti Martini*).[10] The guild itself, referred to simply as "the exchange of Saint Martin" (*cambium Sancti Martini*), had its office in, or near, the cathedral proper.[11] The guild maintained a small treasury which was entrusted to the incumbent consuls and passed on to their successors. In 1236 Bonconsilius and Ubertus received £21 5s. Lucchese from their predecessors in office; a year later they handed over to Pilius *quondam* Castracanis and Galganectus *filius* Gulielmi Genovensis, the new consuls for 1237, the diminished sum of £11 19s., "since no more remained after the old consuls had paid all expenses" ("cum non essent plures qui remanissent suprascriptis veteris consulibus factis et solutis omnibus expensis ab eis").[12] But in the next year, 1238, Genovese *filius* Gulielmi and Ubertus Maghiari Cipoletta were entrusted with a treasury, probably swelled by dues, fines, or both, of £14 18s.[13]

Unfortunately it is impossible to give any exact figures for the size of the money changers guild. However, the cartulary of Ser Ciabatto, who plied his trade in the environs of Saint Martin and who numbered a host of changers among his clients, records the names of fifty known or presumed money changers for the period 1236–38.[14] Ciabatto's cartularies surviving from the decade of the thirties contain the names of sixty-eight individuals who, even if not explicitly styled *campsor*, nonetheless repeatedly engaged in activities connected with the art.[15] In the forty-one-year period 1230–71,

10. LL 11, fol. 4.
11. LL 11, fol. 67v, 10 Jan. 1236, "Actum Luce ante ecclesiam S. Martini apud cambium"; fol. 28v, 20 June 1236, "Actum Luce sub porticu cambii in Curia S. Martini"; LL 32, fol. 17, 8 Feb. 1259, "Actum Luce apud cambium S. Martini."
12. LL 11, fol. 69v.
13. LL 11, fol. 160.
14. LL 11, passim.
15. LL 5 through LL 11 inclusive.

the names of some 103 campsores turn up.[16] We may surmise
that the number of changers working at any one time was
slightly less than fifty.

Apparently common guild membership and professional
interests were often reinforced by intermarriage between the
families of changers. For example, Castracane *filius* Rugerii
in 1250 married Diamante, daughter of Durassus Durassi
campsor.[17] Felicita, daughter of the changer Gerardus Maghiari, was the widow of another money changer, Perfectus
Schlacte.[18] Genovese Gulielmi, who had been consul of the
money changers guild in 1238, was the nephew of the campsor
Passavante Guidocti, while the latter's son, Genovese, married
the daughter of the changer Genovese Lupardi.[19] The list
is by no means exhaustive, but we may still cite one Jacobus
quondam Gerardi. His half-sister Columba was the daughter
of the changer Arrigus Rape and he, Jacobus, was the nephew
of Gulielmus Genovensis, who apparently belonged to a
veritable clan of money changers.[20]

While the organization of the money changers' business
seems family oriented, individual changers occasionally pooled
their resources in partnership. Such enterprises were also
small, characteristically involving two or perhaps three
changers. The earliest instance of partnership I have un-
covered is dated 27 November 1230 and shows only three
"partners of the table" (*socii tabule*).[21] The term of individual
partnership arrangements was usually short, three months to a
year. But once two changers came together they tended to stay

16. LL 2 through LL 36 inclusive.
17. LL 24, fol. 70.
18. LL 21, fol. 102, 21 Sept. 1246.
19. For Genovese and Passavante, see LL 5, fol. 84, 25 Oct. 1230.
20. Jacobus *quondam* Gerardi was the son of Berta, the widow of
Arrigus Rape: LL 5, fol. 27v, 29 Jan. 1230. Arrigus Rape's daughter,
Columba, was married to Orlandinus Guasconis: LL 5, fol. 27v and
LL 6, fol. 6, fol. 37, 28 Aug. 1230. In LL 8, fol. 4, 11 Jan. 1231, Columba
is described as Jacobus's *sorella* (sister). Jacobus, in turn, was Gulielmus
Genovensis's nephew: LL 11, fol. 71v, 17 Feb. 1237.
21. LL 5, fol. 87v.

together for a considerable time by successively drawing up new partnership arrangements. Thus, Bertaloctus Painella was in partnership with Vethus *campsor quondam* Deotifeci in 1230,[22] and when the two dissolved a partnership in the year 1243 their relationship was described as being of long standing (*per longum tempus*).[23] Similarly, the changers Castracane Rugerii and Genovese Perfectuccii augmented their working capital through a series of short-term partnership arrangements which spanned the period 1256–71.[24]

If the number of partners jointly operating a *tabula* remained small throughout the thirteenth century, their capitalization tended to increase. In 1249 the brothers Guido and Genovese formed a *societatem de arte cambii* with a working capital of £200.[25] But when Guido entered into three successive partnerships with the brothers Castracani and Luccerius Castracanis in 1254, 1255, and 1256, the average capitalization amounted to £936 6s. 8d.[26] And in the last of the known associations formed by Genovese and Castracani in 1271, the capital conferred by the partners amounted to £3,800.[27] Yet even when partnerships had been contracted and considerable capital committed to them, the partners continued to act on their own behalf as well as in partnership affairs. The changers considered themselves essentially individual entrepreneurs, who combined with their confreres when opportunity and circumstances dictated, but they desired above all to maintain their freedom of economic action.

Archival materials tell us something of how the money changers' profession was organized as well as where and under what circumstances they worked. The changers' common non-banking involvements in urban and rural real estate, investment in livestock, and mining or mercantile enterprises must

22. LL 5, fol. 69v, 28 Aug. 1230; fol. 70, 3 Sept. 1230.
23. LL 17, fol. 86, 16 Sept. 1243.
24. Blomquist, "Castracani" (n. 2 above) 464–66.
25. LL 23, fol. 78, 5 May 1249.
26. Blomquist, "Castracani" (n. 2 above) 464–66.
27. Ibid.

have occupied a good deal of time.[28] What were their activities in the field of finance and credit, and what role did they play in the history of early banking?

We need not dwell upon the money changers' function as literal changers of money since there is no way to gauge the extent, and therefore the importance, of this activity; save to say that campsores, stationed at their tables, continued manually to exchange petty foreign coin into legal Lucchese tender. The contracts do, however, show changers occasionally lending sums in foreign coin to clients;[29] unfortunately, we do not know the purpose to which this capital was put before being repaid to the changer. At the same time, the money changers dealt extensively in gold and silver, either worked into leaves and thread or in bullion form.[30] In this commerce they co-operated closely with the gold-beaters, to whom they sold the refined metal and from whom they also secured for resale the finely worked thread and leaves used to enhance the more luxurious of Lucchese silk cloth.[31] Some changers were also

28. See ibid. for the "outside" business and investments of the Castracani. Their activities appear to have been typical.

29. See inter alia LL 5, fols. 46, 2 April 1230; 47v, 15 May 1230; 69v, 28 Aug. 1230; 85, 26 Oct. 1230; 87v, 27 Nov. 1230; LL 11, fols. 5, 29 Jan. 1236; 16, 26 Mar. 1236; 138, 20 Oct. 1237; 257v, 5 Nov. 1238; 235, 8 Aug. 1238; LL 17, fol. 22v, 19 Mar. 1243; LL 25, fols. 116, n.d., 1250; 125, 1 Dec. 1250; LL 27, fols. 43v, 3 Jan. 1256; 45, 5 Feb. 1256; 48, 17 Feb. 1256; 48v, 8 Mar. 1256; LL 33, fol. 136v, 31 Jan. 1269.

30. LL 11, fol. 165, 17 Feb. 1238; LL 20, fol. 35, 16 Mar. 1245 and 17 Mar. 1245; LL 21, fols. 24, 24 Feb. 1246; 28, 5 Mar. 1246; 39v, 28 Mar. 1246; 41, 28 Mar. 1246; 77v, 25 July 1246; 98v, 15 Sept. 1246; LL 23, fols. 55v, 3 Mar. 1249; 66v, 27 Mar. 1249; LL 24, fol. 95, 2 Sept. 1250; LL 25, fol. 116v, 28 Nov. 1250; LL 27, fols. 31, 13 May 1253; 34, 13 May 1253; 121v, 26 Sept. 1252; LL 28, fols. 3, 2 June 1254; 127, 31 Aug. 1254. Also see LL 20, fol. 74, 20 June 1245, in which Benectus Puliti rented out a silver smelter, *furnum argenti.*

31. In 1259, one Ugolinus Gulielmi *magister* agreed to work all the gold and silver which Castracane Rugerii supplied him. In 1266, Castracane, Genovese Perfectuccii, and Barocchus Barocchi, all three of whom were changers, formed a partnership with the gold-beater Rubertinus Bonaventure who was obliged to work into leaves, *folia*, all the gold and silver supplied him by the partnership: Blomquist, "Castracani" (n. 2 above) 466 n. 33. Also ibid. 467 n. 34, for the dealings of Luccerius Castracanis in wrought gold and silver.

involved in mining silver in the nearby mountains of Versilia.[32]

The evidence is tantalizingly vague regarding the changers' relationship to the mint and hence to the flow of specie. Although a technical knowledge of the minting process is suggested by the Lucchese changer Barocchus Barocchi's undertaking to make dies and strike coins in Arezzo and Perugia,[33] the fact remains that no evidence links the changers to the Lucchese mint. Indeed, the only direct evidence for the operation of the Lucchese mint, the 1308 Statute of the Commune of Lucca, states that the changers were to have nothing to do with the striking of coin;[34] monetary policy was to be defined in the Great Council of the Commune and carried out by the chief executive, the *Podestà*.[35] We must remember, however, that the statute of 1308 was produced by the Black faction which came to power in the wake of the popular rebellion of 1300.[36] Many of its provisions therefore must be interpreted as reactions against the policies of the defeated, merchant banker dominated, regime. Explicitly banning the money changers from the minting process could well have been the response to what the popular regime viewed as an untoward influence by the changers in the administration of the mint. At the same time, vesting the Great Council with the formulation of monetary policy has a populist ring to it, and this accords with the spirit of the document. For in addition to

32. Benectus Puliti possessed an *argenteria* in Versilia as well as a smelter for silver and iron: LL 24, fol. 70v, 25 Jan. 1250. For the Castracani involvement in silver mining, see Blomquist, "Castracani" (n. 2 above) 462–63, 466.

33. LL 33, fol. 66, 3 Oct. 1266, and LL 24, fol. 78, 2 April 1250.

34. Salvatore Bongi and Leone Del Prete, eds., *Statuto del Comune di Lucca dell'anno MCCCVIII* (Lucca 1867) 26: "et nullus campsor lucanus habere debeat in dicta moneta lucana aliquod officium."

35. Ibid. The Statute provides that "dictam monetam laborari faciam [the incoming *Podestà*] continue, exceptis diebus festivis et solepnibus, bona fide, sine fraude in loco Curte Regis, ubi consuetum est fieri, si a maiori parte Consilii et invitatorum fuerit iudicatum."

36. For a contemporary account of the events of 1300, see Bernhard Schmeidler, ed., *Tholomei lucensis annales*, Monumenta germaniae historica, Scriptores rerum germanicarum, n.s. 8 (Berlin 1930) 318–19.

the provisions regarding money, the Black faction brought the
Collegium mercatorum under its scrutiny and sharply curtailed the political prerogatives of those adherents to the defeated White party—to which all the mercantile banking
families belonged—who abjured exile and remained in Lucca.[37]
In other words, it seems justifiable to conclude that the statute
provisions of 1308 reflect conditions somewhat different regarding the mint—and the changers' relationship to it—than those
existing in the thirteenth century. We should not, then, ex-
clude on the basis of the statute the likelihood that the
changers were suppliers of bullion to the mint. Certainly the
very nature of the profession required that they retire worn
or clipped coins, as well as some foreign issues, to the mint.[38]
These responsibilities must have been spelled out in the lost
guild statutes.

But, while the exact nature of the campsores' dealings with
the mint and their role in determining the money supply remain obscure, their activities as bankers in the thirteenth
century are relatively well documented. Our sources show
them regularly accepting deposits from their clients. Deposits,
just as today, took various forms. The changers augmented
their working capital through time and demand deposits, with
a variant on the latter resembling the continental *depôts à
préavis*. The contracts of deposit varied in their terminology:
depositum seu accomandiscia, accomandiscia seu prestantia,
and *mutuum seu prestantia* were used indiscriminately to
describe a deposit with a changer, and the exact character of

37. Bongi and Del Prete (n. 34 above) 153. The guild could meet
only in the church of San Cristoforo or the *Curia mercatorum*. The
merchants could not appear before the *Podestà* or in the Council of
the Commune without the express permission of those authorities. Nor
could the guild have a notary who was not a member of the popular
militia organization, *societas armorum*. Also see ibid. 241–44 for a list
of those families branded *casastici* and *potentes*.

38. Ibid. Changers were required, on pain of a £100 fine, to destroy
false coins. Only coins equal to the Florentine *à piccioli* were allowed
to circulate.

the deposit was spelled out in the details of the contract.

The thirteen contracts of deposit that survive from the decade of the 1230s indicate that persons making deposits at the changers' tables came from the middle to upper range of the social strata. We find two judges and a successful merchant along with an artisan and a *magister scolarum* investing capital through the medium of deposit at a changer's bank.[39] And we also find the changers Arrigus Durassi and Gerardus Arzuri investing a portion of the estates of their respective wards at the banks of Genovese *anticus quondam* Aldibrandini and Talliabove and Marcoaldus Perfecti.[40] The total amount placed in this fashion came to £390, or an average per deposit of £32 10s. By contrast, the eighty contracts reflecting the changer's loans in the same period totaled £489 3s. 3d. and averaged £6 2s. 3d. for each loan. These figures conform to the general pattern of borrowing and lending established by the Castracani family in their exchange dealings between 1254 and 1274, with deposits averaging £96 6s. 6d. per individual deposit and loans amounting to £22 12s.[41] Although the ratio of loan size to deposit is somewhat lower in the case of the Castracani than for the earlier period, it is clear from these figures that the size of deposits consistently averaged about five times that of the loans made by the campsores. Moreover, deposits were held for a relatively long term. Time deposits varied in length from three months to a year, while the term of depôt à préavis and demand deposits depended on the needs and wishes of the depositors. In general, the changers accepted few demand deposits, preferring, it would seem, the more or less fixed terms to the unpredictable demand deposit. The time deposit allowed the changer to gauge his roll-over of capital and thus to maintain a lower fractional reserve than

39. LL 11, fol. 235v, 7 Aug. 1238: Aldibrandinus *judex quondam* Leonardi; fol. 230v, 27 July 1238: Aldebrandinus *judex* Malagallie; fol. 257v, 5 Nov. 1238: *Magister* Guido *quondam magistri* Bonaiuncte; fol. 44v, 7 Oct. 1236: Fiamingus *quondam* Orlandi Mosche; fol. 49, 13 Nov.; and fol. 251, 11 Sept. 1236: Benvenutus magister scolarum.

40. LL 11, fols. 262v, 30 Nov., and 168, 14 Feb. 1238.

41. Blomquist, "Castracani" (n. 2 above) 468.

would have been possible had his funds been subject to recall on demand.

As we have seen, the typical changer's loans were smaller in size but greater in frequency than were his deposit transactions. Loans were also consistently of shorter duration than deposit arrangements: the changers borrowed long and lent short. Contractually, these were straight loans, *mutua*; most were made to socially obscure persons from both city and country. Indeed, the peasantry constituted a favored target of the changers' lending. Loans to the peasantry were relatively safe since they involved the peasants' crops as security—and crops could not disappear. The peasant borrowed cash at the *tavola*, small sums to tide him over or to purchase seed or tools, but obligated himself to repay in kind—either grain or wine—at harvest or vintage time. Such loans were not only safe, they were profitable. Although in the absence of price lists for grain and wine we cannot be sure of the profit on these agricultural loans, the price fixed at the time of the loan was likely to be pegged lower than that expected at harvest.[42] In the Florentine *contado* such lending returned a profit of 30%.[43] This was clearly exploitative and may in part explain the money changers' extensive holdings of rural land.[44] Only one instance survives of a changer foreclosing on a peasant, but we may surmise that some, if not most, of the changers' rural holdings were acquired by seizure for debt or bought on favorable terms from a vulnerable peasantry.[45] But

42. On 20 Nov. 1234, one Albertinus Orsecti appealed to the archdeacon, claiming that he had been usuriously victimized by Biancone Overardi, who may have been a changer, in the sale of grain made to Biancone ("de dando ei granum quod ei vendidit et que venditio facta fuit in fraudem usurarum"). Interestingly, although no details are given, Albertinus's plea was denied and he was ordered to pay £6 and one *modium* of grain to Biancone within four months. See LL 9, fol. 12.

43. David Herlihy, "Santa Maria Impruneta: A Rural Commune in the Late Middle Ages," *Florentine Studies,* ed. Nicolai Rubinstein (Evanston, Ill. 1968) 262.

44. On the rural holdings of the Castracani, see Blomquist, "Castracani" (n. 2 above) 462–63.

45. LL 11, fol. 50v, 18 Nov. 1236.

the impact of urban credit and credit mechanisms upon the structure of the Lucchese countryside is all too seldom visible in our sources.

The occupations of the campsores' debtors in the city are difficult to define since many borrowers appear in the documents only once and are otherwise unidentifiable. Yet their very anonymity suggests that they belonged on the lower rungs of the social ladder. In the city as in the country most loans were straight loans, mutua. But not infrequently the changers accepted articles of clothing, utensils, or even horses in pledge against a loan.[46] To be sure, we are witnessing in these "consumption" loans, credit transfer at a very modest level, yet this aspect of the changers' business must have been, in the aggregate, of considerable economic and social consequence.

On the other hand, the evidence suggests that changers were active in supplying capital, around mid-century, to the nascent mercantile banking organizations. At least some merchants in international commerce used such services.[47] These larger advances to the commercial community reveal the money changers channeling the savings of the non-business sector into the economically productive one of industry and trade. Although no absolute quantitative conclusions can be drawn, I think some examples make the case. On two occasions in 1245, Panfollia and Albertinus *quondam* Rustici Guinigi, founders of the Guinigi family fortunes and the mercantile banking partnership bearing their family name, borrowed £100 and £50 respectively from the money changer Gerardus Arzuri.[48] Similarly, in the same year, Perfectus Ricciardi *quondam* Gratiani, the founder of what at the end of the century would be one of the most powerful merchant banking partnerships in Europe, the *Societas Ricciardorum*, received

46. For loans with a pledge, see inter alia LL 8, fols. 18v, 13 Mar. 1231; 73, 4 April 1231; LL 11, fols. 16v, 4 April 1236; 59v, 3 Jan. 1237; LL 18, fols. 30v, 15 March 1244; 81, 3 Sept. 1244; LL 21, fol. 69v, 28 June 1246; LL 23, fol. 14, 13 Nov. 1249; LL 33, fol. 31v, 10 Dec. 1265.

47. Cf. Blomquist, "Commercial Association" (n. 1 above) for a discussion of the large-scale Lucchese partnerships.

48. LL 20, fols. 74v, 21 June 1245, and 146v, 12 Dec. 1245.

on 27 January and 4 March loans of £100 and £200.[49] Also on 27 January, Perfectus borrowed £150 from the changers Soldanus, Gerardus, and Uguiccione Maghiari.[50] Given the woefully fragmentary nature of our sources, these instances—not in themselves particularly imposing—may be only a small fraction of similar but now lost transactions.

Enough scattered evidence from Lucca exists for us to conclude that the changers paid interest on deposits.[51] The rate is hard to ascertain, since medieval lenders were extremely chary of stating in contractual form the return to be gained from a loan. But one surviving contract shows the money changer Gerardus Arzuri accepting a deposit of £50 on 17 March 1230 from the guardians of the minor heirs of Ubertus *quondam* Bugianese and promising to pay £6, or 12%, annually in interest.[52]

Transfer banking, in retrospect perhaps the most significant of the money changers' activities, is the hardest to detect in the Lucchese sources. My reading of the sources indicates that the money changers did, to a limited degree, clear their clients' obligations by transferring debts on their books. Compared to

49. LL 20, fol. 57.

50. LL 20, fols. 13 and 25v. On the Ricciardi in England, see Emilio Re, "La compagnia dei Riccardi in Inghilterra e il suo fallimento alla fine del secolo XIII," *Archivio della Società Romana di Storia Patria* 37 (1914), and, more recently, Richard W. Kaeuper, *Bankers to the Crown: The Riccardi of Lucca and Edward I* (Princeton 1973). Cf. Thomas W. Blomquist, "Administration of a Thirteenth-Century Mercantile Banking Partnership: An Episode in the History of the Ricciardi of Lucca," *Revue internationale d'histoire de la banque* 7 (1973) 1–9.

51. See my remarks on usury in "De Roover on Business, Banking and Economic Thought," *Journal of Economic History* 35 (1975) 825–26.

52. LL 5, fol. 57. Volume 1 of the *Inventario del Reale Archivio di Stato in Lucca*, ed. Salvatore Bongi (4 vols. Lucca 1872), held by the Newberry Library of Chicago, contains on p. 210 a marginal note, written in a nineteenth century Italian hand, citing a parchment document of 1304 to the effect that 12% was recognized by statute as a legal return ("interesse o benefecio") on a loan: "Da pergamena 5 Dic. 1304 della Certosa si cava che, per lo Statuto vigente allora l'interesse o beneficio del denaro era stabilito al 12% l'anno."

Genoa, however, where as early as 1200 a client could order a banker to settle a debt by merely crediting the amount owed to his creditor's account in bank,[53] in Lucca this clearing function did not become routinized during the thirteenth century. In Lucca such transactions required recourse to a notary rather than simple entry in the banker's books. On 14 October 1245, for example, the changer Albertinus *quondam* Aldebrandini Malagallie acknowledged that he had received from the campsor Genovese Anticus the sum of £15 Lucchese from those £44 which Goldus and Bonagiunta *quondam* Bonaccursi Ronthi owed to him, Albertinus, and his brother.[54] In other words, Albertinus was being reimbursed from the account maintained with Genovese by Goldus and Bonagiunta, which would in this case accordingly be debited in the amount of £15. On 23 January 1245, the changer Soldanus Gerardi paid £50 owed to the cathedral chapter by another changer, Gerardus Maghiari.[55] In neither case was the changer acting explicitly as an agent for his client. This business indicates that the changers kept drawing accounts with one another in order to facilitate settlement of debts through bank transfer.

The conclusion that settlement by transfer was becoming increasingly common is supported by evidence that the changers posted credits to clients' accounts from payments by third parties at the changers' banks. In 1256 Castracane Rugerii, mentioned earlier, stipulated in a notarial contract to Savariscius Ubaldi Rainerii that he, Castracane, had received on behalf of the notary £84 from the *sindicus* of Controne, £30 from the Commune of Lucca, £21 from one Bonaccorsus de Batone, and £30 as partial payment due from Custor Battosi; and that he, Castracane, was as a result in the debt of

53. Robert S. Lopez, *La prima crisi della banca di Genova (1250–1259)* (Milan 1956) 28–29, and R. L. Reynolds, "A Business Affair in Genoa in the Year 1200; Banking, Bookkeeping, a Broker and a Lawsuit," *Studi di storia e diritto in onore di Enrico Besta* (4 vols. Milan 1939) 2.7–19.

54. LL 20, fol. 116v.

55. LL 20, fol. 12.

Savariscius for £165, the total of these sums.[56] Although
nothing directly indicates that the campsores routinely allowed
overdrafts to their clients, given the existence of transfer it
would be logical for a changer to permit such credit extension
by merely posting an entry to the client's debit column. In
fact, some of the notarial contracts recording the existence of
debt to a changer may have arisen from a prior overdraft. In
any case, the activities of the Lucchese changers—acceptance of
deposits, supplying "consumer" and commercial credit, facilitating debt clearance through transfer, and (possibly) creating
credit by allowing overdrafts—clearly served to rationalize the
distribution of credit and to focus purchasing power where it
was needed.

The field of the money changers, as they provided credit
services to the populace at large, was essentially local. Some
campsores, however, such as Gerardus Arzuri or Aldebrandinus Malagallie, did leave their native city for extended so-
journs north of the Alps to engage in petty moneylending and
pawnbroking among the cash-poor inhabitants of the smaller
rural towns and settlements, principally in the county of
Champagne.[57] But Italian international commerce in the
course of the thirteenth century was becoming ever more
concentrated in the hands of "big business"—that is, the large-
scale, centrally directed mercantile banking partnerships that
were making their appearance in all the major towns of north
and central Italy around the mid-thirteenth century. Lucca
was no exception in the willingness of her merchants to explore new ways to respond to the challenges of economic opportunity. By 1284 there were twenty-two identifiable large-
scale partnerships engaging in international trade and commerce through partners or agents representing them in foreign
markets.[58] Eleven of these organizations were designated by
the papacy as depositories of papal funds collected abroad and

56. Blomquist, "Castracani" (n. 2 above) 468.
57. LL 30, fol. 94v, 2 Dec. 1245, and LL 31, fol. 164, 4 Dec. 1258.
58. See Blomquist, "Commercial Association" (n. 1 above) for these
partnerships.

as such were among the wealthiest and most powerful business organizations operating in the West.[59]

Here we can deal only with the banking and credit functions of these large-scale partnerships, putting aside the more detailed study of their complex business with the reminder that in the unspecialized Middle Ages commerce and finance went hand in hand. Among the fragmentary and scattered references to international exchange banking in the surviving notarial materials, one piece of evidence stands out. In 1284 the notary Bartolomeus Fulcieri and his two sons Tegrimus and Fulcierus were active among a clientele drawn almost exclusively from the ranks of international merchants and financiers of Lucca.[60] The cartulary which they produced, chronologically complete for the year, numbers among its 506 folio pages and thousands of individual agreements some 205 rough drafts of contracts, *instrumenta ex causa cambii*, reflecting foreign exchange dealings of Lucchese merchant bankers in the great cycle of Champagne fairs. Representing only a fraction of the total banking business between Lucca and Champagne, these documents provide the fullest, most concentrated, and earliest evidence for the workings of an international banking place.

International banking developed in tandem with international money markets and the techniques of foreign exchange. Lucchese merchants as early as 1200 had developed considerable skill in financing commerce by recourse to foreign exchange. As an industrial center, Lucca was particularly dependent upon Genoa as port of entry for raw silk and dye stuffs to feed her burgeoning silk industry.[61] In order to ex-

59. Ibid. 159.

60. On the Fulcieri, see ibid. 172–73.

61. For the Lucchese in Genoa: Florence M. Edler, "The Silk Trade of Lucca during the Thirteenth and Fourteenth Centuries" (Ph.D. diss. University of Chicago 1930) 116–23; Domenico Gioffrè, "L'attività economica dei Lucchesi a Genova fra il 1190 e il 1280," *Lucca archivistica, storica, economica: relazioni e comunicazioni al XV Congresso Nazionale Archivistico, Lucca, Ottobre 1969* (Rome 1973) 94–111; and M. Baldovini, "Santa Croce di Sarzano ed i mercanti lucchesi a Genova (sec. XIII–XIV)," *Atti della Società Ligure di Storia Patria* n.s. 2 (1962) 76–96.

pedite this traffic, a group of Lucchese resident in Genoa
began to advance Genoese funds to their conationals visiting
the Ligurian port to secure silk, dyes, and other wares for export to their city. In return, the visiting merchant would hand
over a notarial instrument in which he promised repayment
in Lucca to the lender's agent or partner, usually within two
or three weeks, of a sum in Lucchese coin equivalent to that
received in Genoa.[62]

The other major terminus of Lucchese trade and finance
was the entrepôt centered upon the annual cycle of six great
fairs held in the county of Champagne at the towns of Troyes,
Provins, Bar-sur-Aube, and Lagny.[63] The Lucchese were the
first Tuscan merchants, and among the first Italians, to be in
regular contact with ultramontane Europe. As early as 1153,
Genoa granted to the merchants of Lucca the privilege of
traversing Genoese territory on their way to and from the
"northern fairs."[64] We may assume a traffic already in existence, perhaps of long standing, in which Lucchese silks constituted the bulk of wares moving north, with cloth of
northern manufacture the dominant commodity on the return
journey. In this early commerce, the merchant customarily
accompanied his wares and was able to supervise their sale
and the reinvestment of the proceeds for export to Italy. But
by the late twelfth century, merchants were beginning to rely
upon partners or agents to handle their affairs abroad. In the
following century these practices were institutionalized by the
emergence of the large-scale international mercantile banking
partnership which maintained permanent foreign representa-
tion through partners or employees, termed *factors* in the
Lucchese sources, stationed abroad.[65]

Accompanying the expansion of international commerce
between Lucca and northern Europe was the development in
Lucca of an organized money market based upon the fairs of

62. Blomquist, "Castracani" (n. 2 above) 471–72.
63. Gioffrè (n. 61 above) 95–96.
64. The treaty is published in Cesare Imperiale, ed., *Il Codice diplomatico della Repubblica di Genova* 1 (Rome 1936) no. 238.
65. De Roover, "Organization" (n. 1 above) 70–76.

Champagne. It should be emphasized, perhaps, that Lucchese merchants dealing in Lucca with northern Europe did so exclusively through the fairs. Exchange transactions drawing upon other places are extremely rare in the Lucchese material. Furthermore, the Lucchese international money market served the needs of the Lucchese mercantile community and, unlike Genoa, did not attract many foreign merchant bankers.

Although the primary function of exchange was the transfer of funds from one place to another, medieval dealings in foreign exchange were also by their very nature credit transactions, and they were to become the principal means by which international merchant bankers secured short-term funds and invested capital. In other words, as Raymond de Roover so effectively demonstrated, international mercantile banking rested squarely upon negotiating short-term exchange transactions.[66] The buyer, or giver, of exchange delivered funds in Lucca and received from the seller, the taker, a notarial instrument promising repayment at one of the Champagne fairs in an equivalent amount of money of Provins.[67] But repayment at one or another of the fairs inevitably meant repayment at some time in the future and hence the buyer was in effect a lender, the seller a borrower, with interest on the buyer's capital built into the fluctuating rates of exchange.

Our contracts reveal that in 1284 Lucchese merchant bankers negotiating among themselves purchased through 205 contracts a total of £44,941 *provinois* payable at one or another

66. De Roover made this point repeatedly in discussing early banking history, but for convenience I will cite only *The Bruges Money Market Around 1400*, with a Statistical Supplement by Hyman Sardy (Brussels 1968) 21–30, and *The Rise and Decline of the Medici Bank, 1397–1494* (New York 1966) 9–14. For a full bibliography of de Roover's work and reprints of ten of his articles (an eleventh, "Gerard de Malynes as an Economic Writer: From Scholasticism to Mercantilism," was published posthumously), see Raymond de Roover, *Business, Banking, and Economic Thought in Late Medieval and Early Modern Europe: Selected Studies of Raymond de Roover*, ed. Julius Kirshner (Chicago and London 1974).

67. Raymond de Roover, *L'évolution de la lettre de change (XIVᵉ–XVIIIᵉ siècles)* (Paris 1953), and *Money, Banking, and Credit in Mediaeval Bruges* (Cambridge, Mass. 1948) 52–55.

of the fairs, with £171,244 Lucchese disbursed in Lucca.[68] These truly impressive figures represent only a fraction of the total exchange business conducted in Lucca. Although no comparable data survive from other banking places for the year 1284, Pierre Racine, using Genoese notarial materials, has shown that in 1288 the sum of recorded exchange transactions concluded in Genoa drawing upon the fairs amounted to at least £60,190 provinois, or a volume roughly one third greater than that recorded for Lucca in 1284.[69] Of course, Genoa as an entrepôt drew representatives of mercantile banking houses from the whole of north Italy. The same material reveals that in 1291 the Lucchese mercantile bankers were the most active in Genoa in dealing on the fair money market, with total transactions of £40,737 3s. 4d. provinois, or 36.30% of the volume in that year.[70] And the Lucchese maintained their leadership in the years 1293–94 with 34% of the market for provinois in Genoa.[71] Thus the £44,941 provinois traded in Lucca in 1284 are likely to have been considerably augmented by the dealings with the fairs of Lucchese bankers situated in Genoa.

The exchange transaction encouraged international commerce by facilitating international payments without requiring large movements of specie. Indeed, the greatest of the Lucchese partnerships—the Bettori, Paganelli, Cardellini, Tignosini, and Honesti—regularly drew upon their assets at the fairs in an obvious effort to repatriate their northern profits. Lucchese importers of northern cloth, too, could avail themselves of the international banker's services and secure capital to pay for cloth purchased in the north. But the exchange transaction was also a credit instrument, and the bankers profited as they bought and sold northern credits for delivery

68. *ASL, Archivio dei notari,* no. 15 (notaries Bartholomeo Fulcieri, Tegrimo Fulcieri, Fulciero Fulcieri), passim.

69. Pierre Racine, "I banchieri piacentini ed i campi sulle Fiere di Champagne alla fine del Duecento," *Studi storici in onore di Emilio Nasalli Rocca* (Piacenza 1971) 481.

70. Ibid. 483.

71. Ibid. 483–84.

at the fair. The bankers' profit derived from interest built into the rate of exchange rather than from discounting.

The movement of the exchange rates on the Lucchese money market confirms for our period what de Roover showed was the case in the fifteenth century: the shorter the term of the transaction the lower the interest charges as expressed in the rates.[72] This may be seen in the movement of exchange rates in contracts drawing upon the May fair of Provins, expressed in so many Lucchese *denarii* to one *solidus* of Provins. The May fair opened, in 1284, on 16 May and closed either 30 June or 6 July.[73] Trading in provinois payable at the May fair began in March and continued into June.[74] If we average the rates for each month, a clear rising pattern of Lucchese against provinois emerges: the seven transactions negotiated in March show an average of 43.43d. Lucchese for one *solidus provinois*; seventeen documents from April indicate a rate of

72. De Roover, *The Bruges Money Market* (n. 66 above) 32–37.

73. The May fair of Provins, according to the texts published by Paul Huvelin, *Essai historique sur le droit des marchés et des foires* (Paris 1897) 600–03, began on the Tuesday before Ascension Day, or 16 May. For the opening dates of the fairs, see Félix Bourquelot, *Études sur les Foires de Champagne* (Paris 1865) part 1, 80–83; Charles Alengry, *Les Foires de Champagne: Étude d'histoire économique* (Paris 1915) 96–98; Levin Goldschmidt, "Die Geschäftsoperationen auf den Messen der Champagne," *Zeitschrift für das gesamte Handelsrecht* 40 (1892) 8–10. According to Goldschmidt, p. 9, the May fair of Provins lasted 46 days. Elisabeth Bassermann, *Die Champagnermessen. Ein Beitrag zur Geschichte des Kredits* (Tübingen and Leipzig 1911) 13–15, and Elizabeth Chapin, *Les villes de Foires de Champagne des origines au début du XIVᵉ siècle* (Paris 1937) 107 n. 9, concur; whereas Richard Face, "Techniques of Business in the Trade between the Fairs of Champagne and the South of Europe in the Twelfth and Thirteenth Centuries," *Economic History Review* 10 (1958) 427 n. 2, and "The Vectuarii in the Overland Commerce between Champagne and Southern Europe," *Economic History Review* 12 (1959) 240 n. 8, following Bourquelot, argues a 52-day cycle. A 46-day duration would have closed the May fair, in 1284, on 30 June, and a 52-day cycle on 6 July. The fair of St. John at Troyes, following Huvelin's texts, opened the first Tuesday a fortnight after St. John's Day, or 11 July.

74. *ASL, Archivio dei notari*, no. 15, fols. 205v, 15 March 1284, and 324v, 6 June 1284.

43.86d.; eleven from May give a rate of 45.95d.; and in June, seven documents yield an average rate of 46.59d. As the rates rose, the seller, that is the borrower, received more in Lucca for a promise to pay a given amount of provinois at the May fair.

Thus, if a merchant sold one solidus of Provins in March for delivery at the May fair, he received, on the average, 43.43d. Lucchese from the buyer, that is, the lender. In June the same merchant received 46.59d. Or, to put it another way, the borrower taking funds in Lucca in June was able, due to the shorter term of the transaction, to borrow 7% more for the same price. Of course, as de Roover also pointed out, other factors besides interest moved the rates of exchange, but given the evidence of Lucca from the year 1284, it seems clear that interest was indeed a powerful element in determining the international rates of exchange.[75] Barring wild fluctuations, the merchant banker could be certain of a profit on his exchange dealings; and the decade of the 1280s does not seem to have been one of turmoil in the monetary relations between Lucca and Champagne.

The evidence for years other than 1284 is sparse indeed, but from what has survived the rates appear remarkably steady. In 1279 the rate was 40.87 denarii Lucchese per shilling of Provins—only slightly below the range of rates for 1284.[76] Only one contract survives from 1294, but it provides a rate of 45.5 denarii per shilling, well within the range of the 1284 figures.[77] The information appended by the notary in the margin of his cartulary, indicating the circumstances under which each obligation was satisfied and rendering the contract void, demonstrates that these transactions were, for the most part, fulfilled in Champagne. In other words, the contracts are genuine and do not represent efforts to avoid the taint of

75. De Roover, *The Bruges Money Market* (n. 66 above) 31–50.
76. *ASL, Archivio dei notari,* no. 13, reg. 1 (notary Armanno di Armanno), fol. 9v, 31 Jan. 1279.
77. *ASL, Archivio dei notari,* no. 29, reg. 1 (notary Gregorio Paganelli), fol. 21v, 11 Feb. 1294.

usury by disguising straight loans as legitimate—in the eyes of the canonists—exchange transactions.

Of the 205 instrumenta ex causa cambii, the cancellations reveal that 111 were actually fulfilled in accordance with the contractual terms, another 34 were cancelled with no information as to where the contract was settled, 35 were not cancelled at all, and 25 were settled in Lucca. I suspect these last were concluded in Lucca as a convenience to the contracting parties and not because of any predetermined agreement on their part. In short, I do not believe that they were set up as fictitious exchanges in order to avoid a nearly unenforceable usury prohibition. But if evasion were intended, the notary would hardly be expected to state in the cancellation that the debt had been liquidated in Lucca. Rather, he would have simply ignored the place of cancellation and the suggestion of a fictitious exchange.

What, then, were the economic consequences of this traffic in foreign exchange? Perhaps the most obvious is the expediting of foreign balances of payment without recourse to large movements of specie. But the existence of an institutionalized money market such as Lucca's, sustained international commerce by giving merchants access to capital in the north as well as a routine means of returning their profits from abroad. Similarly, the exchange market allowed merchant bankers to raise commercial capital at home, which stimulated industry and so animated the entire economy of thirteenth century Lucca.

4 Italian Merchants in Late Thirteenth and Early Fourteenth Century England

MICHAEL PRESTWICH

IN 1306 THE CHIEF ITALIAN COMPANIES IN ENGLAND were summoned before the exchequer to provide assurances that they would not leave the realm or remove their assets, under pain of confiscation. The immediate cause of this incident was the flight of the Pulci and Rimbertini from the country,[1] but in a wider perspective it shows that, despite some mutual suspicions, both government and bankers were anxious that the latter should continue their financial and trading operations in England. What role did the Italians play in England, and what were the resultant benefits and disadvantages?

The traditional view is that the Italians brought to England sophisticated techniques of finance and commerce which spurred the development of the state and the economy. With their substantial resources of capital they could take a powerful position in the most important English trade, the export

---

1. London, Public Record Office (hereafter PRO) E 159/79, m. 34d.; Richard W. Kaeuper, "The Frescobaldi of Florence and the English Crown," *Studies in Medieval and Renaissance History* 10 (1973) 63 n. 71.

of wool. Massive loans to the crown gave the financial machinery of government new strength and flexibility, although
the successive failures of the Ricciardi, the Frescobaldi, the
Bardi, and the Peruzzi showed the danger of extending credit
too far to improvident rulers. Recent researches by Fryde and
Kaeuper have emphasized the importance of the Italians in
royal finance: significantly, only when temporarily without
the backing of an Italian company did Edward I face a major
political and constitutional crisis, in 1297.[2] Postan expressed
a much more critical view of the Italians. He argued that they
contributed little to the productive capacity of agriculture
and industry, and that they brought little capital into England. As crown bankers they were "helping the king to un-
settle the economic life of the country," for much of the money
they advanced was spent on foreign wars and was diverted
from productive investment. He concluded that the part
played by the Italians was "very secondary and relatively
unimportant."[3]

2. There is a considerable literature on the Italians in England. See
in particular Edward A. Bond, "Extracts from the Liberate Rolls, relative to Loans supplied by Italian Merchants to the Kings of England,
in the Thirteenth and Fourteenth Centuries," *Archaeologia* 28 (1840)
207–326; Robert J. Whitwell, "Italian Bankers and the English Crown,"
Transactions of the Royal Historical Society n.s. 17 (1903) 175–233;
Walter E. Rhodes, "The Italian Bankers in England and Their Loans
to Edward I and Edward II," *Historical Essays by Members of the
Owens College, Manchester,* ed. T. F. Tout and James Tait (London
and New York 1902); C. Johnson, "An Italian Financial House in the
Fourteenth Century," *Transactions of the St. Albans and Hertfordshire
Architectural and Archaeological Society* n.s. 1 (1901–02) 230–34; Armando
Sapori, *La compagnia dei Frescobaldi in Inghilterra* (Florence 1947);
idem, *La crisi delle compagnie mercantili dei Bardi e dei Peruzzi* (Flor-
ence 1926); E. B. Fryde, "Loans to the English Crown, 1328–31," *English
Historical Review* 70 (1955) 198–211; E. B. and M. M. Fryde, "Public
Credit, with special reference to North-Western Europe," *Cambridge
Economic History of Europe,* ed. Michael M. Postan et al. 3 (Cambridge
1963) 430–553; Richard W. Kaeuper, *Bankers to the Crown: The Riccardi
of Lucca and Edward I* (Princeton 1973).

3. Michael M. Postan, *Medieval Trade and Finance* (Cambridge 1973)
335–41.

How significant were loans to the crown? The sums involved were impressive. The Ricciardi of Lucca advanced some £400,000 between 1272 and 1294, and the Frescobaldi of Florence about £150,000 between 1296 and 1310. Under Edward II and in the early years of Edward III regular advances from the Bardi were an essential lubricant of government machinery, and with the outbreak of the Hundred Years War, loans from them and the Peruzzi reached an extremely high level: over £125,000 in 1338–39.[4] The normal technique was to repay the Italians from the proceeds of customs duties. In this way revenues could be anticipated, and the cost of an expensive campaign spread over several years; an intolerable burden of taxation over a short period might thus be avoided. Many examples can be provided of the value of this system, which worked at its best during Edward I's Welsh wars. One campaign, that of 1287, was financed almost exclusively by the Ricciardi, who provided £8,288 out of a total expenditure of about £10,600. That was perhaps exceptional, for the king and his household staff were in Gascony, but in the more normal circumstances of 1282–83 the company still advanced about two fifths of the funds allocated for the campaign.

The great castles that Edward I built in Wales were only made possible by foreigners: Savoy provided the chief masons, notably the great James of St. George, while Lucca provided the bankers who made some of the payments to the workmen and gave the government the financial stability needed for such a major project to be carried through smoothly.[5] When money was needed in Scotland in 1303, £666 13s. 4d. was transferred from London to Durham by the Bellardi, and the money taken on north by the cofferer of the king's wardrobe. In 1315 the Bardi were advancing sums to the earl of Pembroke and Lord Badlesmere for their efforts in Scotland.[6] With their

4. Kaeuper, *Bankers* (n. 2 above) 129–31; Michael C. Prestwich, *War, Politics and Finance under Edward I* (London and Totowa, N.J. 1972) 211; Kaeuper, "Frescobaldi" (n. 1 above) 71; *Cambridge Economic History* (n. 2 above) 3. 457–60.

5. Kaeuper, *Bankers* (n. 2 above) 183, 191–94, 198.

6. PRO, E 101/364/5, fol. 34; E 101/14/5.

widespread international affiliations, the Italians were ideally placed to make payments on the Continent. Walter Langton's diplomatic mission of 1296–97 was partly financed by more than £5,000 in loans from Italian firms.[7] Climaxing the provision of credit overseas was the major part the Italians played in financing Edward III's initial ventures in the Hundred Years War. The use of loans to finance war made possible what arguably amounted to a military revolution. Edward I's armies were much larger than those of his predecessors, up to 30,000 strong, with a greater proportion of paid men among them. Forces could be kept in the field much longer, as in Wales in 1282–83 or Scotland in 1303–04.[8] An obvious comparison is the "Dutch finance" in the late seventeenth century, which made possible the great armies led by Marlborough in the War of the Spanish Succession.[9]

Although remarkably willing to promise advances to the crown, the Italians were not invariably ready to pay out as requested. Where the companies had no established relationship with the government, with revenues pledged securely to them against their loans, they might prove far from obliging. In February 1298, Edward I received a letter from Thomas Paynel, acting on behalf of John de St. John, then a captive in France. Arrangements had been made to ransom him for £5,000, but the government could not spare such a sum. Paynel had been authorized to ask Italian merchants residing in London for a loan on royal security. This was unacceptable, and the merchants asked instead for guarantees from the archbishop of Canterbury and various monasteries. Paynel commented that if this had occurred in France, Philip IV would have punished the merchants harshly, and he asked that they be "menaced as they have deserved." The king considered the matter an outrage, but although a powerful group of officials expressed his displeasure to the merchants, they

7. George P. Cuttino, *English Diplomatic Administration, 1259–1339* (2nd ed. Oxford 1971) 248–49.
8. Prestwich (n. 4 above) 91, 113.
9. Geoffrey Parker, "The 'Military Revolution,' 1560–1660—a Myth?" *Journal of Modern History* 48 (1976) 212–13.

won their point. The money was provided on security given reluctantly by a group of religious houses.[10] The incident shows the need for adequate guarantees of repayment, and reveals that the companies were unwilling to assist the king when his financial standing was weak, as it undoubtedly was in the aftermath of the Flemish expedition of 1297–98. The comparison Paynel made with Philip IV is interesting, for as he became less reliant on the services of the Italians, Philip could put them under greater pressure, notably by taxation, than Edward I could afford to do.[11]

The Italians were unhelpful on other occasions. In 1301 the keeper of the wardrobe, John Droxford, was appointed to approach five companies, but no loans were forthcoming. A similar approach in 1302 yielded only a limited response of about £2,000 from the Frescobaldi.[12] A file of negative responses has been preserved from this period. In one, the Bellardi stated that they had nothing to lend, and that they were owed about £7,000; in another, the Spini pointed out that they were owed over £3,333.[13] In many cases the companies genuinely did not have large sums of ready cash on hand: only when they were in receipt of the customs duties were the Ricciardi and Frescobaldi able to make substantial advances to Edward I. Even the Ricciardi were not always able to provide funds immediately: a demand for £1,000, probably made in 1284, produced the answer "we have no money at present, nor can we raise any so hastily," though they then

10. PRO, E 159/71, mm. 20v., 43. The monasteries were compelled to make the payments they had pledged in 1306. Six Italian companies were involved: E 159/79, m. 35.

11. Joseph R. Strayer, "Italian Bankers and Philip the Fair," *Economy, Society and Government in Medieval Italy,* ed. David Herlihy, Robert S. Lopez, and Vsevolod Slessarev (Kent, Ohio 1969) 113–21.

12. *Calendar of the Close Rolls, 1296–1302* (hereafter *CCR*) (London 1906) 463; *Calendar of the Patent Rolls, 1301–1307* (hereafter *CPR*) (London 1898) 153; PRO, E 101/126/23. PRO, E 101/126/21 shows that the Frescobaldi did advance £266 13s. 4d. in 1301, but not as result of Droxford's mission; it was paid to Ralph Manton at Newcastle-upon-Tyne.

13. PRO, E 101/127/24, nos. 13, 17.

added that with the aid of their overseas partners they should be able to provide it in fifteen days.[14] Once a company had decided to lend to the crown—and by no means all did—it would naturally be as obliging as possible in order to protect its investment. New loans would be made to retain royal favor. The Frescobaldi regretted their initial decision to lend, judging by a petition they presented in 1302,[15] but once begun, the relationship with the crown was hard to withdraw from.

The baronial opposition's demand in 1311 that the Frescobaldi be expelled suggests that the Italians, like international bankers today, influenced government policy. Yet although Orlandino da Pogio had a unique relationship with the department of the wardrobe early in Edward I's reign, and Edward II made first Berto Frescobaldi and then Antonio Pessagno royal councilors,[16] it is not easy to determine the extent and direction of Italian influence. The export duty on wool, a pillar of the English financial system in the later Middle Ages, owed much to Italian advice. The Ricciardi played a major role in setting up the Ancient Custom in 1275.[17] A curious memorandum dating from 1294, which advised the king how best to finance his wars, may have been the work of an Italian. It advocated a heavy increase in export duties, the *maltolt*, which was levied, and the introduction of sumptuary legislation and an internal sales tax.[18] There is no evidence so clear as the French memorandum which shows how Musciatto Guidi of the Francesi helped postpone debasement of the coinage and assisted in the conduct of French diplo-

14. PRO, SC 1/48, no. 74; Kaeuper, *Bankers* (n. 2 above) 83–84.

15. PRO, SC 1/47, no. 120. For a translation, see Whitwell (n. 2 above) 198; a fuller version of the petition is in PRO, C 47/13/1, no. 28.

16. Prestwich (n. 4 above) 206–07; *CPR, 1307–1313* (London 1894) 305; Alice Beardwood, *Alien Merchants in England, 1350 to 1377* (Cambridge, Mass. 1931) 64. Berto's appointment was largely honorific.

17. Kaeuper, *Bankers* (n. 2 above) 148–51.

18. C. V. Langlois, "Project for Taxation Presented to Edward I," *English Historical Review* 4 (1889) 517–21.

macy;[19] but it is clear that the English government welcomed advice from the Italians.

One possible area of Italian influence on government was the drawing up of accounts. Under Edward I, and later, the department of the wardrobe, which controlled the bulk of royal expenditure and received most of the funds advanced by the Italians, used books rather than the conventional rolls for its accounting. Advances were recorded in books of prests, *jornalia* books provided a daily cash record, and debts were recorded in separate volumes. The final account, a substantial volume, would be submitted to the exchequer for audit.[20] The system has resemblances to Italian commercial accounting. The surviving account book for the small firm of the Gallerani of Siena's London branch is termed a *libro dell'entrata e dell' escita*; there was also a *grande libro* and a *libro de' conti*. From the Paris branch a book of debts survives.[21] In the multiplicity of account books, and their format, lie similarities between the practices of the merchants and the wardrobe clerks. Orlandino da Pogio was certainly in a position to suggest how royal clerks might best draw up their accounts. Even earlier, Henry III's influential clerk, John Mansel, had kept various royal documents in the Ricciardi's document chests in the company's office.[22]

Italian expertise was widely used in England in coinage matters. William de Turnemire of Marseille bore the main responsibility for the great recoinage of 1279, but Orlandino da Pogio was a joint warden of the mint in the vital years

19. Frantz Funck-Brentano, "Document pour servir à l'histoire des relations de la France avec l'Angleterre et l'Allemagne sous le règne de Philippe le Bel," *Revue historique* 39 (1889) 328–34.

20. For a discussion of some of the wardrobe books of this period, see *Book of Prests of the King's Wardrobe for 1294–5*, ed. E. B. Fryde (Oxford 1962) ix–xxvi.

21. *Les livres des comptes des Gallerani*, ed. Georges Bigwood and Armand Grunzweig, Academie Royale de Belgique, Commission Royale d'Histoire (2 vols. Brussels 1961–62).

22. *The London Eyre of 1276*, ed. Martin Weinbaum, London Record Society 12 (1976) no. 521.

1279–81. Amerigo Frescobaldi was likewise warden of the mint from Edward II's accession until the expulsion of his company. The highest paid mint official under Edward I was Boniface Galgani, whose two nephews shared his offices between them when he returned to Italy, one of them eventually marrying an Englishwoman. In the fourteenth century, Italians played an important part in the introduction of a gold coinage; Percival Porche of Lucca and two Florentines, Giorgio Chierichini and Lotto Nicholini, acted as masters of the mint.[23] The gold coinage was initially based on the florin, and Edward III's plan to make it an international currency that could be freely exported may have owed something to the advice of Italian merchants as well as to that of London goldsmiths.[24] The Frescobaldi had even been briefly involved in bullion production, when they received custody of the royal silver mines in Devon, but the venture was unsuccessful.[25]

What did the merchants gain by lending to the crown? The traditional view was that no interest was paid on crown loans, though grants to cover expenses and losses might be made. Fryde has argued, however, that the Bardi received 26% interest on loans made between 1328 and 1331, and Kaeuper has suggested that interest payments formed part of the rewards received by the Ricciardi.[26] Earlier in the thirteenth century, interest rates had been explicit, as in the case of loans raised by Frederick II in Italy in 1239–40.[27] In England in 1232, Henry III agreed to repay a loan within a year, and he

23. Mavis Mate, "Mint Officials under Edward I and II," *Edwardian Monetary Affairs (1279–1344),* ed. N. J. Mayhew, British Archaeological Reports 36 (1977) 23–44; C. G. Crump and C. Johnson, "Tables of Bullion Coined under Edward I, II, and III," *Numismatic Chronicle* 4th ser. 13 (1913) 200–45.

24. Thomas F. Reddaway, "The King's Mint and Exchange in London, 1343–1543," *English Historical Review* 82 (1967) 1–3.

25. Kaeuper, "Frescobaldi" (n. 1 above) 60–62.

26. Fryde, "Loans" (n. 2 above) 210; Kaeuper, *Bankers* (n. 2 above) 118–21.

27. Jean L. A. Huillard-Bréholles, *Historia diplomatica Friderici Secundi* (6 parts in 12 vols. Paris 1852–61) 5.654 ff.

consented to a scale of payment for damages amounting to 120% per annum if the term was not met.[28] In the course of the century attitudes changed. In 1240 Henry forbade usury, and the records of Canterbury Cathedral Priory show that whereas interest payments had been made openly up to that date, they were later concealed. The accounts suggest that from 1270 the merchants even stopped imposing hidden interest, although penalty charges might be imposed for late repayment.[29] It seems that the merchant bankers who lent to Edward I and his son expected no more than payment for damages and costs incurred as a result of their loans. An agreement made by the Frescobaldi with the crown on 30 August 1309 is illuminating. The company promised £6,666 13s. 4d., of which £1,000 was to be paid immediately at London, and £1,000 at Boston. On 8 September, £1,333 6s. 8d. was due at London, and in mid-October, £3,333 6s. 8d. in the north. Repayment was to be prompt: half in late November, and the rest by Easter 1310 at the latest.[30] Kaeuper has argued plausibly that short periods for repayment were often a device to facilitate the levy of damages, since the crown would be unable to meet the term set.[31] In this case, however, payment for damages was promised at the same time as the repayments were due.

A system for the payment of damages which did not specify a precise rate does not properly qualify for the term *interest*, although it did offer the merchant bankers the promise of some returns. The Frescobaldi were granted in all £11,533 6s. 8d. by the crown in compensation for losses incurred as a result of their loans, while in 1338 the Bardi and Peruzzi were promised £30,000 and £20,000 respectively to cover their labor and expenses.[32] In practice, however, the Italians were

28. Whitwell (n. 2 above) 194–95.

29. Mavis Mate, "The Indebtedness of Canterbury Cathedral Priory, 1215–95," *Economic History Review* 2nd ser. 26 (1973) 183–97.

30. PRO, C 49/4/7.

31. Kaeuper, *Bankers* (n. 2 above) 120.

32. PRO, E 372/154, Frescobaldi accounts; *CPR, 1338–1340* (London 1898) 388.

fortunate if they even recovered the principal from the crown. An accurate balance sheet for the Ricciardi cannot be calculated, but they estimated that they were owed over £26,666 by Edward I in 1295, after he had dispensed with their services.[33] The crown probably owed the Frescobaldi a total of at least £150,000, and repaid them only about £125,000.[34] Although Fryde has shown that the Bardi made a profit between 1328 and 1331, the company was owed £9,533 by the crown early in 1333,[35] and with the onset of the Hundred Years War huge loans were not remotely matched by repayments. Firms less deeply involved in crown finance fared little better; the Bellardi of Lucca advanced £7,493 between 1298 and 1307, but were repaid only £4,021.[36] It is true that in accounting with the crown it was in the companies' interest to prove that they received less than full payment. The Frescobaldi did not include all their receipts from the crown in their final accounts.[37] But it is still hard to see how lending to the English crown at this period could have been directly profitable to the Italians.

Only when in acute financial straits in the Low Countries were Edward I and Edward III compelled to raise loans that involved the payment of interest on a true percentage basis. In 1297 a group of Lombards from Asti advanced 4,600 li. tur. to Edward I on security of jewels and plate worth an estimated 7,015 li. tur. The Frescobaldi repaid the money on the king's behalf eight months later, with interest amounting to at least 560 li. tur.[38] The great Bruges financier and pawn-

33. Kaeuper, *Bankers* (n. 2 above) 225.

34. Prestwich (n. 4 above) 211.

35. Ranald Nicholson, *Edward III and the Scots* (London 1965) 115.

36. PRO, E 101/127/7. The Bardi fared best under Edward I; PRO, E 372/158 shows advances of £3,906 from 1294 to 1309, with all but £431 repaid.

37. Kaeuper, "Frescobaldi" (n. 1 above) 71. In addition, they did not account for £6,000 assigned to them from taxation in 1301: PRO E 159/75, m. 10.

38. PRO, E 159/71, m. 36; E. B. Fryde, "Financial Resources of Edward I in the Netherlands, 1294–98: Main Problems and Some Comparisons with Edward III in 1337–40," *Revue belge de philologie et d'histoire* 40 (1962) 1178.

broker Simon de Mirabello took the great crown of England as a pledge for a loan he made to Edward III, on which 35% interest was charged. A loan from the Leopardi of Asti bore charges of 42% for late repayment, and Russell has cited it as "a very definite example of the payment of interest."[39] In these cases, however, the money was advanced by authorized usurers in the Low Countries, not by merchant bankers. De Roover made a clear distinction between the two, which the evidence bears out.[40] A comparison with the sixteenth century is interesting. Loans raised at Antwerp in the middle years of the period bore substantial interest charges, whereas most of the funds later borrowed at home carried no such burden.[41]

It is curious that the Italian companies should have lent so much to the crown when the financial returns were so poor, particularly when they may well have had to pay substantial charges to raise the money themselves. In 1302 the Frescobaldi estimated that loans totaling £32,886 had cost them £15,245 in Florence and at the Champagne fairs.[42] There were, however, advantages to be gained from royal favor. Under Edward II the Frescobaldi were showered with grants. In 1309 Amerigo received six manors for a nominal rent, and in the next year orders were issued to give preference to the firm's nominees for ecclesiastical offices. Exemptions from such burdens as jury service and taxation were also given. Court life seems to have appealed to the Italians. The Frescobaldi processed in full

39. E. B. Fryde, "Financial Resources of Edward III in the Netherlands, 1337–40," *Revue belge de philologie et d'histoire* 45 (1967) 1165–90; the quotation is from Ephraim Russell, "The Societies of the Bardi and the Peruzzi and Their Dealings with Edward III," *Finance and Trade under Edward III*, ed. George Unwin (Manchester 1918) 115.

40. Raymond de Roover, *Money, Banking and Credit in Mediaeval Bruges* (Cambridge, Mass. 1948) 99–139. Fryde (n. 39 above) suggests that the distinction was blurred in the early fourteenth century. Yet although some moneylenders traded on a larger scale than they did later, no evidence suggests that the merchant bankers were able to impose interest rates comparable to those of the Lombard moneylenders.

41. R. B. Outhwaite, "The Trials of Foreign Borrowing: The English Crown and the Antwerp Money Market in the Mid-Sixteenth Century," *Economic History Review* 2nd ser. 19 (1966) 301–05.

42. Whitwell (n. 2 above) 198.

finery at Edward II's coronation and maintained close relationships with such courtiers as Henry de Beaumont and the
notorious Piers Gaveston.[43] A poem written by a member of
the family after their expulsion from England pointed the
moral: Italians should wear drab, inconspicuous clothing and
avoid the court.[44]

More important were the commercial advantages to be
gained by lending to the government. In reviewing Kaeuper's
work, Goldthwaite suggested that merchants were able to take
advantage of exchange rates, while the grant of the customs
revenues in repayment for loans gave them capital to invest
in the wool trade.[45] Foreign exchange was certainly one means
of obtaining profits without taint of usury, and when the
English government employed fixed rates which did not cor-
relate exactly with those prevailing commercially, the Italians
could benefit. In 1297 the value of sterling was rising as a
result of French debasement, but the official rate was held at
the traditional one sterling to four petit tournois. When the
Mozi lent 1,000 li. tur. in Flanders and received £250 at the
exchequer, there was a profit to the crown of £12 10s.[46] The
Frescobaldi put their profit from the exchange on their overseas loans of about £7,000 at £666 13s. 4d.[47] Such gains could
only be made if funds were advanced abroad and repaid in
England. In practice, the bulk of Edward I's overseas expenditure on war from 1294 to 1298 was financed by means of coin
taken by sea from England.[48] In 1286 even the Ricciardi had
carried coin abroad to lend to the king in France, rather than

43. *CPR, 1307–1313* (n. 16 above) 152, 305, 321; Kaeuper, "Frescobaldi" (n. 1 above) 72–73, 82; *Les livres des comptes des Gallerani* (n.
21 above) 1. no. 402.

44. Sapori, *La compagnia* (n. 2 above) 76–77.

45. R. A. Goldthwaite, "Italian Bankers in Medieval England," *Journal of European Economic History* 2 (1973) 769.

46. Cuttino (n. 7 above) 249.

47. Whitwell (n. 2 above) 199.

48. Prestwich (n. 4 above) 172–73; idem, "Edward I's Monetary Policies and Their Consequences," *Economic History Review* 2nd ser. 22
(1969) 411.

make use of letters of exchange.[49] Edward III, in contrast, borrowed huge sums in the Low Countries, with repayment promised in England. It would have been easy to disguise interest payments by fixing an artificial exchange rate, and the king did indeed use a standard rate of 3s. to the florin in his dealings with the Italians. However, when it was introduced in the late 1330s, this rate stood substantially below the normal level. The accounts of the transfer of funds to the Curia in 1337 and 1338 show the florin valued at 3s. 4d. By the early 1340s the value of the florin had fallen below 3s., however,[50] so that the crown's fixed rate, once unfavorable for the Italians, came in time to be favorable.

Fluctuations in exchange rates could bring losses as well as profits. In 1302 the Frescobaldi claimed that when £7,333 6s. 8d. had been assigned to them in the previous year, the mark had been worth five florins, but that it had since fallen to below four, with a consequent loss to the firm of £1,333 6s. 8d. This implies a change in the value of the florin from about 2s. 8d. to 3s. 6d.[51] Such a startling range was indeed possible: the Gallerani accounts for March 1305 show the florin valued at 2s. 4½d., while by the following December it stood at 4s. A table in Pegolotti's handbook shows a similar potential range of movement.[52] With rates as unstable as these, the merchants were in a precarious position.

In their petition of 1302 the Frescobaldi further complained of losses from poor wool sales, which probably resulted from the disturbed situation in Flanders. Trade in wool was the

49. Kaeuper, *Bankers* (n. 2 above) 93–94.

50. *Accounts Rendered by Papal Collectors in England, 1317–1378,* ed. William E. Lunt and Edgar B. Graves (Philadelphia 1968) 65; *Calendar of Entries in the Papal Registers Relating to Great Britain and Ireland: Papal Letters,* ed. William H. Bliss (London 1893–) 2.572; 3.13–14. See also Paul de Monte Florum's account at the Curia, PRO, E 101/311/25.

51. Whitwell (n. 2 above) 198.

52. *Les livres des comptes des Gallerani* (n. 21 above) 1. nos. 5, 13, 101, 137; Francesco Balducci Pegolotti, *La pratica della mercatura,* ed. Allan Evans (Cambridge, Mass. 1936; rpt. New York 1970) 202–03.

chief commercial activity of the Italians in England, and merchants who lent to the crown were at a clear advantage. If they were being repaid out of the customs, the company representatives at the ports were assured of substantial funds, which could be used to buy wool. This helps to explain the Ricciardi's dominant position in the wool trade while they were crown bankers. The Frescobaldi received over £85,000 from the customs during their association with the crown.[53] Other companies may have invested in trade receipts from papal taxation. In 1283 no less than £70,152 was deposited with the leading companies in England,[54] and in 1290 the merchants of the Cerchi commented on the effect the new papal tenth would have on wool prices, as the receipts would be placed with the Italians.[55]

One important way in which the crown assisted the merchant bankers was by making full legal facilities available to them. The Italians accepted English law readily. In contrast to their custom on the Continent, they made little use of public notaries. Instead, they used the system of enrolling recognizances of debt at the chancery or exchequer.[56] It is tempting to see Italian influence behind the reform of the debt collection process in the early 1280s, with the statutes of Acton Burnell and *De Mercatoribus*. However, the case that probably inspired these changes involved a Flemish merchant, not an Italian, and in their dealings with the great monastic houses the Italians made little use of the new procedures. More important to them was the opportunity given to favored com-

53. Whitwell (n. 2 above) 198; Frescobaldi accounts in PRO, E 372/154.

54. William E. Lunt, *Financial Relations of the Papacy with England to 1327* (Cambridge, Mass. 1939) 665.

55. Paolo Emiliani-Giudici, *Storia dei comuni Italiani* (3 vols. Florence 1866) 3.421. By the fourteenth century the merchants were not obtaining much advantage from the deposit of papal taxes: Yves Renouard, *Les relations des papes d'Avignon et des compagnies commerciales et bancaires de 1316 à 1378* (Paris 1941) 527–36.

56. For a rare example of the use of a notary, see *Les livres des comptes des Gallerani* (n. 21 above) 1.267–69; and nos. 113 and 333 for recognizances at the exchequer.

panies of using the exchequer's machinery against clients who defaulted on their obligations. In the 1280s only the Ricciardi made regular use of the exchequer memoranda rolls for recording the debts of monastic wool producers; the value of their special position as crown bankers is clear.[57] Late in Edward I's reign the Spini were granted the privilege of using the exchequer for debt recovery,[58] while in the case of the Frescobaldi, Edward II stated that their debts were to be collected as if they were owed to the king himself.[59] Some Italians were given the title of treasurer's *vallettus*, which appears to have allowed them to receive preferential treatment. Coppuccio Cotenna, one of the Frescobaldi, was so termed in the later years of Edward I.[60] In general, the Italians were sympathetically treated in their legal dealings in England. A case between a Lucchese merchant and his agent involved technicalities of commercial practice beyond the comprehension of the exchequer barons; the account books which they could not follow were submitted to a group of expert arbitrators, and a satisfactory conclusion reached. The most remarkable instance of an Italian's faith in English justice is that of the Florentine Hugh la Pape, who appealed to Edward I to obtain restitution for losses incurred when his property in Florence was destroyed by the Ghibellines. His plea, not surprisingly, was unsuccessful.[61]

What sorts of commercial operations required the Italians to turn to the royal courts? The most important was the provision of loans on security of future wool crops. In 1284 the prioress of Arden in Yorkshire agreed to sell the house's wool production for the decade from 1291 in return for an annual

57. F. Maurice Powicke, *The Thirteenth Century, 1216–1307* (Oxford 1953) 623–25; T. H. Lloyd, *The English Wool Trade in the Middle Ages* (Cambridge 1977) 293.

58. PRO, E 159/79, m. 21.

59. Kaeuper, "Frescobaldi" (n. 1 above) 72.

60. Prestwich (n. 4 above) 211.

61. *Select Cases concerning the Law Merchant, A.D. 1239–1633*, ed. Hubert Hall, Selden Society 46 (2 vols. London 1929) 2.34–39, 53–62, 148–50.

advance of £10. The price was set at £7 13s. 4d. a sack. The merchants came to collect the wool for three years, but then ceased coming. They claimed that the nuns should have sent it to their agents at Thorpe, rather than allowing it to deteriorate in storage. A compromise was reached in court in 1303, with the prioress agreeing to hand over two sacks of wool, valued at £5 6s. 8d. each. An interesting, though not abnormal, feature of the original agreement was the Italians' insistence that the wool be properly sorted and packed; this was one reason for the high price they agreed to pay. Another case in the same exchequer roll concerned the abbey of St. Osyth in Essex. The Frescobaldi sued for five sacks of wool, worth £8 each. Again the price was high, for in 1294 the Cerchi Bianchi had contracted for ten sacks at £5 each. The abbot agreed to deliver the wool and to pay £3 in damages. These are small examples, but the scale of Italian investment in the wool trade was immense. In the early 1290s they were buying wool from forty-nine of the seventy-four Cistercian houses in the country.[62]

The Italians' trading techniques had important consequences. Repayment of advances in wool at fixed prices offered the merchant bankers the chance of high profits without the stigma of usury, while meeting the urgent need of monasteries for cash.[63] In some cases, such as that of St. Swithun's, Winchester, ably analyzed by Kaeuper, the house was unable to escape from a vicious circle of indebtedness, being forced to pledge its wool crop for longer and longer periods.[64] As the former abbot of Pipewell was to complain in the 1320s, "Leger est a prendre, mes fort est a rendre."[65] In such cases, the Italians were not performing a beneficial function, for

62. PRO, E 13/26, mm. 15, 23; *Select Cases* (n. 61 above) 2.69–71; T. H. Lloyd, *The Movement of Wool Prices in Medieval England, Economic History Review* Supplement (Cambridge 1973) 10, 53.

63. In only one case was usury alleged where a loan was repaid in wool; see Bond (n. 2 above) 226, and Lloyd (n. 57 above) 291.

64. Kaeuper, *Bankers* (n. 2 above) 38–41.

65. Eileen E. Power, *The Wool Trade in English Medieval History* (London and New York 1941) 43–44.

their loans were merely used to cover excessive expenditure and to finance earlier advances, and not to improve the estates. Smith suggested that at Canterbury Cathedral Priory the estates prospered as a result of the injection of Italian capital, but recent work has shown that the monks were only borrowing to cover extraordinary expenditure. Land improvements were paid for out of normal income. Here, however, there was a real value in being able to borrow to meet such heavy but intermittent costs as those of archiepiscopal elections. Under the direction of the great Henry of Eastry, loans were repaid on time, so that no penalty charges were incurred.[66]

In some cases Italian loans were used productively. At Kirkstall, scab had reduced the sheep flocks to nothing by 1284, while debts stood at over £5,000. Without loans, recovery to the position reached by 1301 would have been impossible; at that date there were over 4,000 sheep, and the debt had been reduced to £160.[67] At Bolton in Yorkshire the priory borrowed extensively from Italians: £200 in 1293–94, £359 in 1298–99, £241 in 1302–03, and £301 in 1303–04. Income averaged about £360 a year at this time. Some payments for damages and gifts were made, but it was only in the event of a total crop failure, as in 1315–16, that the amount of debt approached unmanageable levels. Improvements to the estate in the first half of the fourteenth century were assisted by loans, and the financial position was clearly strengthened by the use of the Italian credit facilities.[68]

While it is true in general that the Italians contributed little to the improvement of agricultural techniques in England, their insistence, as at Arden Priory, on wool being properly packed and graded forced producers to improve their methods. A contract made by the Bettori with Kirkstall in

66. Reginald A. L. Smith, *Canterbury Cathedral Priory* (Cambridge 1943) 18; Mate (n. 29 above) 183–94.
67. Noël Denholm-Young, *Seignorial Administration in England* (London 1937) 61.
68. Ian Kershaw, *Bolton Priory: The Economy of a Northern Monastery* (London 1973) 90–93.

1292 is significant: the firm was to receive the total crop for ten years, and while it could be delivered unsorted for the first three, it was thereafter to be provided in three qualities.[69] Further, it is unlikely that English wool exports would have reached such high levels in the early fourteenth century without the injection of Italian capital into the trade. Much wealth was brought to the country as a result; and we can show a direct correlation between imports of bullion and exports of wool.[70]

The Italians did not confine their attentions as traders to the religious houses. They dealt widely with great lay estates, notably those of Holderness. Roger Bigod, earl of Norfolk, was deeply involved with the Ricciardi, to whom he owed over £1,000, and in 1294 four other earls were in the firm's debt.[71] A list of debts to the Bettori of the same date totaled £3,312 and included only two monasteries. The firm's main dealings were with Robert FitzRoger, one of the opposition in 1297, his son John de Clavering, and Adam Cretyng.[72] Clavering's further loans from Italians late in Edward I's reign mark him as an improvident landlord, struggling to maintain his status.[73] Earlier in the thirteenth century such men had borrowed from Jewish moneylenders, frequently sinking so deep into debt as to lose their estates. But few, apparently, were impoverished as a result of loans from Italians in the late thirteenth and early fourteenth centuries. It was men such as Walter Langton, the treasurer, who gained substantial estates by lending money on security of land and by manipulating legal processes.[74]

The Italians were not anxious to acquire estates in England.

69. R. A. Donkin, "Cistercian Sheep-Farming and Wool-Sales in the Thirteenth Century," *Agricultural History Review* 6 (1958) 7–8.

70. Prestwich, "Edward I's Monetary Policies" (n. 48 above) 408, 414.

71. Kaeuper, *Bankers* (n. 2 above) 32, 34.

72. PRO, E 101/126/12.

73. *CCR, 1296–1302* (n. 12 above) 297, 476.

74. Alice Beardwood, *The Trial of Walter Langton, Bishop of Lichfield, 1307–1312*, Transactions of the American Philosophical Society n.s. 54, pt. 3 (1964) 32–36.

Their loans to private individuals, like those to the crown, did not bear specific rates of interest; profits were taken in the form of damages for late repayment. In a case between Henry de Bray and the Buonsignori, a loan of £6 13s. 4d. was acknowledged in court, and duly repaid, with the company remitting any claim for damages. In another case, a debt of £8 to the Frescobaldi was recognized, but the company's claim for £5 damages was reduced by the exchequer to 13s. 4d.[75] It is striking that whereas the Italians had been very unpopular earlier in the century, when their loans bore interest openly, by the reign of Edward I their moneylending activities did not incur the same dislike. There were, however, strong feelings when a company defaulted, as the Pulci and Rimbertini did late in 1305.[76]

As bankers, the Italian companies naturally received deposits, and much of their strength rested on the funds invested with them in Italy. The extent to which they accepted deposits in England cannot easily be determined. The best-known example is that of the money placed with the Peruzzi and the Bardi by the Younger Despenser, a story ably elucidated by Fryde.[77] There is some earlier evidence. A few references to deposits with the Ricciardi survive, such as that showing that Reginald de Gernyn had £120 *in deposito* with the firm.[78] The earl of Lincoln placed appreciable funds with the Frescobaldi, and the chief creditors of the Pulci and Rimbertini at the time of their failure—the earl of Hereford, Isabella de Vescy, Guy Ferre, and Adam de Osgoteby, an exchequer official—were presumably depositors.[79] The Bellardi

75. PRO, E 13/26, mm. 13, 60.

76. Matthew Paris, *Historia Anglorum*, ed. Sir Frederic H. Madden (Rolls Series, 3 vols. London 1866–69) 2.382; Powicke (n. 57 above) 626.

77. E. B. Fryde, "The Deposits of Hugh Despenser the Younger with Italian Bankers," *Economic History Review* 2nd ser. 3 (1950–51) 344–62.

78. PRO, E 405/1/10, 2 July. For other deposits, see Kaeuper, *Bankers* (n. 2 above) 28; Gwyn A. Williams, *Medieval London, from Commune to Capital* (London 1963) 66.

79. Fryde (n. 77 above) 355–56.

owed Walter Langton over £2,000 by 1307. These are not, however, examples of simple investment with the Italians. When the Bellardi were questioned, they explained that Langton had entrusted them with money so that they could make payments on his behalf,[80] and the Peruzzi were likewise acting as Despenser's agents. One instruction to them asked them to pay £1,000 "of our money" to Despenser's clerk, Richard de Naceby.[81] Fryde has cited a splendid example of the use made of Italian banking facilities. Despenser owed the earl of Norfolk £1,000, and of this, £300 was simply transferred from the Peruzzi to the Bardi, acting for the respective parties.[82] In the thirteenth century the countess of Aumale had used the Ricciardi to transfer funds from Holderness to the Isle of Wight, in lieu of transporting cash at considerable cost.[83]

In most cases, apparently, money was placed with the Italians so that they could make payments on behalf of the depositor. These were not long-term deposits made on the grounds of security or profit, and in England the Italians' role as deposit bankers was not considerable. The Gallerani account book reveals only one deposit, of £19 6s. 8d. made by another Sienese, for which they gave him presents worth 26s.[84] The dangers of handing money over to Italians are revealed by a privy seal writ of 1304 to the company of the Great Table of Siena, in which the king ordered them to release money they were holding on behalf of John Russell; they were detaining it to his great detriment, as he wished to depart for Gascony.[85] Piers Gaveston was strongly criticized for paying money over to Italian merchants,[86] and the normal practice

80. *Records of the Trial of Walter Langeton, Bishop of Coventry and Lichfield, 1307–1312*, ed. Alice Beardwood, Camden Society Publications 4th ser. 6 (1969) 185–86.

81. PRO, SC 1/49, nos. 146, 147.

82. Fryde (n. 77 above) 348.

83. Denholm-Young (n. 67 above) 65–66.

84. *Les livres des comptes des Gallerani* (n. 21 above) 1. no. 419.

85. PRO, SC 1/14, no. 49.

86. *Johannis de Trokelowe, et Henrici de Blaneforde, Monachorum S. Albani, necnon quorundam anonymorum Chronica et annales*, ed. Henry T. Riley (Rolls Series, London 1866) 64–65, 68.

was still to use the security of religious houses for cash deposits. When Edward I decided to appropriate private deposits in 1294, it was the monasteries that were searched, not the lodgings of the Italians.[87]

Foreign exchange was an important part of the Italians' business. Churchmen in particular made much use of the companies to transfer funds overseas. The crown imposed stringent prohibitions on the export of coin, and letters of exchange were a simple alternative. The Gallerani accounts are dominated by such transactions. When Thomas of Savoy wanted to export the proceeds of his living in York, he handed over £38 19s. 4d. to the company in London and received 555 li. tur. in Paris. In 1305 the prior of Bermondsey used the firm to transfer £116 in two transactions to Paris. Many exchange dealings involved other Italian companies, but no English merchants used the Gallerani's services. These transfers were profitable, though with the fluctuations in exchange rates gains cannot be calculated precisely. Two dealings of 8 July 1305 are suggestive. Money was transferred to Paris at 8 li. tur. to the mark sterling (13s. 4d.), while funds sent from Paris to London were exchanged at 9 li. 9s. tur. to the mark; this indicates a profit of some 10% on each transaction.[88] Besides providing profits, the letters of exchange enabled the Italians to compensate for their visible trade imbalance: they were exporting large quantities of wool and importing little by way of goods. By one estimate, £10,000 a year was transferred overseas by means of letters of exchange in the early fourteenth century.[89]

Problems inevitably occurred in the use of letters of exchange. In 1297 the bishop of Winchester attempted to transfer £2,000 abroad by using the Spini, but the king seized the money from the company and summoned the bishop's clerk to explain why the letter of exchange had been sent

87. Prestwich (n. 4 above) 214–15.

88. *Les livres des comptes des Gallerani* (n. 21 above) 1. nos. 47, 96, 229, 339, 340, 342, 343.

89. T. H. Lloyd, "Overseas Trade and the English Money Supply in the Fourteenth Century," *Edwardian Monetary Affairs* (n. 23 above) 102–03.

overseas contrary to royal orders. The accusation was denied
and the letter eventually produced for inspection.[90] In 1300
the Pulci and Rimbertini accepted £18 for transfer to Paris,
but the money proved to have been stolen, and the London
authorities forbade the sending of the letter. It was not, however, until much later in the fourteenth century that the
systematic licensing of letters of exchange began. In some
cases, letters were not honored. In 1304 Amanieu de la Bret
lost £500 when the Mozi failed, and under Edward II two
Italian spicers in London paid £133 6s. 8d. to the Cornacchini,
to be spent on goods at the Champagne fairs. The Cornacchini
failed to pay and left the country secretly.[91] Partly as a result
of the failure of the Buonsignori, the papacy under Clement V
ceased using the Italians to transfer funds to the Curia.[92]

Letters of exchange did not wholly supersede cash payment.
In 1284 the Ricciardi had £1,000 sent in coin from France;
and in the years 1294–97 Edward I exported huge sums to his
troops and allies on the Continent, as when a convoy of
seventeen ships took £25,000 to his agent Robert de Segre in
Holland in 1294. In 1299 the Frescobaldi were permitted to
export up to £1,000 in cash on the king's business.[93] On a
smaller scale, some travelers took small quantities of coin
overseas, either illicitly or with permission. In 1331 John
Middleton of Merton College, Oxford, went to the Curia. He
took £10 in cash, and when that proved insufficient, met his
expenses by selling a cloak, a fur coat, and a horse.[94] Yet undoubtedly foreign exchange was a most important part of
the business of the Italian merchant bankers. Not, perhaps,
their prime function at this period, as it was to be for the

90.   PRO, E 368/69, m. 18v; Kaeuper, "Frescobaldi" (n. 1 above) 49.
91.   *CCR, 1302–1307* (London 1908) 431; Lloyd (n. 89 above) 103,
115–18. For a full discussion of the licensing of letters of exchange, see
John H. Munro, pp. 198–215 below.
92.   Renouard (n. 55 above) 94–98.
93.   Prestwich (n. 4 above) 173; *CCR, 1296–1302* (n. 12 above) 246–47.
94.   James E. Thorold Rogers, *A History of Agriculture and Prices in
England* (7 vols. Oxford 1866–1902) 2.631–34.

Alberti in the late fourteenth century,[95] it was nevertheless an integral part of their complex operations.

The opportunities for the Italians to profit from money changing within England were more limited than elsewhere in Europe. Tight royal control over the currency provided that foreign coin could only be exchanged for sterling at the royal exchange at the Tower or at its branches in various ports. The kind of banking based on money changing which de Roover has depicted for Bruges could not develop in England.[96] In 1301 the exchanges were put in the hands of Italians, but such grants were not particularly profitable. The highly disturbed state of the currency at the outset of the fourteenth century, resulting from the importation of imitation sterlings known as pollards and crockards, provided them briefly with the opportunity for some lucrative, if legally dubious, dealings.[97] In the 1320s the circulation of gold coin in England, some of it Florentine, was turned to advantage by the Italians. The Younger Despenser on one occasion made what amounted to a *cambium* contract with the Bardi and Peruzzi, giving each firm £1,000 to be repaid later in florins.[98] In 1326 the treasurer suggested that an appropriate action to take against the Bardi for their decision to lend to Queen Isabella in Paris would be to recall money given them in sterling for similar repayment in florins.[99] Both bankers and depositors were presumably confident that fluctuations in exchange rates would ensure them a profit.

In addition to lending money, trading in wool, and transmitting funds abroad, the Italians were engaged in a wide range of miscellaneous enterprises in England. They bought

95. George A. Holmes, "Florentine Merchants in England, 1346–1436," *Economic History Review* 2nd ser. 13 (1960–61) 196.

96. De Roover (n. 40 above) 171 ff.

97. *CPR, 1301–1307* (n. 12 above) 61; Kacuper, "Frescobaldi" (n. 1 above) 59–60; N. J. Mayhew and D. R. Walker, "Crockards and Pollards: Imitation and the Problem of Fineness in a Silver Coinage," *Edwardian Monetary Affairs* (n. 23 above) 137.

98. Fryde (n. 77 above) 346.

99. PRO, SC 1/49, no. 106.

and sold plate, jewels, and precious stuffs. The Bellardi supplied the Great Wardrobe under Edward I; between March and May 1298 they provided twenty-four pieces of cloth of gold and one gold cup, and they later supplied the elaborate trappings for the king's funeral.[100] The Gallerani accounts show that they dealt in English lead and Gascon wines, while a joint subsidiary company was set up with the Frescobaldi to trade in horses. Each firm put up capital of £133 6s. 8d., and a profit was made of £23 8s. 2d. (Curiously, none of the horses they bought were very valuable. On one occasion they took a horse worth £2 18s. to Scotland to sell to a client, and this at a time when the best animals might cost over £40.)[101] Such trading activities were relatively unimportant when set against the major concerns of the companies.

No substantial body of letters and accounts survives for the English branch of one of the major companies. The bulk of the surviving correspondence of the Ricciardi and Frescobaldi dates from the years of the companies' collapse and reveals little about the normal conduct of their affairs.[102] Much, therefore, remains obscure. Little is known of the internal organization of the companies, and while it is possible to distinguish the chief personnel, there are few clues as to their personalities. Most of the leading members of the companies remained in England for a considerable time. Orlandino da Pogio can be traced from 1275 until 1309, long after the fall of his company, the Ricciardi.[103] In the case of the Frescobaldi, Taldo Janiani was joined in the late 1290s by Coppuccio Cotenna, and as the relationship with the crown

100. PRO, E 101/127/6, E 101/127/7; E 101/356/2.

101. *Les livres des comptes des Gallerani* (n. 21 above) 1. nos. 91, 201, 216, 357, 377, 398.

102. For the Ricciardi letters, see Emilio Re, "La compagnia dei Riccardi in Inghilterra e il suo fallimento alla fine del secolo XIII," *Archivio della R. Società Romana di Storia Patria* 37 (1914) 87-138; Kaeuper, *Bankers* (n. 2 above) 71–73. For the Frescobaldi, see Kaeuper, "Frescobaldi" (n. 1 above) 93–95.

103. Kaeuper, *Bankers* (n. 2 above) 56.

developed, Amerigo and Bettino, the sons of Berto Frescobaldi, took over in England.[104]

One interesting minor figure emerges more clearly than most. Biagio Aldebrandini was head, with Nicoluccio di Cante, of the Gallerani's London branch from 1304 to 1308. The surviving accounts make it possible to trace his frequent travels to Paris and his many purchases of horses. He showed political acumen in giving spices and confectionery to Piers Gaveston, the heir to the throne's favorite. The small firm of the Gallerani was not sufficient for Biagio's ambition, and in 1308, at Edward II's coronation, he took his place in the retinue of the Frescobaldi, dressed in a splendid robe.[105] But Biagio did not associate himself exclusively with the Frescobaldi, and he avoided exile when disaster struck the Florentine firm in 1311. A letter he wrote in 1313 to Bettino and Pepe Frescobaldi shows him trying to salvage what he could from their business. His political skill is shown by his having obtained royal letters to ensure that he could not be held responsible for Frescobaldi debts, and he stressed that he would not go to such lengths on their behalf as might incur royal displeasure.[106] In 1312, 1315, and 1319, Edward II employed Biagio, now described as "the king's yeoman," to buy horses and goods overseas. The Gallerani accounts do reveal one embarrassing incident: £2 had to be paid to a Londoner to persuade him to withdraw a charge that Biagio "aveva sforçata la mollie" ("had done violence to his wife").[107] The last mention of Biagio in England is in 1322, when he witnessed a lease made by the bishop of Durham to the Peruzzi.

---

104. Kaeuper, "Frescobaldi" (n. 1 above) 63.

105. *Les livres des comptes des Gallerani* (n. 21 above) 1. no. 400; 2.107–09.

106. PRO, SC 1/58, no. 6. Part of this letter is translated in Kaeuper, "Frescobaldi" (n. 1 above) 82–83. Kaeuper suggests that the Ser Manente mentioned in it was a leading partner of the Manenti company; a more probable alternative is Manente Francheschi of the Cerchi Bianchi; see *Les livres des comptes des Gallerani* (n. 21 above) 1. nos. 210, 371.

107. *Les livres des comptes des Gallerani* (n. 21 above) 1. no. 379.

The determined man was again linking his fortunes to a great Florentine company.[108]

The late thirteenth and early fourteenth centuries were the high point of Italian achievement in English finance and commerce. The disastrous failures of the Bardi and Peruzzi in the 1340s did not mark the end of Italian activity, but the pattern for the rest of the Middle Ages was to be rather different. The Italians did not become crown bankers again, preferring to lend to the government through such English intermediaries as William Latimer and Richard Lyons.[109] In the mid-fourteenth century, typically Florentine business acumen was displayed by Nicholas Bullieti, the one known dealer in wardrobe bills; but his operations were on a small scale.[110] The old trading and banking connections with the great religious houses disintegrated, and English merchants took an increasingly important part in the wool trade.

By the fifteenth century the Italians were still exporting wool, but they were buying in the Cotswolds for direct shipment to the Mediterranean via Southampton, abandoning the abbeys of Yorkshire and Lincolnshire and the ports of Hull and Boston. The author of the *Libelle of Englyshe Polycye* (1436) described the Florentines as importers of "apes and japes and marmusettes taylede," a very different role from that of their heyday.[111] The use of Italian exchange facilities by English ecclesiastics continued, however, with such payments as the £1,333 6s. 8d. made by the Strozzi on behalf of Cardinal Langham at Avignon in 1372.[112]

How far do these considerations affect the negative arguments set out by Postan? It is not possible to argue that the Italians caused major improvements in agriculture or industry,

108. *CPR, 1307–1313* (n. 16 above) 492; *1313–1317* (London 1898) 265; *1317–1321* (London 1900) 408; *1321–1324* (London 1902) 401.

109. George A. Holmes, *The Good Parliament* (Oxford 1975) 88–90.

110. G. Sayles, "A Dealer in Wardrobe Bills," *Economic History Review* 3 (1931–32) 268–73.

111. *The Libelle of Englyshe Polycye,* ed. Sir George F. Warner (Oxford 1926) 18.

112. Holmes (n. 109 above) 86.

though their insistence on high quality when buying wool had some effect. The credit they supplied to landowners was normally used to cover extraordinary expenditure, not to improve estates. This was not, however, a period when much capital investment took place,[113] and the loans from Italians enabled some landlords to survive crop failures and heavy financial impositions. The Italians made a significant contribution to trade, handling at least a quarter of the main export commodity, wool. Their business techniques were not closely copied by English merchants, however; and the letters of exchange that the latter used in the 1340s were not based on Italian models.[114] It is probably true that the Italians did not import much capital directly to England, but with their wide resources they were able to accumulate funds in a way that no Englishmen could match, and the way they deployed those funds was largely beneficial. Their exchange facilities were very important, particularly to the church. The use of letters of exchange made it easier for the government to maintain its bullionist policies by providing for payments abroad, an alternative method to the shipment of specie.

The central contribution of the great Italian companies, however, was to state finance. The system of lending on the security of the customs was of inestimable value, for it provided an essential degree of flexibility and enabled the crown to anticipate revenues in time of need. Only in 1294 was Edward I able to accumulate sufficient funds to plan a war without Italian financial aid, but the unforeseen events of a Welsh uprising and trouble in Scotland compelled him to turn to the companies.[115] The king's difficulties in the years after 1294, when he had lost the support of the Ricciardi, provide eloquent testimony to the importance of their loans.[116] Postan has few favorable words about a system primarily intended

113. Rodney H. Hilton, *The English Peasantry in the Later Middle Ages* (London 1975) 174–214.

114. Fryde (n. 39 above) 1187–88.

115. *Book of Prests* (n. 20 above) 1–li.

116. Richard W. Kaeuper, "Royal Finance and the Crisis of 1297," *Order and Innovation in the Middle Ages,* ed. William C. Jordan, Bruce McNab, and Teofilo F. Ruiz (Princeton 1976) 103–10.

to finance war,[117] but the Italians enabled the crown to pay for wars without imposing intolerable burdens of taxation over short periods. The cost of campaigns could be spread over many years, and the system was not expensive, particularly since the loans were not repaid in full. Nor was the impact of war wholly negative. Some wars financed by the Italians were profitable in terms of territory, as in Wales, or in plunder and ransoms, as in France. Only in Scotland did the losses clearly outweigh the gains.

The achievements of the Italians were impressive. Despite the fact that they were hampered by prohibitions on usury and using many techniques strange to modern bankers, the companies provided essential facilities of credit and exchange in a social and legal environment very different from their own Italian background. They were merchant bankers in a full sense. Commodity trade was important to them, but it is also more than coincidence that the Ricciardi and Gallerani should have rented counting houses in Walbrook near Lombard Street in the heart of the City of London, so long unrivaled as a banking center.[118] In an very untypically ill-chosen phrase, Powicke referred to Edward I as "strangely entangled" with the Florentines in his later years.[119] Without that entanglement, the history of England in the late thirteenth and early fourteenth centuries would have been a far more somber one.

117. Postan (n. 3 above) 341.
118. *The London Eyre of 1276* (n. 22 above) no. 521; *Les livres des comptes des Gallerani* (n. 21 above) 1. no. 374.
119. Powicke (n. 57 above) 643.

5   From the Fifteenth Century in
    Italy to the Sixteenth Century
    in Germany: A New Banking
    Concept?

Jean-François Bergier

BANKING WAS ITALIAN BY BIRTH and remained so up to the end
of the fifteenth century. Or perhaps it would be more accurate
to say Mediterranean, to allow for its early (from about 1240)
and steady development in Catalonia, as described some years
ago by A. P. Usher[1] and examined here in more detail by
Manuel Riu. For nearly three centuries, through all the vicis-
situdes of an eventful evolution, the private banks, particularly
those of Florence and Genoa, or the semipublic ones such as
the Casa di San Giorgio, followed or joined one another,
growing ever more numerous. They offered their services to an
Italian and foreign clientele of rapidly increasing diversity.
Princes, merchants, and simple citizens began to turn to the

Translated from the French by Stanley Mason.
    1. Abbott Payson Usher, *The Early History of Deposit Banking in
Mediterranean Europe* (Cambridge, Mass. 1943; rpt. New York 1967)
part 2: "Banking in Catalonia: 1240–1723."

banks to obtain credit, to pay bills for goods, to transfer funds, or to deposit moneys at interest. In other words, Italian banks from the first assumed the essential functions which customers of banks in the following centuries were to expect from institutions of this kind. The merchant bankers developed for this purpose—and perhaps helped to diffuse, a point to which I shall return later—carefully worked out techniques (simple and double-entry bookkeeping, bills of exchange, insurance systems), some of which also safeguarded them from the charge of usury.

The more enterprising of these businessmen did not hesitate to settle outside their own country or far from their native city in order better to satisfy the wishes of their customers abroad, to simplify the transfer of funds, to meet more efficiently the requirements of an international trade which had expanded greatly since the thirteenth century, and to profit as much as possible from the differences in the rates of exchange of the currencies in use. Numbers of large companies, most of them from Florence, some from Genoa and a few from Venice, set up branches in other Italian cities and later abroad. The most striking and best-known example was that of the Medici,[2] with their banks in Rome, Venice, Avignon, Catalonia, Geneva, and later in Lyon, Bruges, London, and elsewhere. Some even had offices still farther off, from Seville or Lisbon to Lübeck or Danzig. Other merchant bankers moved abroad altogether.[3] All this has been well established by the historians of banking, and it is not my purpose to linger over it here.

Then, rather suddenly, in the last few years of the fifteenth century and still more markedly after 1500, a new phenomenon

2. Raymond de Roover, *The Rise and Decline of the Medici Bank 1397–1494* (Cambridge, Mass. 1963).

3. Examples abound, whether at Avignon, London, or Bruges. For an exceptionally well-documented instance, see Michele Cassandro, *Il Libro Giallo di Ginevra della Compagnia Fiorentina di Antonio della Casa e Simone Guadagni, 1453–1454* (Prato 1976); idem, "Banca e commercio fiorentini alle fiere di Ginevra nel secolo XV," *Schweizerische Zeitschrift für Geschichte* 26 (1976) 567–611.

set in, a shift and transfer of banking institutions which took place in less than a single generation. The Italians, it is true, did not freely give up an activity which they had been almost the sole masters of for so long, from which they had made enormous profits, and on which they had founded a kind of hegemony over European commerce and finance. But all at once they were not alone; and they were not to stand up very long to the competition which now arose. By 1520 they would hold only a secondary position in the international money market. We should, however, make an exception for the Genoese: they regained their standing from about the 1530s onward, and they were destined to triumph after 1557–60, a triumph which brought the bankruptcy of Spain and the financial downfall of the Germans; but that was to take place in the shadow of the Spanish king and with the accompanying glint of American "treasure"—in conditions, that is, very different from those prevailing in the centuries before.[4]

The fact remains that there was some sort of gap between about 1490 and 1520. Or was it rather a breakdown in the dynamism of Italian banking? Who was going to take advantage of it? Who was going to leap into the breach and quickly establish his own position? It might have been expected that the French would do this, and specifically the bankers of Lyon. The kingdom of France had regained real prosperity, and Lyon was, before and around 1500, one of the big centers of fairs and of money transactions in Europe. But the inhabitants of Lyon, like the Genevese before them, had only a very limited part in the business that was done in their city. Banking, in particular, was entirely in the hands of the Italians, and for the most part it was to remain so in the sixteenth century.[5]

Then there were the Flemish. But Bruges was in a similar

4. Fernand Braudel, *La Méditerranée et le monde méditerranéen à l'époque de Philippe II* (2nd ed. 2 vols. Paris 1966) 1.454 ff.; Felipe Ruiz Martín, *El siglo de los Genoveses en Castilla (1528–1627): Capitalismo cosmopolita y capitalismos nacionales* (in preparation).

5. Richard Gascon, *Grand commerce et vie urbaine au XVIᵉ siècle: Lyon et ses marchands* (2 vols. Paris 1971) 1.357 ff.

situation to Lyon, occupied by bankers who mostly hailed from Florence. It was also in this period that the famous transfer of activity from Bruges to Antwerp[6] took place; but the boom in Antwerp's economy that Herman van der Wee places between 1493 and 1520[7] was the result of a new dealing of the cards of big business. The best trumps went to the Portuguese, with their pepper, and to the Germans, particularly with their copper, but not to the Flemish or Brabantines with their textiles. Moreover, between the ruin of the financial market of Bruges, its progressive liquidation from 1493 onward,[8] and the emergence of a similar market at Antwerp about 1510–15, there was a time lag, a caesura in the money trade in the Low Countries.[9]

It was precisely in this comparatively short interval of some twenty years that the "irresistible rise" of the German banks took place. In 1487 Jacob Fugger arrived in the Tyrol, where he began to amass his fabulous fortune; in 1490 he became Maximilian's principal moneylender; and from 1494 on he was active in the Antwerp money market. In 1498 Anton Welser founded, with his brother-in-law Conrad Vöhlin, a company destined to achieve remarkable prosperity. The Hochstetters had set themselves up in Antwerp even a little earlier, just prior to 1486, and may thus be considered pioneers. But there is no need to list here all the examples that serve to illustrate the rise of the financial power of the citizens of Augsburg, Nuremberg, and numerous other less

6. Jan A. van Houtte, "Bruges et Anvers, marchés 'nationaux' ou 'internationaux' du XIVe au XVIe siècle," *Revue du Nord* 34 (1952) 89–108; idem, "Anvers aux XVe et XVIe siècles: Expansion et apogée," *Annales: Economies, Sociétés, Civilisations* 16 (1961) 248–78, reprinted in his *Essays on Medieval and Early Modern Economy and Society* (Louvain 1977) 143–79.

7. Herman van der Wee, *The Growth of the Antwerp Market and the European Economy (Fourteenth–Sixteenth Centuries)* (3 vols. The Hague 1963) 2.113 ff.

8. Ibid. 2.111.

9. Ibid. 2.140 ff.

important towns of upper Germany,[10] that is to say, south
Germany and Switzerland (Basel, Bern, Schaffhausen, St. Gall),
and their spectacular appearance on the international scene.

It is at this point that the problems begin and questions
arise. The purpose of this account is to formulate some of
these questions and to suggest some possible answers—hypotheses only, for only hypotheses are permissible at the
present stage. We now have a good knowledge of the medieval
Italian banks, which left behind a fairly rich documentation.
We are fairly well informed about the merchant bankers of
Germany, or at least about the most famous of them, Fugger
and Welser; there is still scope for intensifying our research
into the activities of their lesser colleagues. By contrast, the
phenomenon of the transfer taking place from one group to
the other has, to my knowledge, scarcely attracted the attention of specialists. Arbitrary as it has always been, the distinction between the Middle Ages and the modern era, the traditional break that textbooks place around the year 1500, seems
to have diverted the attention of banking historians from this
question.

Yet it is a question of some importance. Might it not be
that the whole future of banking in the sixteenth century and
even up to our own times was involved in this switch from
Italy to Germany? It is certainly not immaterial whether there
was any real continuity between the activities carried on over
such a long period in Italian cities and those that now began
to take place north of the Alps. It is admittedly a very complex
question, and in fact a whole knot of questions here awaits an
answer.

I have spoken of a shift and a transfer. Are these the correct
terms? It was certainly no transfer if we take that to mean that
by some coincidence or miracle the same banking activities

10. Richard Ehrenberg, *Le Siècle des Fugger* (translated from the
German, Paris 1955) 35 and 36 (Fugger) and 87 ff. ("Les autres puis-
sances d'argent en Allemagne"); Léon L. Schick, *Un grand homme
d'affaires au début du XVI siècle: Jacob Fugger* (Paris 1957); and all
the literature on the Fuggers, Welsers, etc.

faded out at one place only to reappear at another. This was obviously not the case. The Italian banks lost their universality, their exclusive character; but they did not disappear at one fell swoop. The German banks, on the other hand, were not born out of a vacuum, in the midst of an economic and financial void. Yet I think we may talk of a shift, since within a very short space of time—a single generation—the center of gravity of European banking (judged by its turnover, which we can well imagine even if we cannot reconstruct it, and by its influence) moved from the south to the north of the Alps; and we may even speak of a transfer, insofar as German banking[11] assumed the same functions that had previously belonged to Italian banking.

This said, we are faced by the following problems:
—Under what conditions did Italian banks pursue their activities, albeit on a reduced scale, after 1500 (if we disregard, as suggested above, the Genoese enterprises engaged in cooperation with Spain)?
—Under what circumstances did German banking institutions emerge?
—Did the German banks perform the same functions as their predecessors, and did they satisfy analogous requirements?
—Did they operate in the same way? Were they inspired by Italian models, and if so to what degree? In other words, was there what we should now call a transfer of know-how from Italy to Germany?
—Did they introduce any important and decisive innovations, and in answer to what factors?
—Finally, what was the structure and what the role of public banking institutions, alongside the big private houses, to the north of the Alps in the sixteenth century?

In setting off the Italian banks of the fifteenth century against the German banks of the sixteenth we run the risk of

11. The term "German bank" is not altogether satisfactory, although it is correct to talk of an "Italian bank"; this is due to a difference in structure that I shall return to later. With this reservation, however, the expression is a convenient one.

oversimplifying the issue. Yet it seems legitimate to pose the question in these terms. On the other hand, it is apparent that the "transfer" we are discussing is directly connected with the structural mutations of the European economy at the end of the Middle Ages and the beginning of modern times, with the displacement of many activities from the Mediterranean to the Atlantic seaboard, with the substitution of the Antwerp market for that of Bruges, and with numbers of other similar phenomena well enough known to us. Nor was the transfer unconnected with the political upheavals of the time, the aftereffects of the Burgundian wars, the beginning of the Italian wars, the self-affirmation of the Habsburgs with Maximilian (elected in 1486) on the imperial throne and Charles on that of Spain (1516).

These are considerations that we should not overlook. But it would be too simple to leave it at that. Neither the failing vigor of the Italian companies nor the impressive expansion of German capital can have been due solely to the economic conditions prevailing at the time. We have to look beyond them for a new pattern of decision, a slipping of the will to dominate: in short, a double mutation in business mentality. The merchant bankers of Italy had long held the lead as a result of their consummate banking techniques and their flair for grasping opportunities, and of course because they were up against no serious competition. It seems, however, that from the middle of the fifteenth century, if not before, they had settled down into a comfortable routine. The forms of their undertakings show all the signs of a smoothly operating capitalism, but the spirit is lacking. Meanwhile, to the north of the Alps certain entrepreneurs not as yet drugged by profits were looking for a breakthrough. They were to find it around 1500, not in comparatively rough techniques or organizational structures but in their fierce will to win the big markets and to dominate international commerce and finance—in a word, to succeed. They invented capitalism in the full modern sense of the word, a capitalism that is not merely a system but a state of mind.

Persistence of Italian Banking after 1500

It will be worthwhile to outline the general situation of Italian banks in the early sixteenth century.[12] The eminent place occupied by the Medici throughout the fifteenth century is well known, and so are the reasons that led to the final ruin of their enterprise in 1494: the bad business conducted by Portinari, head of their Bruges branch, with the Habsburgs; the poor management of the Lyon branch; and, more generally, a growing lack of interest in business on the part of the responsible principals, Lorenzo and his right-hand man Francesco Sassetti, who was old (he died in 1490) and was, like his master, more inclined toward the arts and belles lettres.[13]

A certain slowing-down of the rhythm of business and profits had been manifest since the middle of the century, and the main branch's move from Geneva to Lyon in 1464–66[14] had taken place in a general atmosphere of recession. Business at Lyon had been affected by, among other things, the transfer of the fairs for ten years or so to Bourges and Troyes,[15] and it no longer reached the same volume or importance it had had in Geneva. The fate that thus overtook the most powerful of the Florentine banks did not spare the majority of the smaller companies.

At the beginning of the sixteenth century, however, a new generation of active Tuscan bankers came to the fore. While they continued their traditional commercial and financial

12. The subject would deserve a careful monograph. Material will be found in the works of Ehrenberg, Gascon, and van der Wee cited above and in the relevant writings of Armando Sapori, Federigo Melis, Raymond de Roover, Henri Lapeyre, etc.

13. De Roover (n. 2 above) 358 ff.; Florence E. de Roover, "Francesco Sassetti and the Downfall of the Medici Banking House," *Bulletin of the Business Historical Society* 17 (1943) 65–80; Jean-François Bergier, "Humanisme et vie d'affaires: La bibliothèque du banquier Francesco Sassetti," *Mélanges en l'honneur de Fernand Braudel* (2 vols. Toulouse 1973) 1.107–21.

14. Jean-François Bergier, *Genève et l'économie européenne de la Renaissance* (Paris 1963) 374 ff. and passim.

15. Gascon (n. 5 above) 2.677–80.

operations in Florence, at the court in Rome, and in other Italian cities, they did most of their business in Lyon, and there can be no doubt that they achieved a considerable and lasting prosperity there, their colony remaining the most numerous until Lyon ceased to be a great center of finance, at the time of the crises of 1573–80. The Florentines, it is true, lost some ground to their compatriots from Lucca. Milanese and Genoese were also active there (though more in trading than in banking). And above all, Germans and Swiss took over a good part of the market. But business at Lyon was thriving; it grew rapidly at the beginning of the sixteenth century, and it remained at a high level, except for a few minor setbacks, from 1520 to 1570.[16]

In the sixteenth century, however, Lyon was no longer able to set the standard for the whole of the West. Its financial market was limited to the kingdom of France and to a country which, though close at hand, was of secondary importance, the duchy of Savoy. The area was far from negligible, and the reviving prosperity of France enabled a large group of businessmen to make good profits. Yet it was not at Lyon that the really big business was being done, either in the commercial or in the financial field. It was being done at Antwerp, and the decisions were being made at Augsburg and Nuremberg, in Spain and Genoa.

And in Antwerp, the Italian businessmen, mostly Florentines, who were following in the tradition of their predecessors, had already for the most part lost the battle. What had happened?

We have seen that from the 1480s onward the money market at Bruges had been deeply affected by its excessively heavy commitments to the house of Burgundy and, soon afterward, to Maximilian, "the worst payer in Christendom." After 1488, most of the bankers stationed at Bruges began to move to Antwerp, particularly the Florentine companies Frescobaldi and Gualterotti, which still held pride of place, the Balbani of Lucca, and the Doria of Genoa. Van der Wee infers from

16. Ibid. 1.357 ff., and 2 part 2: "Conjonctures," 459 ff.

the presence of these latter, who were new arrivals, that the Florentines had already suffered grave losses.[17] However that may be, most of the Italians returned to set up shop at Bruges again a few years later, and there clung desperately to a declining market. Even in 1501, when the supremacy of Antwerp was quite evident, the Florentines of Lyon persisted in seeing Bruges as the principal money and exchange market for the whole of northwest Europe.[18]

How are we to explain this attachment to a place where the Florentines had registered such successes but which was now at its last gasp? Was it perhaps fear of facing new competitors—the Germans—whose ambitions and working methods were different from their own and whose mentality they had difficulty in understanding, as van der Wee suggests?[19] Hardly, for the Florentines showed elsewhere—at Lyon—that they were quite capable of adapting to this foreign presence. Was it a result of the setbacks suffered by the Italian economy in the East? In part no doubt it was: their commercial position (spices, silks) had been weakened by this development. But they had succeeded in finding substitute markets and activities. Was it not, rather, a simple lack of imagination, a habit that had grown up during more than a century of good business, of easy business on a short-term basis, whereas now it was suddenly becoming necessary to plan for the long term?

This momentary blindness did not last long. When Portuguese spices began to arrive in the Low Countries around 1501, they were unloaded in the port of Antwerp, a sign that was the more unmistakable because this new trade was set up at the expense of the Venetians, though it also had repercussions on the other Italian centers. The Frescobaldi and Gualterotti hastened to try to recover so important a market, but it was too late. They succeeded only in a few isolated ventures before finally foundering: the Frescobaldi in 1518, the Gualterotti in 1523.

17. Van der Wee (n. 7 above) 2.111.

18. Emile Coornaert, *Les Français et le commerce international à Anvers, fin du XVe–XVIe siècle* (2 vols. Paris 1961) 1.95 n. 1.

19. Van der Wee (n. 7 above) 2.111.

It is consequently no exaggeration to say that the fate of European banking was decided at Antwerp, and by pepper. The strong position the Italians had built up in Lisbon, the port of arrival of the fleet from the Indies, was here of no use to them: they had made a strategical error. It was the distribution market they ought to have held. And a money changing service. The Italians had little but their credit system, and even that had lost its cutting edge.

There was still the skill of the Genoese. Their situation was different: the course they steered ran counter to that of their Florentine colleagues. Dominated through the fifteenth century by the Casa di San Giorgio, which remained a local institution, Genoese banking did not take the same "multinational" line. Its expansion beyond Italian frontiers was on a modest scale and marked by reserve. It took hardly any part in the great speculations of the century, but first and foremost served specifically Genoese interests: the silk trade, and exchange operations conducted with a degree of sophistication unknown elsewhere.[20] The Genoese had been very much to the fore in Geneva. They left it for Lyon, but only after great hesitation and later than the other Italian merchant bankers.[21] Their ups and downs at Lyon, and the coquetry they continued to display there, are too familiar to need telling here.[22] It is also well known that the Genoese, exposed to a good deal of worry on the banks of the Rhone yet dependent on fairs for their exchange operations, finally decided to go it on their own: from 1512 on they held their own fairs at Montluel, not far from Lyon but outside the kingdom of France, and later at Chambéry. On several occasions (1513, 1522) they considered returning to Geneva.[23] Then in 1534 they

20. Jacques Heers, "Gênes, Lyon et Genève: Les origines des foires de change," *Cahiers d'histoire* 5 (1960) 7–15; idem, *Gênes au XVᵉ siècle: Activité économique et problèmes sociaux* (Paris 1961) 74 ff.

21. Bergier (n. 14 above) 312 ff.

22. Domenico Gioffrè, *Gênes et les foires de change de Lyon à Besançon* (Paris 1960).

23. Jean-François Bergier, "Marchands italiens à Genève au début du XVIᵉ siècle (1480–1540)," *Studi in onore di Armando Sapori* (2 vols. Milan 1957) 2.893–94.

gave serious thought to Lucerne, on the northern slopes of the St. Gotthard route to Germany. And they finally opted for Besançon in 1535.

Montluel, Chambéry, Geneva, Lucerne, and Besançon are all cities of the Empire. Might this not indicate that the Genoese, sooner and clearer than the merchant bankers of the other Italian cities, sensed the changing weather? They did not settle in Germany itself, where they would scarcely have been tolerated. But they chose a territory which was under the same sovereign authority and situated so as to leave open the doors of both Germany and France. The area, or rather the line, along which Genoese exchange fairs oscillated from 1512 to 1535, between Montluel and Lucerne, seems to me significant: always within the Empire, always on a land route directly connecting Genoa with the northern countries by one or another of the best passes in the western or central Alps: the Mont Cenis pass to Montluel and Chambéry, the St. Gotthard to Lucerne, the Simplon or the Great St. Bernard to Besançon.

Was this chance, or a necessity realized in time? Political circumstances no doubt contributed to these successive choices, but they cannot explain them alone. I detect here the workings of a strategy dictated by the new balance of forces: already perceptible in 1512 when the Genoese withdrew from Lyon, it became evident in 1535 when they established themselves in the Franche-Compté.

The Irresistible Rise of German Banking

From the 1480s onward, German businessmen began to spring up wherever profitable operations were possible, wherever large-scale business projects were afoot in the merchandise area, in the money market, in mining, in industrial manufacture. In the space of a generation or less, they moved into all the important commercial and financial centers of Europe, they entered all the channels of business—and nearly always with success. They were the first to recognize the possibilities of the Antwerp market and to show faith in its future, at a time when its chances of success were not at all obvious. Between 1480 and 1510, the first generation of big merchant bankers from Augsburg and Nuremberg established themselves there: Ludwig Meuting, the first of them, in 1479,[24] then the Hochstetters (1486) and Jacob Fugger (1494). The Welsers followed only in 1507; they had first put their money on Lisbon (1503), but had realized sooner than their Italian colleagues that Antwerp was the place for spices and credit banking, from now on to be closely linked. It was also in the 1480s that German merchants—mostly from Nuremberg—invaded the Geneva fairs, taking the place abandoned by the Italians some fifteen years earlier and reviving the languishing trade,[25] though here they were, in the strict sense of the word, less bankers than merchants. From this time on, Geneva acted mainly as a relay station on the way to Lyon, but it would have provided a place to withdraw to if the capital of French trade had ceased to give satisfaction. These are simple examples of the German "diaspora"; I wish only to point out its almost explosive nature and to add a few comments.

First of all, these southern Germans did not come from nowhere. They lived in a remarkably prosperous country, where the agricultural surplus had permitted the development of a relatively dense urban network (though it was not comparable with that of the Low Countries or northern Italy). In the cities a sound artisan tradition had grown up with a fairly wide range of products: textiles (wools, fustians, linen cloth) south of the Danube and around the Lake of Constance, metalwork around Nuremberg, woodwork, and so forth. At the end of the thirteenth and in the fourteenth century, a complete commercial and financial system had developed around this production. In the fifteenth century it expanded in all directions: from Poland to the Iberian peninsula, from the Low Countries to the valley of the Po; even in Italy, in Venice,

24. Ehrenberg (n. 10 above) 88.
25. Jean-François Bergier, "Recherches sur les foires et le commerce international à Genève, principalement de 1480 à 1540," *Ecole des Chartes: Positions des thèses* . . . (1957) 31–36.

Milan, and Genoa, at the very heart of the leading economic power, the German presence very soon made itself felt.[26] Thus, by the end of the fifteenth century, the Germans had at their disposal a network of connections and agencies covering the whole of Europe. It was a network mainly commercial in character; but they had only to transform it into a financial and banking system.

A second consideration was southern Germany's geographical location: a central position nearly equidistant from the great European centers of production and consumption. This meant that the businessmen of the region were admirably placed for the role of intermediaries. That was certainly the main reason why most of the firms originating in Augsburg and Nuremberg kept their headquarters there and sent their middlemen and agents to all the peripheral markets, from Antwerp to Rome, from Seville or Lisbon to Danzig or Prague. Ports, on the other hand, were far away; most German trade was by land (maritime ventures on the Atlantic and from the Iberian ports nearly all ended in failure). It was a trade in luxury or semiluxury goods requiring the investment of considerable funds. It was thus based on the existence of substantial capital, without which the German breakthrough at the end of the fifteenth century would not have been possible. The birth of German banking around 1500 in fact depended on the partial transfer of capital from commercial to financial operations. Finally, by way of the Alpine passes, southern Germany was very closely connected to Italy, with which it had entertained close and privileged relations for a long time, at least since the thirteenth century. If Italian banking moved over to Germany, it was not by any detour over the sea but

26. It should suffice to recall the classic works of Aloys Schulte, *Geschichte des mittelalterlichen Handels und Verkehrs zwischen Westdeutschland und Italien* . . . (2 vols. Leipzig 1900; rpt. Berlin 1966), and *Geschichte der Grossen Ravensburger Handelsgesellschaft, 1380–1530* (3 vols. Stuttgart and Berlin 1923; rpt. Wiesbaden 1964); those of Hektor Ammann (too numerous and scattered to be listed here); and more recently those of Wolfgang von Stromer, particularly *Oberdeutsche Hochfinanz 1350–1450* (3 vols. Wiesbaden 1970).

by the direct road over the Alps, without any French or Flemish halfway stations.

Thirdly, the lucky chance of the Germans, the great opportunity so quickly seized by their merchant bankers, lay in metals, particularly silver and copper. Nuremberg businessmen made profits from the resources of Saxony, Moravia, and Silesia, and in turn they stimulated improvements in ore mining and metal working methods from the mid-fifteenth century onward. The Tyrol played a part in the rise of Fugger and several other Augsburg companies. The monetary situation was decisive in this context; the "squeeze" which prevailed in Europe at the end of the fifteenth century and the beginning of the sixteenth gave the systematic exploitation of these resources obvious importance. But here again substantial investments were needed for the undertaking, and for the first time in the history of capital in Europe they had to be long-term investments. In this immobilization of funds, this extension of the risk over a period of time, I see the reason for a concept of finance quite different from that of the Italians, and the source of a new approach, a different view of money, its use and its anticipated profits. "Banking bridging time": the merchant bankers of southern Germany were certainly the first to grasp the truth contained in Martin Mayer's phrase, and it was not the least of their contributions to the development of banking economics.

From trade, mining, and industrial undertakings to the German banking activities was only a step, a mere change of approach which it is difficult to follow in the documents but which was certainly rapid. To pinpoint it exactly, we should have to make a detailed chronological inventory of all important operations carried out by the Germans in the second half of the fifteenth century. Even without these data, we may assume without much risk of error that such a change of emphasis took place in the last twenty years of the century. We should be clear that it was not a single event but rather a trend among a group of businessmen, few in number and, if I am not mistaken, all from Augsburg, who now directed their transactions mainly toward the handling of capital, that is, toward banking. But it was only in the reign of Charles V that their convincing example was to be followed by many others and that a veritable class of bankers was to develop. It is important to add that such business was not terra incognita for most of them, since they had practiced it occasionally, on a more or less large scale, for two or three generations, though never outside German territory.[27] Conversely, banking in the sixteenth century was never to be their sole activity; even at the highest level, that of the Fuggers or the Welsers, they were all merchant bankers. In this respect, the private German banks did not differ from the Italian model.

Such a change of emphasis can be accounted for only by the conjunction of three different needs: the need of princes—particularly the Habsburgs, Maximilian, and Charles V—for readily available means, that is to say, for credit; the need for finance on the part of industrial entrepreneurs, especially in mining; and the need to place capital, which was being amassed by trade, the handicrafts, agriculture, civil service officers, war chiefs, soldiers, and so on. The function created the instrument: those merchants who had some money of their own, some good relations or means of applying pressure, and above all had a keen sense of initiative, could set themselves up as intermediaries between these complementary needs. After all, when Jacob Fugger began his profitable Tyrolean operations, he possessed only a small part of the necessary capital: he had to collect the rest from his compatriots in order to make his loans to Sigismund of Austria and later to Maximilian, receiving in return the right to work the mines of the Tyrol.

Italian Model or Original Construct?

The question of function remains: did German banking play a similar role in the economy of the early sixteenth century to that which Italian banking had played a few decades earlier?

27. Von Stromer (n. 26 above) has called attention to several exceptions, notably credit operations in favor of the house of Savoy. They are, however, limited and not very significant.

And there is also the question of means: was the structure of the companies of Augsburg and its environs analogous to that of the older but still existent companies of Florence, Genoa, or Lyon? Did they use the same techniques? These two questions are basically one.

Let us begin with structure. One resemblance is evident: on both sides of the Alps, banking firms had a very marked family character. Almost all consisted of a small number of associates who were close relatives or members of the same family clan—witness the Medici in Italy and the Welsers in Germany, the constitution of whose personnel was almost the same. At most, women played a more prominent role in the German companies: not that they were themselves active in the management, but through them brothers-in-law, sons-in-law, and nephews were brought into the enterprise. Jacob Fugger, who worked alone and then made his nephew Anton his sole heir, was an exceptional case: elsewhere, the clan ruled. The analogy, however, did not result from any continuity, from the intentional imitation of an established pattern, but was an arrangement that came naturally—family ties are the best guarantee of a community of interests. This phenomenon can be observed in the history of banking up to the opening of the big business banks in the nineteenth century, and even up to our own day in private banks (public banks being, by definition, exceptions to the rule).

There is another similarity in the contracts of incorporation, particularly in their duration.[28] We know that Florentine companies were rarely formed for more than three, four, or five years.[29] This was probably because the companies were originally founded with a specific operation, of limited duration, in view. It was also a way of guarding against risks in the absence of any clause about breaking the contract. And

---

28. The German contracts have recently been analyzed in a work by Elmar Lutz, *Die rechtliche Struktur süddeutscher Handelsgesellschaften in der Zeit der Fugger* (2 vols. Tübingen 1976), where the details can be found.

29. Cf. the example of the Medici as presented by de Roover (n. 2 above) passim.

thirdly, the life expectancy of the partners was often brief, and death with its concomitant inheritance problems might well compromise the success and even the existence of a company. But it was always possible to renew the contract for one or more additional periods, when its terms could be modified as required. These successive *rinnovi* gave the companies great flexibility. This system persisted and was still practiced by Florentine companies in the sixteenth century.[30] The Germans adopted the same policy. Practically all the articles of association of German companies which have come down to us from the fifteenth and sixteenth centuries are limited to periods ranging from one to twelve years; most often they were drawn up for four, five, or six years.[31] Yet the majority of these companies lasted much longer—several decades, or even a whole century, with repeated renewals and the modifications imposed by circumstances.

There is hardly any doubt that such contracts were directly inspired by Italian models, as was all common commercial law in South German cities. The same customary arrangements are found in them, and in the same order. The definition of the company's goals is couched in similar and equally vague terms—perhaps even more vague in German contracts, where the banking function of the company is never explicitly stated. In Italian: "mestiero del canbio, come usati siamo, e così anchora se di merchatantia deliberasimo trafichare";[32] "per intraprendere . . . mercantie, camby, spedizioni di bonefizi, chonmessione e altre facciende."[33] In German: "hanntierung und gesellschaft ains kauffschlagen-

30. See as an example the contract signed in 1521 for three years by Lorenzo and Filippo Strozzi on the one side, Piero and Giovanfrancesco Bini on the other, for a company domiciled in Lyon. Published by Federigo Melis, *Documenti per la storia economica dei secoli XIII–XVI* (Florence 1972) 342.

31. Lutz (n. 28 above) 1.210–11.

32. Contract signed by the Medici for their Venice branch, 1406: Melis (n. 30 above) 336.

33. Strozzi-Bini contract, 1521: Melis (n. 30 above) 342.

handels";[34] "bruderlichen handl und gesellschaft, gewerbe und hantierung";[35] "gesellschaft, hantyrung und gewerbe kauffmannshendell und sachen."[36] Thus, on a formal level, there seems to be a direct relationship between Italian and German companies. Moreover, mixed companies, consisting of both Italian (mostly Milanese) and German merchants, were not unusual in the fifteenth century or at the beginning of the sixteenth.[37]

The outer form, then, was the same. The contents, however, differed in several essential points. The great Italian firms were subdivided into branches that were constituted as autonomous companies (Medici, Strozzi, etc.). Nothing of the kind occurred in Augsburg or Nuremberg, where the organization of the companies was much more centralized. The Italian division of duties and responsibilities contrasts with the German cohesion, unity of management for all current business, and, despite the formal brevity of the contracts, real continuity of the activities. Was this an answer to the need for much longer-term operations? Probably, but I cannot say so positively.

There is a fundamental difference on another level, this time a structural innovation made by the Germans—the formation of cartels and monopolies.[38] Not that monopolies were unknown to the Italians: we may think of Genoa and Venice,

34. Imhof company, Nuremberg, 1481 and 1490: Lutz (n. 28 above) 1.205.

35. Fugger, 1494 and 1502: Lutz (n. 28 above) 1.205.

36. Grander, Rehlinger & Hanolt, Augsburg, 1503, 1507, and 1511: Lutz (n. 28 above) 2.28–29.

37. Schulte, *Handel und Verkehr* (n. 26 above) 1.586 ff.; and 2.269 ff., example of a contract between two merchants of Nuremberg and one of Milan: "im handel . . . es sey an barm gelt, an güten, schulden oder pfenbarten im zimlichen rechten gelt geschäczt. . . " (1506).

38. See the literature on the German companies and on the Fuggers; furthermore, Fritz Blaich, *Die Reichsmonopolgesetzgebung im Zeitalter Karls V. Ihre ordnungspolitische Problematik* (Stuttgart 1967); Heinrich Lutz, *Conrad Peutinger: Beiträge zu einer politischen Biographie* (Augsburg 1958).

of the monopoly of papal alum held by the Medici or by
Agostino Chigi at the beginning of the sixteenth century. Yet
with the exploitation of Tyrolean and Central European
mines, the role of metals (silver and copper) in German enterprises, or the Spanish farms, a new dimension was added
to the monopoly system in the financial and commercial
economy of the sixteenth century: they became an instrument,
privileged in all respects, of the merchant bankers' activities.
Cartels and monopolies depended upon a jurisprudence particular to the Empire. But above all, they represented a new
concept in business strategy: they expressed the capitalist
mentality of their members. That is why monopolies were the
object of violent criticism and of suits before the Diet, conducted by business circles (such as the Hanseatic League) which
had not absorbed the modern capitalist spirit.

"Technological" Backwardness and Innovations

We know that German companies clearly lagged behind
their Italian predecessors in accounting and banking techniques. The bookkeeping, some of it double-entry, which
every fifteenth century Italian accountant had at his finger-
tips was introduced slowly and belatedly into the offices of
Augsburg and Nuremberg and their agencies at Antwerp. The
first manual to explain its mysteries to the German-speaking
public, that of W. Schweicker, was not printed until 1549—a
very revealing delay. Not all businessmen north of the Alps,
however, were ignorant of the technique; Jacob Fugger had
acquainted himself with it at the beginning of his career,
when he was studying in Venice. It looks very much as though
its use was not considered necessary. The same applies to
the principal banking techniques. Genoese virtuosity in exchange transactions remained foreign to German manage-
ments; if they sometimes did exchange business, they never
made it an end in itself. The bill of exchange was used less
regularly and more straightforwardly—that is, in its original
function as a means of deferred payment or transfer. The

Germans seemed to prefer simpler but less flexible expedients: I.O.U.'s and promissory notes.

It appears from this that the shift of banking toward the centers of upper Germany was accompanied by only a partial transfer of know-how. Even at Antwerp, where Italian influence was still manifest in the early years of the sixteenth century, there was a regression, or perhaps it would be wiser to say a certain hesitancy, in this domain. Must we, then, question the modernity of German banking in the sixteenth century?

We cannot deny the business acumen and the imagination of the Fuggers, Welsers, Hochstetters, Imhofs, and their colleagues. The dimensions they gave to their ventures within a few decades are there to be seen. If they did not adopt all the range and refinements of the techniques and methods developed in two or three centuries of Italian experience, it was not out of ignorance—their personal contacts with Italian businessmen were too close for that—nor for any lack of mental ability, and still less because of any moral scruples. It was because they deliberately rejected them, judging them unsuitable for the management of their affairs. The problem must be considered from two different angles: that of the mentality of German businessmen, and that of their specific requirements. But both aspects allow of the same interpretation.

When I speak of mentality, I mean that the Germans did not rise to the same level of abstraction as their Italian colleagues. Credit for credit's sake, or even gain for the pleasure of gain, did not enter to the same extent into their conception of business. They always looked for a concrete base: the trade in goods, the working of mines, industrial production. Every sizable medium- or long-term credit was covered, if possible, by a specific security. Of course, the risks were no less great—bankruptcies occurred from time to time. But before the Spanish collapse of 1557, the bankruptcies all seem to have been the result of wrong calculations in dealings with merchandise, and not of imprudent banking operations.

We can therefore formulate the hypothesis that the financiers of southern Germany at the beginning of the sixteenth century, drawing upon both the technical apparatus inherited from preceding generations and the well-stocked arsenal of Italian banking, kept those instruments which they felt most capable of handling and which most aptly answered their needs. These needs, however, derived from the specific functions of banking as developed by the people of Augsburg.

At first sight, these functions do not differ fundamentally from those of Italian banking. Credit was still credit. It seems at most to have rid itself in Germany and Antwerp of the burden of church prohibitions against usury which the Italians had used such ingenuity to circumvent. Perhaps it was for this reason that German money exchange speculations were no longer of the same kind or on the same scale. On the other hand, the Germans were less involved in transferring capital on commission. And above all, the German merchant bankers understood their role as agents of economic life in general: they placed themselves, far more clearly than the Italians did, as intermediaries between the available capital—now more abundant than in the previous century—and those who needed it, whether princes or entrepreneurs. They were less the inventors of capital (as the Florentines had been in a high degree) than its go-betweens. The fact that they grasped the need for this mediation and assumed the role is what constituted the "modernity" of these businessmen. They scarcely invented techniques; they rather refined them. In return, they conceived of banking on a broader basis, both economic and social. It suffices to mention the initiative of the Hochstetters in the 1520s, when they called on people to save, even on the most modest scale. Through them the whole economy and a large sector of society were integrated into the capitalist system, won over by its spirit.

Public Banks

Here we may recall, as a sort of revealing corollary, the example and the role of certain "public" banks (i.e. banks dependent on the state) in German countries in the sixteenth century. They were not large enterprises. No doubt that is why banking historians have generally disregarded them, although several old works pointed out their existence.[39] A young Swiss historian, Martin Koerner, has recently turned his attention to the bank of Basel.[40]

In the first few years of the sixteenth century there appeared on the banks of the Rhine, in Strasbourg and Basel simultaneously, the so-called *Stadtwechsel,* or municipal bill of exchange. While this term is current, we should not be misled by it: the activities of the two establishments quickly exceeded the mere exchange of moneys and embraced all the services of a bank. The Basel bank (founded by the city in 1504) accepted deposits from public bodies (from the city itself, from Strasbourg, Bern, etc.) and from private persons; it offered credits to public and private clients; it carried out transfers; and later (1574) it even took over the administration of fortunes. It was, of course, not comparable with the great houses of Augsburg. The operations of the bank of Basel were limited to the surrounding region (Switzerland, Alsace, southern Germany). Its clients were neither other financiers nor Europe's great debtors. The amounts on its balance sheet were hardly impressive. Above all, the bank rigorously eschewed all speculation: its statutes were very clear on this matter, and the municipal authorities watched over the morals of its management. In return, the city was able to offer guarantees to numerous depositors.

These banks seem to have been a purely original creation: they owed nothing to older or to Mediterranean models. They were intended to handle local needs—originally, no doubt, to

---

39. Richard Hallauer, *Der Basler Stadtwechsel 1504–1746* (Basel 1904); Julius Cahn, "Der Strassburger Stadtwechsel: Ein Beitrag zur Geschichte der älteren Banken in Deutschland," *Zeitschrift für die Geschichte des Oberrheins* N.F. 14 (1899) 44–65. More recently, Hans Mauersberg, *Wirtschafts- und Sozialgeschichte zentraleuropäischer Städte in neuerer Zeit* (Göttingen 1960) 287–91.

40. Martin Koerner, *Solidarités financières suisses au XVIe siècle* (thesis, University of Geneva 1976, typescript) 401 ff.

put to good use the financial resources of a rich city which did not know how to invest its capital so as to retain control of it and to be able to mobilize it easily in case of need. In this they contrast markedly with the Catalan public banks, as described here by Manuel Riu, which were meant to find capital when it was in short supply. In any event, the example of Basel and Strasbourg was not much followed elsewhere.[41] The phenomenon is consequently interesting not for its breadth or its diffusion, but only for its function, which was to meet the need felt by at least two cities for the flexible disposition of local or regional capital. On its own small scale, it thus demonstrates the new role of the bank that was developing north of the Alps around and after 1500.

This essay has only scratched the surface. The subject of banking in the fifteenth and sixteenth centuries deserves an entire book, but it would call for much more research, and in particular comparative analyses of the balance sheets and accounts of some of the great banking firms on either side of the Alps. Banks from other parts of Europe—Spain, the Low Countries, France, and England—ought also to be included in the survey. I have merely suggested some lines of approach and put forward some hypotheses, while recalling certain facts which might be susceptible to new interpretations. My purpose has been primarily to establish a connection between two already well-researched areas, Italian banking at the end of the Middle Ages and German merchant banking at the beginning of the modern era.

The decline of Italy's banking activity, of her hegemony in the financial life of Europe, is one of the facts just mentioned; the sudden rise of the Germans is another. Between the two, there is no direct or obvious causal relationship: each must be considered in its own context. Yet the coincidence of these two

41. At Geneva in the second half of the century, but it was a failure. William Monter, "Le change public à Genève, 1568–1581," *Mélanges d'histoire économique et sociale en hommage au professeur Antony Babel* (2 vols. Geneva 1963) 1.265–90; and Koerner (n. 40 above) 151 ff., 283 ff.

things could not have been fortuitous. For it was, after all, the position partially vacated by the Italians that the Germans resolutely and sometimes brutally filled, so that within a few decades—between 1480 and 1520 or 1530—they became its masters.

In taking it over, the Germans remodeled banking to suit the needs of their economy and the new spirit that animated them. Between the Italian fifteenth century and the German sixteenth century, there was no interruption in banking. But there was a shift, a transfer; and there was a change in the nature of the institution. The Italians had given banking its name and its instruments. The Germans gave it its place in the economy and in society.

6 Banking and Society in Late Medieval and Early Modern Aragon

MANUEL RIU

IN THE STUDY OF THE ECONOMY AND SOCIETY of the states under the crown of Aragon—Catalonia, Aragon, Valencia, and Majorca—almost everything remains to be done. Abbott Payson Usher's book,[1] a general analysis of banking and credit in the western Mediterranean, is still the most important work on the rise of banking in Catalonia.[2] Most of the financial

Titles listed in the Bibliography are cited here in shortened form.

1. Abbott Payson Usher, *The Early History of Deposit Banking in Mediterranean Europe,* part 1: *The Structure and Functions of the Early Credit System;* part 2: *Banking in Catalonia, 1240–1723* (Cambridge, Mass. 1943; rpt. New York 1967). Idem, "Deposit Banking in Barcelona, 1300–1700," *Journal of Economic and Business History* 4 (1931) 121–55, translated (Catalan with Spanish title) as "La Banca de Depósito en Barcelona (1300–1700)," in *Cuadernos de Historica Económica de Cataluña* 3 (1969–70) 157–81.

2. Usher noted *(Early History* [n. 1 above] xi): "Full analysis of the material collected has confirmed the impression formed at an early stage. The conditions in Barcelona were in many respects more advanced, and the documents supply more specific evidence of primary functions than is available elsewhere. The prominence given the description of banking in Barcelona can thus be justified in terms of its intrinsic

connections between the medieval crown of Aragon and the rest of Western Europe still need to be studied, mainly through documents available in other European countries. Usher pointed out the similar origins of banking institutions in northern Italy and Catalonia. De Roover observed that Italy was on the debit side, Catalonia on the credit side, of the commercial balance in Flanders in the fourteenth and fifteenth centuries: the account books and correspondence of Francesco Datini (d. 1410) and the Medici bank show that their agents in Bruges were constantly accumulating credits in Barcelona in order to transfer funds to Italy, and money changers and bankers in Barcelona did the same, using letters of exchange. In fact, at the end of the Middle Ages, Barcelona, Valencia, and Palma de Majorca were among the most important banking centers of Western Europe, maintaining relations not only with Bruges but also with Palermo and mainland Italy.[3]

But I shall concentrate on the domestic history of banking in Aragon, for it is even less well known. Within Spain, various royal, municipal, and ecclesiastical archives hold a wealth of unpublished source material on virtually all aspects

---

importance, as well as upon the mere practical fact of the amount of material now available." It is important to keep in mind the difference between Aragon itself, where banking remained exclusively in the hands of the Jews until the end of the fifteenth century, and Valencia, Majorca, and the principality of Catalonia, where Christians took an active part in banking and money changing from the time of Jaime I on.

3. Raymond de Roover, "New Interpretations of the History of Banking," in *Business, Banking, and Economic Thought in Late Medieval and Early Modern Europe,* ed. Julius Kirshner (Chicago and London 1974) 200–38, especially 204–05. See also Ramón Carande, "Comercio, banca y crédito medievales según De Roover," in *Moneda y Crédito* 40 (1952) 9–23. On Sicily and Italy, see Carmelo Trasselli, *Note per la storia dei banchi in Sicilia nel XV secolo* (Palermo 1958) and "Sul debito pubblico in Sicilia sotto Alfonso V d'Aragona," *Estudios de Historia Moderna* 6 (1956–59) 69–112; Henri Lapeyre, "Alphonse V et ses banquiers," *Le Moyen Age* 67 (1961) 93–136; Alfonso Silvestri, "Sull'attività bancaria napoletana durante il periodo aragonese: Notizie e documenti," *Bollettino dell'Archivio Storico del Banco di Napoli* 6 (1953) 80–120.

of banking and foreign exchange. To suggest how such materials can be exploited, I shall first briefly describe some archival and other sources and then survey the rise of private banking in Catalonia, before examining in greater detail the first *taules de canvi,* or municipal banks, in Barcelona and other cities of Aragon.[4]

In Barcelona, the royal house's banking activities are revealed in the archives of the crown of Aragon, the records of the *Maestro Racional* (Archivist of the Royal Patrimony) and the treasury, and records of taxes levied by the crown. Through the capitular archives of the cathedral, through diocesan, episcopal, and parish records, we can study the property and business of all social classes: dowries, wills, legacies, and pious foundations record a complex economy of contracts, mortgages, loans, rents, and annuities. The Notarial College houses the *Archivo Histórico de Protocolos*; there, though the records seldom reveal the daily activities of banks, we can study some important dossiers, such as those of bank defaults, that permit us to gauge the volume of business carried on by private bankers like Pere dez Caus and Andreu d'Olivella in 1381.

Barcelona's municipal Archivo Histórico offers abundant documentation on the Taula de Canvi, which has been only partly explored.[5] The *Llibres Majors* of the bank for the years 1401–07 are preserved, in five volumes; notebooks contain indexes or *rúbricas* to them (green box no. 1) listing the names and professions of depositors and borrowers in alphabetical order. Also preserved are the deposit books *(capbreus)*, with their *rúbricas*, of the first administrators *(regidors)* of the

---

4. Basic bibliographical information on Spanish archives can be found in the *Censo-guia de Archivos Españoles,* listed in the general bibliography appended to this essay. For the ecclesiastical archives, see the entries there under Mateu y Llopis. All of the important archives have printed guides, catalogues, or published or unpublished inventories.

5. The Archivo Histórico has a manuscript inventory of the holdings from the Taula, made by the archivist José Serra Roselló. Any in-depth study of the Taula should begin with a review of Usher's investigation. See also the relevant entries in the Bibliography.

Taula. Other documents include accounts of redemptions, reductions and sales of mortgages (*censals*), daily records of
receipts (*rebudes*), records of payments, and lists of embargoes
(*emparas*) for 1430 and 1455. Judging from an inventory of
the Taula's records taken in 1458, there were once many more
volumes dating from 1401 stored away.

It would be especially important to make a thorough study
of the five volumes of *Llibres Majors* from 1401 to 1407. For
example, even though it has been said that the municipal
bank was not authorized to make loans to private citizens,
such loans appear among the very first entries: £6 were lent
to a priest to buy ornaments for the altar, and a loan of £50
was made to a merchant from Barcelona to pay for the linen
cloth from Alexandria which he had purchased from Juan
Asopardo of Pisa and Escará Figa of Genoa. Money was also
lent to execute wills and to build churches.

The *Levament* or balance of the Taula prepared in 1433
(inventory no. 17), which has not been investigated either,
would offer the names of all 1,460 clients of the bank, reflect
their comparative wealth, and reveal the relationship between
the Taula de Canvi and the people of Barcelona. Among the
debtors and creditors of the Taula were the king and Queen
Violante, scribes and notaries, nobles and knights, merchants,
money changers, wool carders, artisans of various trades—
silversmiths, goldsmiths, tailors, weavers, glassworkers—cathedral canons, priests and friars, butchers, innkeepers, ship-
owners and sailors, peasants, widows, and young women. The
amount of money deposited or borrowed usually ranged from
£2 to £150.

Similar materials, equally interesting but also unpublished,
are preserved in other archives, such as those of Gerona and
Vic, the various towns in the old kingdom of Valencia, or
the municipal and historical archives of the kingdom of
Majorca.

I know of only two literary sources that could contribute to
a study of banking: the words which Ramon Llull (d. 1315)
addressed to the *canviadors* (money changers) in his *Libre de
contemplació*, and the commentary by José María Ainaud on

a few fragments of the poem *Lo Canviador* by the poet Jordi de Sant Jordi.[6] The poem is a fine satire on the activities of an unknown money changer who lived somewhere in Aragon in the fifteenth century. Although the poem was first published around the beginning of this century, it has never been studied in depth. More generally, careful review of the vernacular prose and poetry of the fourteenth and fifteenth centuries would reveal the importance of money in that society. Very often such words as *mogobell* and *remogobell* appear, referring to usurious loans at 20–30% interest and to loans with compound interest. Bernat Metge (d. 1413) says in his *Libre de Fortuna e Prudència* (verses 564–81) that the money changers "have changed gold into lead" and "they do not feel satisfied unless they can change twenty *sous* into five hundred." Such comments are obviously significant.

Private Banking in Catalonia

In Aragon, the existence of money changers is attested at Jaca in the middle of the eleventh century, and in Saragossa at the beginning of the twelfth. The Christian money changers Ramon and Esteve competed with Jewish bankers like Bon Judà in Barcelona in the twelfth century.[7] The financial records of Jaime I and his immediate successors contained in the *Aureum Opus*, a collection of royal decrees, shed some light on the birth of banking in Valencia in the thirteenth

6. Jose María Ainaud de Lasarte, "Cambistas y banqueros en la Barcelona medieval," *Divulgación Histórica de Barcelona* 9 (1959) 214–18. Josep Romeu i Figueras has recently republished the poem *Lo Canviador* ("Comentaris al cançoner de Jordi de Sant Jordi," *Serra d'Or* 19 [1977] 25–28) with a commentary which I consider superficial and erroneous. He believes that "the money changer was so kindly and simple that he could not distinguish between what was proper and what was not, between good and evil."

7. Ruiz Martín, "La Banca," 6. I owe the information on the money changer Esteve to Dr. Carmen Batlle, who found his wife Guilleuma's will, dated 5 January 1212, in the Capitular Archive of Barcelona, Diversorum D, box 9, 175.

century.[8] It was in the thirteenth century that Christian banking developed in earnest, in the hands of private money
changers, or *de menuts*, aided by licensed public exchanges.
Even though the Catalonian changers had to compete with
Italians (mainly from Pisa, Genoa, and Florence), they made
considerable gains throughout the thirteenth century. In
Barcelona, their shops or *taules*—referring to the wooden
board, folding table, or bench on which the transactions took
place—could be found near the harbor, located in the square
called Canvis de la Mar and along the adjoining streets,
Canvis Vells (Old Exchanges) and Canvis Nous (New Exchanges). These streets still exist, in the neighborhood of Santa
Maria del Mar.[9] The *Llotja* or *Lonja* (Exchange) was built in
the Plaça dels Canvis de la Mar starting about the middle of
the fourteenth century (it was completed in 1392); its fine
Gothic hall is still preserved inside a later neoclassical building. Twenty-five exchange offices were functioning in Barcelona in the fourteenth century: ten on Canvis Vells and fifteen
more along Canvis Nous.

Our present knowledge about the thirteenth century is little
more than fragmentary, though it could easily be amplified
by consulting the abundant source material available. On 13
October 1217, Jaime I authorized the citizens of Lérida and
all other towns and villages of his royal domain to lend money
at interest (*dare pecuniam mutuo*)—confirming what they had
already been doing since the time of his great-grandfather
Ramón Berenguer IV (d. 1162).[10] The Christian subjects of
the counts of Barcelona and the kings of Aragon had been
engaged in legal lending transactions within the Catalonian

8. Arcadio Garcia Sanz, "La banca en los siglos XIII y XIV según el
Aureum Opus," *Boletin de la Sociedad Castellonense de Cultura* 33 (1957)
201–05.

9. Lluis Almerich Sellarés, *Història dels carrers de la Barcelona vella*
(3 vols. Barcelona 1949–50) 1.55–58. In 1328 there was still one street
called "Dels Canvis." See also Carrère, *Barcelone*, 1.50 n. 1.

10. Ambrósio Huici Miranda and Maria de los Desamparados Cabanes
Pecourt; *Documentos de Jaime I de Aragón*, I: *1216–1236* (Valencia 1919;
rpt. 1976) 29–30, doc. 5.

territory of the royal dominions, in competition with the Jews, since the middle of the twelfth century. In 1220 Jaime I himself named Friar Guillem of the Order of the Templars to administer the royal income in Catalonia, and he appointed another Templar friar to administer the financial affairs of the kingdom of Aragon. These officials were authorized to collect rents, fix payments, and cancel debts, all actions that required experience in monetary matters. It was probably his new administrators who advised Jaime I to obtain from Bishop Guillem of Vic permission to open a taula de canvi in Vic for forty days in 1222, in order to pay off his debts.[11] By the middle of the thirteenth century, at least one Christian moneylender, named Vila, was in business in Vic alongside the Jewish lenders and money changers. In June of 1256 he lent 159 sous to Berenguer, the abbot of Sant Joan de les Abadesses, at a monthly interest rate of four *diners* per pound (1.66%, or 20% annually).

The frequent mention of a "silver mark of the board of exchange of Barcelona," whose value was fixed at 88 silver sous between 1223 and 1238,[12] confirms the existence of various exchanges in Barcelona with at least some degree of organization among them. The circulation of money increased significantly during this period. On 31 March 1229, Jaime I had to order notaries and Jews in Gerona and Besalú not to lend money at rates higher than 20% and to give interest "only on the amount lent, not on the proceeds, as some do."[13] Some lenders demanded interest on the profits made with the money that was borrowed from them, or else they recorded higher

11. Ibid. 86, doc. 35. On the money changers in Vic, see Francesc Carreras y Candi, "Notes dotzecentistes d'Ausona," in *Miscelánea Històrica Catalana* (2 vols. Barcelona 1905–06) 2.361–463, especially 388–89 (though this work affirms that the Jews still had a monopoly on lending in 1277).

12. Sayous, *Els mètodes,* 147, doc. 6, and 149, doc. 9. The second document shows that Esteve Scasset had to pay to the Jew Astrug Rubén, also from Barcelona, interest consisting of four diners per pound per month (20%). In 1358 the mark was set at 72 sous in silver *croats* and the ratio of silver to gold was established at 13 : 1.

13. Huici (n. 10 above) 221–22, doc. 117.

amounts than were actually lent so as to cover the expected gains. It seems clear, then, that money was borrowed for business purposes and that some attempt was being made to clamp down on usury.

There is no doubt that the money changers received deposits to negotiate with in genuine banking transactions. Two documents of Joan de Banyeres, a money changer from Barcelona, show that they obtained higher profits this way.[14] The documents date from 1261 and 1264. Both times he formed a partnership (*societat*) with his relative Ramon de Banyeres. Two thirds of the capital belonged to Ramon, the other third to Joan. Joan promised to obtain a profit by putting the money to work in his money changing business (*in office tabule*). After discounting 36 sous for the yearly rent of his taula, they would divide up the profits in proportion to the capital invested. The 1261 contract totaled £128 10s., for a period of one year; in 1264 the amount was £202 10s., to be returned in two years. Joan de Banyeres is an example of how a Barcelona money changer turned into a banker in the mid-thirteenth century, without the name of his profession changing. The same could be said of the merchant banker Jaume Ferràn, who invested money from his taula in commerce with North Africa.[15] These money changers were actually private bankers, though the term *banquero* or *tauler* never appears in any documents from this period.

In 1235 the Cortes had decreed that Christian subjects of the crown could lend money at 12% interest and Jews at 20%, a measure which tended to favor Christian money changers and lenders. But the benefits which the king obtained from the Jews enabled them to negotiate the special statute of 1240. Although this statute has sometimes been identified as the beginning of Christian banking in Catalonia, it was actually no more than a means of maintaining a balance between the Jewish and Christian communities at a time when the latter were beginning to offer serious competition to the former. The

14.   Sayous, *Els mètodes,* 146, doc. 4, and 146–47, doc. 5.
15.   Ibid. 34–35.

Jews continued to lend money, protected by the crown, but their Christian rivals grew in strength and power, especially after they began to participate in the municipal government of the principal cities. In Barcelona, between 1254 and 1270, twenty-two money changers were members of the Consell de Cent (city council), and several later figured among the five *consellers* who ruled the city.

As Usher observed, the privileges granted by the kings to various cities such as Barcelona, Valencia, and Tortosa served to obviate differences between them that could have interfered with financial operations. The privilege of Barcelona granted on 11 January 1284 decreed that money changers' books would be considered reliable proof of payment for credit transfers, as long as their authenticity had been sworn to before the *veguer*.[16] A month earlier, when Pedro III confirmed the laws and liberties of the kingdom of Valencia, he ordered the Valencian money changers to have their *taules* or banks insured with the curia to guarantee the money left on deposit or *en comanda*. Similarly, the *jurats* of Majorca in 1288 obtained from Alphonso II a decree that no money changer could operate without having insured his taula at the Majorcan court; a tapestry spread over the table served as a sign that the taula was insured, and all operations were to be recorded in a *Llibre registre*. In Valencia, Catalonia, and Majorca alike, it was felt that banking operations should be insured, precisely because the same person could engage in both banking and industry or commerce.

Irresponsibility, speculation, and lack of foresight on the part of some money changers doubling as bankers led to the first failures during the last third of the thirteenth century. The high clergy were very much involved in financial business by the end of the thirteenth century. In a document dating from 1299, a money changer from Barcelona named Tomàs de Vic, a creditor of the king, confessed to receiving 2,000 sous from Eymeric Bou, a canon of the cathedral of Barcelona, by order of Bishop Bernat; the royal counselor Bernat de Sarrià

16. Usher, *Early History* (n. 1 above) 238–39.

was to have received this amount from the bishop, who had obtained a fifth of the profits from an illegal business venture in Egypt (*ad partes Alexandrie*).[17] In 1298 the important monastery of Santa María de Poblet had 6,440 sous deposited in the *Tabula pensi* of Valencia (which had had charge of the salt tax since before 1283) and 3,300 sous with Pere de Reguer of Tarragona ex comanda.[18]

Some more or less fraudulent bankruptcies around the beginning of the fourteenth century led to the first laws governing banking in Catalonia,[19] passed by the Cortes of Barcelona in February 1300 and by that of Lérida in March 1301. By the former, which some authors date to 1299, Jaime II decreed that the money changer who went bankrupt (*abatut*) should be publicly denounced, not only in the streets of Barcelona but also in all the towns where he had done business. He could not open any exchanges or banks thereafter, and would be imprisoned and kept on bread and water until he paid off all his creditors. The money changer was declared responsible for all entries (*dites*) made for his clients, just as if they were deposits or *comandas* (money to be used for investment). All entries were to be recorded in his *Capbreu major jurat* or *Libro Mayor*, and not in other books or documents, and henceforth no one, not even the king, could postpone settlement of credit beyond the set time. In Lérida, the king decreed that money changers were responsible to their creditors and that their goods could be confiscated in cases of default. In the future, no one would be allowed to open a taula de canvi in Catalonia without first submitting a deposit as guarantee: 1,000 silver marks in Barcelona and Lérida and 300 marks in all other towns and cities in Catalonia—obviously

17. Sayous, *Els mètodes*, 167–68, doc. 28.
18. Luis Altisent, "Administración del monasterio de Poblet durante la Edad Media: La descentralización administrativa interna" (doctoral thesis, University of Barcelona 1976) 309.
19. José María Madurell Marimón, "Quiebras en la Vida Mercantil Catalana," *Anuario de Historia del Derecho Español* 59 (1969) 577–670, with documentation for Barcelona and notarial documentation on some cases between 1300 and 1761.

Barcelona and Lérida were the most important centers of monetary circulation at this time. Only after the deposit was paid could the money changer place the tapestry bearing the shield of the city on his table, indicating that his office was guaranteed. Those who did not pay the fee had to leave the wooden top of their tables bare, without tapestries or other cloths, as a warning to their clients.

All kinds of tricks were used to evade the law. Ponç Fibla, a money changer from Valencia, declared bankruptcy and was thrown in prison by his creditors. To escape trial he cut his hair in a tonsure and claimed to be a priest. He was set free, but the Council of Valencia brought a complaint before the king on 4 February 1318 insisting that he had lived and dressed as a layman until the time of his imprisonment.[20]

Laws to guard against this sort of abuse would continue to be in effect for centuries; many appear in the *Constitutions y altres drets de Catalunya*[21] drawn up by Philip IV in 1702. But this and other similar frauds made it necessary to formulate new and stricter laws to prevent fraudulent bankruptcies and protect creditors. King Sancho I of Majorca decreed in 1314 that money changers who concealed resources and escaped to avoid payment of debts brought ill fame to Majorca and would henceforth be condemned to death and executed *sens tota mercé*, without mercy.[22] Such drastic measures were not limited to Majorca. In 1321 the Cortes of Gerona decided that the money changer who declared bankruptcy should be brought to justice after his infamy was proclaimed and his goods sold at auction to repay his creditors.[23]

The *cambiadors* had become a necessity, not only for

20. Heinrich Finke, *Acta Aragonensia* (3 vols. Berlin and Leipzig 1908–66) 2.852–53, doc. 533.

21. *Constitutions y altres drets de Catalunya* . . . (Barcelona 1704) 350–51 (book IV, title 35) and 420–21 (book IX, title 10); *Cortes de Cataluña* 1 (Madrid 1899) 170 and 186–87.

22. Pons Pastor, "La banca mallorquina" 173. Archivo Histórico de Mallorca, *Cedules reials*, fol. 142v, 15 July 1314.

23. *Constitutions* (n. 21 above) 420. *Cortes* de Gerona, cap. 13, tit. 10, 3.

merchants (who sometimes doubled as money changers) and
rich burghers, but also for the royalty, high clergy, and
universitats or urban municipalities. In 1301 Jaime I released
Berenguer de Finestres, Bartomeu Cendra, and Pere Sentpere
from infamy on condition that they pay off their creditors
before Christmas, since the king himself was in debt to them.
Various money changers who served as fiscal agents in the
royal treasury appear in the records from 1302 to 1304. Bernat
Cavaller, a changer active in Barcelona in 1315, spent some
years in the service of Frederick of Sicily in the kingdom of
Trinacria, and returned in 1318 with a recommendation to
Jaime II.[24] The taula of Bernat Llorenç was used by
Barcelona in 1328 for its financial transactions.[25]

For the unscrupulous, this could be a very profitable investment. The cities needed cash for payments and often requested loans from the money changers, agreeing to return
the money within a limited time and at correspondingly high
interest rates. But cities were not the only speculators. The
desire to get rich quick led a lot of people to *fer dites en les
taules,* to take out loans or deposit money in order to receive
interest payments a certain number of times a year. This type
of speculation led to the bankruptcy or near bankruptcy in
Majorca of the money changers Francesc Renovart, Pere de
Castelló, and Jaume de Condomines in September 1329, an
event so serious that by a royal decree the king appointed six
inspectors to examine the bankers' books, hear their oaths,
count the money on hand, and make an inventory of the
merchandise held in deposit and a second, general inventory.
Then they were to seek an agreement with the creditors. If
this proved impossible, they were to sell both the property of
the money changers and the merchandise held in deposit, to
pay off the creditors. Not even these transactions would be
free from speculation, since they involved the exchange of

24. Archivo de la Corona de Aragón, Barcelona, Cancilleria, reg. 214,
fol. 57.

25. Jean Broussolle, "Les impositions municipales de Barcelone de
1328 à 1462," *Estudios de Historia Moderna* 5 (1955) 1–164.

Majorcan *reials* for currency from Barcelona and the sale of minted gold and silver for more than its legal value (special laws prohibiting this practice had to be passed in 1329). On the same day the royal decree was issued in 1330, the money changers in Majorca who were not insured (*sens tapit*, or without tapestry) were warned not to buy or sell any currency except in cash—*nengún cambi a escrita de taula*; that is, they were authorized to deal solely in hard currency, so as to avoid fraudulent transfers and speculation. The money changers who were insured could *fer dita e escritura en la sua Taula*. Anyone who acted on his own, without the necessary guarantees, would be at the king's mercy.

It would be hard to explain the growth of the taules de canvi in Barcelona between 1340 and 1360 if it were not for the practice of short-term transactions lasting only a few months. From this time on, the city itself began to deposit rents and incomes not needed for immediate use, and in this way the taules came to serve as a municipal treasury.[26] In 1342–43 the bankers handled the city's floating debt by issuing loans and accepting transfers between one taula and another at an annual interest rate of 20%: the 50,000 sous (£2,500) that Roger Sant Vicens lent to the city in 1342 were deposited in the taula of Francesc Castanyó and Pere dez Caus.[27] Hence Barcelona's interest in obtaining from the king the right to certify persons who wished to operate as bankers and to inspect the books of private exchanges—privileges granted in 1349.

The abuses perpetrated by the city of Barcelona in demanding advances from the money changers who held public funds led to the bankruptcy and execution of some in 1345. Francesc Castelló was beheaded in front of his taula in the Plaza de los Canvis de la Mar the evening of 10 November 1360. The fact that the economy had been severely affected by the Black Plague between 1348 and 1350—that prices and wages had

---

26. Yvan Roustit, "La dette publique à Barcelone au milieu du XIV⁰ siècle," *Estudios de Historia Moderna* 4 (1954) 13–156.

27. Ibid. 35–36, 149.

tripled and credit plummeted—does not seem to have been taken into account.

The grave crisis at mid-century forced the city of Barcelona to borrow from the Jews, to request new loans and advances from the money changers, and to adopt an economic policy more heavily dependent on credit, which the monarchs also adopted. When money could not be repaid on time, another money changer intervened and paid, receiving a "wage for the job" which actually amounted to interest on interest. Jaume dez Vilar, for example—probably the most important banker in Barcelona at this time—paid back £4,500 to the Jews on behalf of the city in 1359. (In 1357 he had advanced to the king's administrators £20,000 granted by the Cortes of Lérida, a sum repaid the following year.)[28] Later he had to declare bankruptcy, and the city councilors ordered Aymeric d'Usay and Jaume de Gualbes, whose family had already bought £2,310 of the city's credits, to take over Vilar's accounts with the city, offering them £100 as payment.[29]

Because of the rise in prices and salaries following the Black Plague, in 1359 the Cortes of Cervera decided to double the deposit required of the money changers to insure their taules. Those who wanted to go into business in the cities of Catalonia and in Perpignan would have to pay 2,000 silver marks, or 1,000 marks to open an exchange in other cities or towns; money changers already in business should have their taules fully insured within two months. The Cortes warned that any money changer who claimed bankruptcy and fled to cities or lands under either lay or ecclesiastical rule to escape royal justice would be judged by the authorities in that place; no one, not even the king, could pardon him unless he first paid back his creditors.[30]

Following the bankruptcy of three changers in 1360,[31]

28. Ibid. 139, 154–55, 136, and 137.

29. Ibid. 139, 150.

30. *Constitutions* (n. 21 above) 351, 421; *Cortes de Cataluña* (n. 21 above) 1.51.

31. *Crònica del Racional de la Ciutat de Barcelona (1334–1417)* (Barcelona 1921) 133. Archivo Histórico of the city of Barcelona, Clavaría, reg. 2, fol. 277v.

Bernat Bertrán bought the *imposició de la farina* (flour tax) from the city council, obtaining £300 in interest from this single operation;[32] and Arnau and Berenguer Bertrán became more firmly established as the great bankers of Barcelona along with Aymeric d'Usay and Jaume de Gualbes. These men did not run the risk of bankruptcy, because they demanded solid guarantees before they would grant credits or advances, even if it meant getting lower returns. The Bertrán brothers made over £1,000 in interest in 1361, when a municipal councilor's yearly salary was only one tenth of that amount.[33]

The private bankers acted as fiscal agents for the city of Barcelona and the Generalitat of Catalonia, which served as the financial organ of the Cortes from the time of Pedro IV.[34] They also served as a vehicle for paying the royal troops, and they could advance large sums of money to the king or other governmental agencies. These amounts were probably not as great as one might suppose, however, for in 1364 Berenguer Bertrán was not able to raise the 50,000 florins needed for an advance of half of the property tax specified by the Cortes and no one could be found to take his place. In 1365 four money changers from Tortosa were called upon to lend £2,500 apiece to the Generalitat in order to pay the soldiers defending the Valencian border. This was granted with "certain conditions" (meaning interest payments) not specified by the Cortes of Tortosa.[35]

Christian bankers and money changers had taken over the important role, formerly held by the Jews, of supplying the king's subsidies from the Cortes. The coordinated action of a group of money changers was fundamental. They included Ramon Medir in Gerona, Berenguer Bellmunt in Tortosa, Guillem Roger Suay and Armengol Martí in Perpignan, Pere Arús in Manresa, Jaume d'Urg in Puigcerdà, Antoni Bertrán and Guillem Togores in Tarragona, and Berenguer Bertrán

32. Broussolle (n. 25 above) 107.
33. Roustit (n. 26 above) 73–74, 140.
34. Pierre Vilar, "Le déclin catalan du Bas Moyen-Âge," *Estudios de Historia Moderna* 6 (Barcelona 1956–59) 1–68.
35. *Cortes de Cataluña* (n. 21 above) 2.231–34.

with his son Antoni, Aymeric d'Usay, and Jaume de Gualbes in Barcelona. The four from Barcelona once lent £26,000 in a single payment to the Cortes of Tortosa.

We still know very little about loans made to private individuals. Parochial and private records give us some clues regarding loans involved in the purchase of *censals* or mortgages (with an interest rate, pension, or *censo* of 7.14%) and *violaris* or life-annuities (at 14.28% interest).

Sometimes bankers intervened on behalf of the public interest. From a document recorded in 1379 we know that Pere and Francesc de Gualbes made a loan of 52,000 sous, by means of a *dita* in their *tabula cambii*, to the administrators of Pere dez Vilar's hospital in Barcelona. The money was to be used to purchase the mills near the monastery of Sant Pere de les Puelles, so that the hospital could substitute the income from the mills for the small censos—hard to collect in times of crisis—deriving from the censals of various donors.[36] The hospital administrators then sold the censals to private citizens through the money changers Pere Brunet and Pere Provençals to pay back the loan made by the Gualbes family. The censals consisted of small revenues from merchants, weavers and tailors, and even farmers, which the money changers would sell to the moneyed bourgeoisie who hoped to be able to live off their censos or fixed annual interest. They were to sell the censals until they collected the 52,000 sous to be turned over to the Gualbes brothers. The actual price of the mills which Bonanat de Pedra sold to the hospital was 50,000 sous in cash. The Gualbes charged only 2,000 sous—a mere 4%—for the "favor," perhaps because of the beneficial civic character of the arrangement.

This step, taken to establish a secure source of income for the hospital by eliminating a large number of small donations by private citizens, might have caused some friction in the following years. But a new crisis was not long in coming, and the financing operation proved to be a wise one after all.

36. Archives of Santa María del Mar, Barcelona, Parchments no. 14,156 (11 August 1372), no. 14,165 (27 March 1376), no. 14,166 (5 May 1376), and unnumbered burnt parchments of 10 December 1379.

The economic crisis already obvious in 1380 worsened in 1383. In these years several private banks went out of business in Barcelona, the nerve center of the Catalonian economy. The first institution affected was that of Pere dez Caus and Andreu d'Olivella.[37] Their books for the years 1377–82 have been preserved, as well as the *capbreu* or notarial register of the taula's creditors for 1381–89. Loans to Pedro IV and his son the duke of Gerona totaled £288,000. This figure alone reveals how important credit was for the economy, the royal family included. The latter, in fact, helped dez Caus and d'Olivella to evade justice during the treasury inspection of 1380: Pere Mayol, the regent assigned to this taula, suspecting that the bankers would "launder their accounts" (*lavarien lurs comptes*), seized their books, promising to give them a hearing before a judgment was made.[38] The capbreu illuminates the activities of the bank's attorneys Mateu Alemany and Joan Vilella, of the Maestre racional and his lieutenant, the money changer Guillem Colom, and the creditors—the royal family, the Generalitat, the nobility, citizens and merchants of Barcelona, the administrators of Pere dez Vilar's hospital, and officials of the crown. Some of them were repaid, by loans from the royal treasury and the nobility, during the nine years the liquidating lasted.[39]

The bank of the Gualbes family, once so flourishing, withstood the crisis until 1405. Perhaps it would be more correct to say "banks," since various members of the family carried on banking operations simultaneously and independently of each other for several generations, maintaining contacts with Francesco Datini, exporting silver and jewels, and so on. Nicolau de Gualbes, for instance, in 1395–97 a leading member of Barcelona's Consell de Cent, formed a banking partnership with his relative Francesc de Gualbes. In 1400 he was

37. Ramón Gubern, "La crisis financiera de 1381 en la Corona de Aragón," X° Congreso Internacional de Ciencias Históricas, *Riassunti delle Comunicazioni* 7 (Rome 1955) 236–38; Jaime Vicens Vives, *Cataluña a mediados del Siglo XV* (Barcelona 1956) 22.

38. Usher, *Early History* (n. 1 above) 258–68; Vilar (n. 34 above) 17–18.

39. Barcelona, Archivo Histórico de Protocolos, not. 22 (F. Ladernosa), dossier 36 (old dossier 7) for 2 July 1381 to 23 April 1389, 148 folios.

accused of fraud in connection with sales of jewelry and dishes and brought to trial.

Other banks were barely able to stay in business. Even guaranteed banks were not considered safe: in 1396 the bailiff of Barcelona was accused of offering unauthorized guarantees to the money changers, and the veguer, the chief civil authority of Barcelona, refused to deposit city money with Pere Burnet in 1399, even though the king had said that this bank was completely reliable.[40] Suspicion and distrust of the banks had become so great in Barcelona that the Consell de Cent had to pass regulatory laws so that people would feel it was safe to make deposits. In 1397, the city decided that the correction of abuses should come under the authority of the Consuls de la Mar rather than that of the veguer or the bailiff, and so ordered the money changers to move their taules into the new Lonja, finally completed in 1392. Some, at least, complied, for we know that in 1397 Joanet ces Anasses and Jaume de Puigdauluch paid an annual rent of 25 Aragonese gold florins for their taula in this building,[41] but others refused, and the order does not seem to have had much force.

Nevertheless, the Lonja now became the center of monetary exchange in Barcelona. Through correspondence in the Datini archives, de Roover traced its links with exchanges in eight other European cities: Avignon, Bruges, Florence, Genoa, Majorca, Montpellier, Pisa, and Venice.[42] Although Barcelona in 1385 contained no more than 35,100 inhabitants—10% of the population of the principality of Catalonia—Barcelona business accounted for half of the £1,500,000 value of Catalonia's foreign trade in 1390, and half of the £2,000,000 in 1402.[43] Her money changers must have had an impressive

40. Marina Mitjà, "La banca barcelonesa de fines del siglo XIV y principios del XV," *Divulgación Histórica de Barcelona* 9 (1959) 235–38.

41. Carrère, *Barcelone*, 1.51 n. 2.

42. Raymond de Roover, *The Bruges Money Market around 1400*, with a statistical supplement by Hyman Sardy (Brussels 1968) 84–87 and 86, tables and a graph showing comparative rates of exchange in Bruges and Barcelona between 1385 and 1416. Equivalencies of the different currencies are given in sous and diners of Barcelona.

43. Carrère, *Barcelone*, 2.532–35.

working knowledge of international exchange rates. It is significant that such modest persons as the dressmaker of a merchant's wife should have invested their small savings—five or six pounds—in business ventures. It is also interesting that when Francesco di Marco Datini was thinking of doing business with the Barcelona money changers in 1397–99, his friend and collaborator Simon Bellardi sought to dissuade him: "a strange idea," he said, "since these money changers are better informed than we are about what is going on everywhere."[44]

With the city's regulatory role increasing, it was not long before the idea arose of setting up a Public Credit Bank in the Lonja. In 1397, in an effort to stabilize the monetary situation, a commission appointed by the city proposed to the Consell de Cent the establishment of a Taula de Canvi, to be insured by the city itself. The public municipal bank was about to be born.

The Taula de Canvi de Barcelona

The public municipal bank emerged in Catalonia at the beginning of the fifteenth century as a result of the private banks' instability and insecurity. The idea was soon extended to Palma de Majorca and Valencia.

The first banking establishment to be created by a city government was the Taula de Canvi de Barcelona. Installed in the Lonja, it began to function on 20 January 1401. It acted as fiscal agent for the city of Barcelona and, from 1413 on, for the Generalitat of Catalonia as well, and it received and administered the savings of private citizens. Guaranteed by the municipality, the Taula de Canvi de Barcelona received surplus taxes, lent money to the city, at moderate rates of about 5%, both for its interest payments and to pay off the public debt,[45] and competed with the private banks. The public bank never overran the private sector, however, because it had not been conceived to supply capital for private

44. Ibid. 586.
45. Broussolle (n. 25 above).

business ventures in an expanding economy, though it did make some attempts in this direction.

The earliest ordinances of the Taula, dating from March and October 1401, are lost. We must deduce its structure from the ordinances of 1412,[46] which entrusted the administration of the Taula to two honorable citizens elected by the city council for two years at an annual salary of £150 each. Each had to deposit 6,000 florins (£3,300) in trust, and their personal belongings could be confiscated if they did not manage affairs properly. A clergyman (two after 1402) was to assist them, and a set of scales and a messenger were also assigned to them. From 1409 on, four books were used in accounting: the *Diari general*, the *Llibre de prèstecs o corrible* (book of loans), the *Llibre de depòsits condicionats* (book of deposits on condition), and the *Registre de joies o penyores* (register of jewelry or pledges); all have been only partially preserved. Accounts were kept in *lliures* (pounds), sous, and diners of Barcelona. The equivalencies in Aragonese florins were established from the outset, one florin being worth 11 Barcelona sous in 1401.

The 1412 ordinances made the Taula independent of the municipal treasury and assigned to it certain fixed revenues due the city; this income was to be used for salaries and public works such as walls, bridges, and roads. The accumulation of capital in the municipal Taula de Canvi produced, as Marina Mitjà observed, "an effect which could not easily be foreseen: the city of Barcelona began to buy up different baronies and became herself a feudal overlord."[47] This process had actually begun in the fourteenth century, but there can be no doubt that the Taula served to aid and stimulate it. Those required by law to place their money in the Taula de Canvi included executors of wills, guardians and administrators of inheritances, and court officials (in cases of dowries, property of minors, sureties, sums in dispute, deposits on company con-

---

46. Usher, *Early History* (n. 1 above) 275–77.

47. Mitjà (n. 40 above) 238. The purchase of the baronies of Elche and Crivillente (Valencia) represented an investment of £27,500 in 1391.

tracts, etc.). Private citizens, communities, and public corporations such as the *bacins* (parish aid to the poor) were free to deposit their funds wherever they wished. A check was issued in exchange for the amount deposited, which could be withdrawn on demand.

With these funds, the city Taula could attend to supplies of wheat[48] and meat, public works, back payments, and the municipal debt. In case of war or other needs, it could offer special services to the king, and it could invest in baronial lands. The functions of the exchange and the city's financial situation were such that between 1410 and 1417 there were, among the persons buying up urban taxes, only six private money changers (2.3% of the investors).[49] A certain stabilization was not long in coming, however, as evidenced by the reduction of the consolidated debt to £125,000 between 1420 and 1429.[50]

The municipal Taula de Canvi was organized with two separate accounting systems. The deposits of a public wary of private bankers were covered by cash on hand, while the assets of regular accounts, subject to the constant deposits and withdrawals of businessmen and professionals, were balanced by the liability of loans made to the state, official organizations, and private individuals. The dual accounting system explains the situation in the Taula de Canvi on 23 January 1433, when the earliest complete balance still preserved was made. The sum of the deposits (£103,275 17s. 7d.) and credits (£254,760 6s. 11d.) equaled the sum of cash on hand (£105,781 15s. 3d.) and liabilities (£252,190 9s. 3d.). The total was approximately £358,000 or 7,160,000 sous, a considerable amount

---

48. Jaime Carrera Pujal, "La Taula y el Banco de la Ciudad," *Divulgación Histórica de Barcelona* 5 (Barcelona 1948) 189–93. It is not easy to calculate what these figures represented. The weekly consumption of wheat in Barcelona (with 35,000 inhabitants) has been estimated at 2,800 *cuarteras*, which at 13 sous per *cuartera* meant a cost to the city of 36,400 sous a week.

49. Broussolle (n. 25 above) 124.

50. Vilar (n. 34 above) 33.

for that time.[51] What is even more surprising is that one man, Pere Ribalta, had over £100,000 in his account—28% of the total. There were 1,494 accounts and 1,460 individual depositors. Most were from Barcelona and the surrounding area, but some came from as far away as Gerona, Lérida, Cervera, and Perpignan.

In spite of the bankruptcies that had occurred in the years preceding the creation of the Taula de Canvi, the bourgeoisie of the city showed a continuing confidence in, and sometimes even preference for, the private banks—whose bankers, it should be noted, deposited their reserves in the municipal Taula. And despite prohibitions repeated throughout the fifteenth century, the private banks continued to do business with each other. More than once the Taula advanced money to private bankers so that they could meet their payments. Fraudulent bankruptcies by private bankers and money changers became a problem after 1429. This time the law was evaded by transferring deposits and comandas to Italian associates—especially in Florence and Lombardy—by letters of exchange. Once the transfer was made, they would claim that the coffers were empty and that creditors could not be paid.[52] To eliminate such fraudulent bankruptcies, an ordinance of 3 March 1436 required that property or funds be surrendered in person. Money orders and checks were evidently used even then for transferring funds from one account to another, both

51. Sayous, *Els mètodes*, 134–37. Usher, *Early History* (n. 1 above) 136–38, 334–39. Archivo Histórico of the City of Barcelona, "Levament fet per En Martí ça Riera," 1433.

52. Carrère, *Barcelone*, 2.739. Mario del Treppo, *Els mercaders catalans i l'expansió de la Corona Catalano-Aragonesa al segle XV* (Barcelona 1976) refers (241–55) to the traffic of gold and silver through Barcelona and Valencia by large Florentine companies with branches in Avignon and Montpellier. During the first third of the fifteenth century a profit of as high as 25% could be made on this trade (255). Furthermore, the Italians leased the royal mints, coined the weaker currencies, and by an intricate system of exchanges made money where currency was sound and paid their debts in the countries where bad currency was in circulation.

within the same bank and between banks, although problems remained to be solved.[53]

Severe measures had to be taken in following years against uninsured money changers, de menuts, who competed with the municipal bank for the right to lend to private parties,[54] and even against cloth merchants who carried on unauthorized banking operations. Despite the fact that certain families could exert pressure on the city government, in 1438 the consellers finally refused to grant permission to private individuals to engage in banking activities.

At about this time the municipal Board of Exchange undertook a commercial enterprise: the Taula began to lend money to buy wool in Flanders and England for weaving in Barcelona. In doing so, however, it was competing with private money changers such as Jaume de Casasagia, who in 1440 invested £3,000 to purchase 500 *quintals* of wool in England.[55] One year later, the Taula paid some £8,000 for the same amount of wool, with a two-year term for the loan—terms not particularly favorable to the success of the venture.

Between 1441 and 1450 appeared a series of laws to protect the city Exchange. Private money changers were forbidden to deposit money or open accounts under the names of executors of wills, minors, hospitals, monasteries, or other charitable institutions. Any such funds not deposited in the Taula within a period of time would be subject to fines of up to 5% of the amount in question. Payment in cash on demand to depositors within twenty-four hours was made obligatory. It was forbidden to offer credit on letters of exchange or other notes. All of these regulations were symptoms of the economic crisis at mid-century that was making it difficult for both private individuals and public entities to pay off the censals or mort-

---

53. The use of the check or *polissa* was sporadic in the fourteenth century and still limited in the fifteenth. It was not legalized until 1527. By 1609 it was in general use.

54. Carrère, *Barcelone*, 1.72–73 and 76–77.

55. Ibid. 2.824–28. Each *quintal* of wool brought from England in sacks was worth £16 6s. 6d. in Barcelona.

gages. Some of the money changers, including Jaume de Casasagia, after holding out as long as they could finally went bankrupt in 1447. Berenguer Vendrell, who had received large amounts en comanda as guardian of the gold coin stored in the royal Ceca, declared himself bankrupt in 1449. (When an attempt was made to prosecute his backers, they claimed to have been promised immunity.[56] Protected by the royal house, Vendrell agreed to return 50% of the money entrusted to him by his imprudent fellow citizens.) In 1457 the canviadors de menuts were informed that they could not charge more than one diner per florin when changing money—or 0.62%.[57]

These measures, however, did not cripple the private bankers. On 15 March 1460, a new bank was organized by Guillem Bages, a merchant from Barcelona, and his partners Galcerà d'Estelrich and his wife Francina. Bages contributed £200 and his partners £600. They planned to exchange florins and other gold coins for silver and copper coins, and to trade in woolen or linen cloth, fish, salt, oil, and other merchandise. Gains and losses would be shared equally and Bages would square accounts with his partners each month. If they decided to increase the capital, the merchant banker would contribute £100 for every £400 added by d'Estelrich and his wife.[58] Commercial ventures were one way of increasing bank profits in a business which had become noticeably restricted by regulation.

But the crisis worsened during the civil war of 1462–72. The consellers prohibited private banking in 1463, though they authorized six money changers to operate as bankers in 1464 and the number rose to eight shortly thereafter. And yet the city Exchange was not able to extricate itself, even by placing such strict limitations on private competition. In 1468 payments had to be suspended temporarily because of excessive

56. Ibid. 1.74–79, 2.737–38 and 784–85.
57. Carmen Batlle, *La Crisis social y económica de Barcelona a mediados del siglo XV* (2 vols. Barcelona 1973) 1.380.
58. Usher, *Early History* (n. 1 above) 251–52.

loans made to the government for war expenses and to the city administration to buy wheat. The city's expenses in that year were 27% higher than its income. This imbalance led to a reorganization of the Taula which seriously affected its depositors: accounts were cut by as much as 12%, and savings deposits were reduced by 15%. The Taula's reorganization was completed in 1476 with the creation of two new offices, those of auditor (*credenser*) and cashier.

Private money changers were also affected by the reorganization. After 1476 they were not allowed to have accounts in the Taula, though they were now permitted to negotiate letters of exchange as long as they employed the same types of exchange as the city bank. Fifteen banks were authorized between 1466 and 1478, bringing the total to twenty-four.[59]

Another reorganization of the Taula under King Ferdinand in the last decade of the fifteenth century was also done at the expense of the private banks. In 1480 he introduced the election by ballot of the Taula's administrators. And in 1493 he decreed that any money changer who fled, hid, or claimed bankruptcy would be declared "without peace or respite" and excluded from every part of the kingdom until he had satisfied his creditors. There was, however, no more talk of applying capital punishment. The new ordinances of the municipal Exchange in September 1499 specified that no private money changer could accept deposits. In 1503, the king confirmed all of the privileges previously granted to the Taula, "from which," he said, "great benefit redounds not only to the principality of Catalonia, but also to many peoples, kingdoms, and seignories." In 1510 he repeated all the old anathemas against money changers and merchants who declared bankruptcy and transferred money to other persons. In the Cortes of Monzon in 1585, it was decreed that any sum greater than 40 sous had to be deposited in the Taula de deposit of the city of Barcelona.[60]

By these and other measures limiting the private sector, the

59. Ibid. 247–49.
60. *Constitutions* (n. 21 above) 421, 398, 350.

Taula was able to withstand even the creation of the first
"Banco de Barcelona" in 1609. The competition between the
two led to a new set of ordinances in 1620 defining their
respective functions. Once again, in 1641, at a difficult time
for Catalonia, the Taula de Canvis had to suspend payments
and undergo a new reorganization. Thereafter it continued
to operate until it was absorbed into the Bank of Spain in
1853.

The Taula de Canvi de Valencia

In 1407, the Consell of the city of Valencia decided to create
a Taula assegurada or Trapezet, in imitation of Barcelona's
municipal bank.[61] The Taula de canvis de la ciutat de Valencia was officially established on 31 January 1408. It was to
be the depository for the city treasury, a "safe and useful
office for merchants and private and foreign businessmen, and
a protector of pilgrims and travelers, widows and orphans,"
who presumably would feel that their savings were secure
there. Public officials and other persons who had money on
deposit elsewhere were given four months to turn over their
funds to the Taula without penalty. But the bank had a very
short life: it was dissolved in April 1416, and not until 1519
was a similar institution, the Nova Taula, established.

No account books from that first period, when the Exchange
operated in the merchants' Lonja, have been preserved. Transactions took place across a large table covered with a cloth
bearing the city's coat of arms; all of the books, scales, stamps,
and weights were in full view of the depositors. Initially, the
bank was run by two officials (*taulagers* or *taulers*) elected
from among the merchant class for two years. They had to pay
a security of 6,000 florins each, and received an annual salary
of £100; they were assisted by two clerks earning £60 a year
each. New ordinances promulgated in June 1409 called for
only one Clavari taulager elected from among the citizens and

61. Most of the facts given here are taken from the documents of
the Municipal Archives of Valencia transcribed by Salvador Carreres in
the appendices of his article "La Taula de Valencia en el siglo XVI"
(see Bibliography).

merchants, and one clerk, now earning £75 a year. Both of them had to be seated at the table morning and afternoon on all working days. They were to report on their accounts every four months, and keep a separate record of deposits and loans to private individuals in one book, and of the municipal funds in another.

Who were the clients of this first Taula in Valencia? There were cities, villages, universitats or municipalities, councils, and schools, and "individuals of every rank, state, condition, and [system of] law," according to the statutes. In other words, anyone could be a depositor. Deposits and payments could be made in gold, silver, or "any other species"; thus even small coins, or *menuts*, were acceptable. Only the mortgages or *censals morts* which the city obtained could be negotiated at interest, not loans. When cash was needed to pay off certain debts, the city could sell mortgages to individuals seeking to invest their capital.

The first ordinances drawn up by the taulagers were approved by the Consell of Valencia on 10 February 1408—after 10,000 Aragonese gold florins had already been lent to the city to cover its debts. It was a bad beginning: most of the money deposited by the bank administrators had already disappeared. In spite of the regulations, it soon became impossible, because of late payments by private borrowers, excessive lending to the city, and negligent administration, to pay the charges on the censales and to meet other expenses. The Taula had to be closed, bringing losses to those who had deposited their capital trusting in the solvency of the institution. The vacuum left by the closing of the Taula de Canvis was filled by private bankers[62] until the Nova Taula opened in 1519. It enjoyed better fortunes, and lasted until 1649.

The Taula de Canvi de Majorca

Before Valencia's Taula de Canvi actually began to function, the city of Palma de Majorca was already planning its own

---

62. Ruíz Martin, "La Banca," 11.

insured Board of Exchange similar to the one in Barcelona.[63] Saragossa was soon to have her *Taula de los comunes depósitos* as well.[64] But, as far as we know, the history of these two Exchanges has never been described in detail. In fact, in the case of Majorca, some have claimed that the Taula did not materialize until the beginning of the sixteenth century, but Majorca, too, had motives for creating a municipal exchange at the end of the fourteenth century.

On 16 February 1399 a municipal proclamation ordered all Majorcans to turn over all their counterfeit Majorcan and Aragonese florins and silver royals and half royals to the taula of Arnau Gener, a private money changer. Anyone who

63. Pons Pastor, "La banca mallorquina"; the documentary appendix, upon which the account which follows in my essay is based, is especially important. For complementary material, see Juan Binimelis, *Nueva historia de la isla de Mallorca y de otras islas a ella adyacentes* (1593; new ed. 10 vols. Palma de Majorca 1927) 3.408–10. He describes the development of the Taula in Majorca from its founding (which he dates in 1507, year of the "founding" ordinances) to the end of the sixteenth century. It is possible that the Taula operated in the first half of the fifteenth century, on the basis of Martín I's authorization in 1401, without ever being consolidated. For the first quarter of the seventeenth century, see Juan Bautista Dameto, *Historia general del reino de Mallorca* (1631; new ed. corrected by Dr. Miguel Moragues and Joaquin Maria Bover, 3 vols. Palma de Majorca 1840–41) 1.119–20. Antoni Pons Pastor, ed., *Constitucions e ordinacions del regne de Mallorca (s. XIII–XIV)* (2 vols. Mallorca 1934) 1.69–73, includes a text from 1329 referring to the circulation of money and the money changers in Majorca. I am indebted to my friend Dr. Alvaro Santamaría for these bibliographic notes.

64. José María Lacarra, *Aragón en el pasado* (Madrid 1972). The epigraph, "El dinero, la usuara y la banca judía," 164–67, shows that Christians in the territory of Aragon were forbidden to lend at interest. Thus the Jews controlled all banking operations until their expulsion in 1492, and there were no Christian bankers as in Catalonia. For Saragossa, see Angel Canellas López, "Estado actual de la historia local de Zaragoza," *X Congreso de Historia de la Corona de Aragón* (Saragossa 1976), 131 mimeographed folios. The presence of Catalonians in the Encomienda de Montalbán and other parts of the kingdom of Aragon in the fourteenth and fifteenth centuries, and the fact that they acted as moneylenders in these places, lead me to suspect that the Catalan money changers competed with the Jews in Aragonese territory. But this is another subject that has not been studied to date.

identified the counterfeiters would be set free if he was a bondsman, or awarded 100 gold florins if he was a freeman. We know nothing of what happened in the intervening months, but on December 16 of the same year another proclamation was made. It stated that any Majorcan possessing, or able to identify others who possessed, goods belonging to the former money changer Arnau "de Ginta" (coins, gold, silver, clothing, jewelry, etc.), should report this to the governor immediately or risk a fine of £500. The same applied to anyone who knew of any settlements (*dites*) or transfers (*transportaments de deutes*) Arnau had made under assumed names as a means of hiding ownership (*per salvataria cuberta*) and thereby doing injury to Ramon Martí and Antoni Miquel, representatives of the merchant banker Llorenç Luques from Barcelona, who had been doing business in Majorca since at least 1392. It would not be stretching the imagination to suppose that these two proclamations referred to the same person, who had gone from trusted money changer to "bankrupt" embezzler within a year.

This was very likely not the only case of its kind, and it is not surprising that the jurats of the Universitat or municipality of Majorca sent a message to King Martín I asking permission to create a Taula like the one in Barcelona "to hold deposits and money." Though Barcelona's Taula had been operating only a few months, its usefulness was manifest. The king agreed, and on 8 July 1401 he granted permission to found an exchange insured by the Universitat of the kingdom of Majorca. Merchants and others could deposit their money, and an accounting system similar to Barcelona's was to be used, so that the profits which previously had been made by private money changers would henceforth benefit "the republic of said kingdom of Majorca."

Although the language of the king's decree was not very explicit, the words *emolumenta et lucra* were clear enough. The new bank was to employ its funds in such a way as to benefit the whole community. The Taula of the city of Majorca would be insured by all the property of the Universitat or "community of the kingdom," and all of the citizens and inhabitants, native and foreign, would be allowed to make deposits without restriction. The city was authorized to issue ordinances, edicts, and other measures and to change them as needed according to "changes of places, persons, or times." The king would confirm these statutes and ordinances and insist that royal officials cooperate in carrying them out.

Some historians, as we mentioned earlier, have argued that a Taula de Canvi did not exist in Majorca at this time. They argue solely from the fact that we have no records or minutes from the city council for the following years. But the lack of records does not in itself prove anything. On the other hand, we know that a Tabula nummularia sive cambii seu depositorum, known popularly as the Taula del General, was operating in Majorca in 1454. The funds of the city were deposited there, and we have no reason to believe this was a different Exchange. We also know that when two taulers or administrators were sworn in by the veguer of the city on 1 October 1454, the office, which was auctioned off, was held for one year. It seems that a merchant named Andreu Soler paid £6,302 in Majorcan *reials de menuts* for the position of tauler. If this was so, and the money was not a deposit in trust, then the disputes that followed should not surprise us. It is possible that the Taula ceased to operate for a few years, but this point needs further investigation.

On 24 December 1472 the jurats asked King Ferdinand the Catholic to confirm the privilege granted by Martín I in 1401 to erect the Taula nummularia with offices and statutes similar to those of the Taula in Barcelona. This fact does not necessarily imply that the Board of Exchange had not been operating throughout the intervening period: it was common to request the confirmation of privileges when a new sovereign came to the throne.

The history of the Taula during these years is still unknown, however. The only thing we know for sure is that it did not eliminate the private money changers in Majorca any more than the Exchange in Barcelona did there. Furthermore, it is quite unlikely that it lasted beyond the end of the fifteenth century. The bankruptcy in 1503 of a private banker,

Joan Angelats, may have led the jurats of Majorca to re-establish the Taula with guarantees in 1506. According to the new ordinances, there would be only one tauler chosen *a sort e a sach* (by lot) every two years. He would have to deposit £25,000 in trust, and would receive a salary of £200 a year.

The Gran e General Consell, anxious to revitalize the economic life of Majorca, determined to create a new Taula in the name of the Universitat, and ordered a new set of *Capitols u ordinacions* drawn up so that "past evils and scandals" might not be repeated. This phrase indicates that such things had happened within the first Exchange and may have led to its ruin. The citizens Pere des Callar, Joan Nicolau Berard, and Joan Vicent de Campfullós, the merchants Mateu Riera and Gabriel Axertell, the carder Gaspar Roig, and the lawyers of the Consell Antoni Sala and Nicolau Montanyans were assigned to draw up the statutes. On 17 April 1507 they finished the thirty chapters of new statutes for the Taula de la Universitat. In the preamble, the economic prostration of the Balearic Islands was attributed to "not having a Board of Exchange." Formerly, they said, there had been a busy trade in the islands, with as many as three hundred *navilis de gàbia*, besides many galleys and other ships, but now there was "hardly any mercantile trade"—and one of the reasons was that there was no Taula. This was the "foundation of business, and like the body without the soul, trade could not exist without it."

The statutes of 1507 specified that anyone could deposit money, coins, gold, silver, pearls, precious stones, jewelry, etc., to negotiate with or simply to keep safe. One could "levar e fer levar, dir e girar a qui volra e usar d'aquelles a son arbitre," withdraw, transfer, send, and freely dispose of his deposits. Three persons would be elected to direct the Taula for a period of two years, and could not be reelected within the following two years. One of the three was the Tauler de la Universitat, who had to belong to either the military or citizens' estate; for a salary of £150 a year, he was to take charge of the books and be responsible for deposits and withdrawals. The second person would be elected from among the merchants; his charge was to record deposits, withdrawals, and transfers in the *Manual* and *Mayor* and draw up the necessary checks, at a salary of £100 per year. The third official would be responsible for weighing coins and precious metals, and would earn £50 per year. All three were to take the prescribed oath on the Bible.

The Taula was to be open to the public on all working days for four hours in the morning and four hours in the afternoon at the home of the tauler, and two hours each morning and afternoon at the Lonja. The tauler was to deposit £30,000, the merchant £2,000 and the weigher £500 with the city notary. The tauler was not allowed to use the funds in his trust for private gain, and the office could not be held concurrently with certain other city functions. The jurats would inspect the funds of the exchange four times a year. At the end of each administration the books would be deposited in the Casa dels Comptes de la Universitat. The Taula was to be secured by the property of the "Universitat e Regne de Mallorca."

In short, a precisely detailed set of ordinances covered all aspects of the Taula's administration. On 7 May 1507 it was announced that the Taula was open for business.

Other Municipal Taules de Canvi

In 1416, the city council of Tarragona decided to create, after the Barcelona model, a general Taula for deposits, its management to be supervised by the *consols* of the town. The Taula would be run by three taulers elected by the council; each tauler would have to post a bond of 2,000 florins, and each would earn an annual salary of £20. Since the councilors doubted that the bank would be profitable enough to cover its costs, it was decided that the bank would function provisionally for one year. The council would ask the archbishop of Tarragona to order the veguers and other officials to deposit the courts' money in the Taula. Implied in the establishment of the Taula, however, was the elimination of the municipal treasurer's position. Finally, in 1420, after much deliberation, the council opted to keep the position of treasurer (*clavario*) as part of the town's financial administration, and gave up the projected Taula altogether.[65]

In Gerona, the jurats of the city obtained a privilege in 1443 from Queen Mary, wife of Alphonso the Magnanimous, authorizing them to organize a bank or Taula de Canvi similar to the one in Barcelona. They decided to set it up in the city hall itself.[66] If the project ever became a reality we have no record of it, but apparently there was an attempt to revive it between 1510 and 1512. It was functioning at the middle of the sixteenth century, though the competition from private bankers was stiff: in 1564 Philip II prescribed how deposits and withdrawals should be recorded in the books of the taulers who ran insured exchanges in the city of Gerona so that they could be legally valid in lawsuits.[67]

The Catalan cities of Vic and Perpignan, which had been prosperous since the thirteenth century, also had their Taules de Canvi. There is abundant documentary material, as yet unpublished, for the first, and also for Cervera, whose Taula de Canvi, created in 1599, was installed over the chapel of Santa Eulalia in the church of Santa María. The windows were protected with iron grates, and a strongbox was built into the thick stone wall of the belltower.

Private banking prospered in eastern Spain during the first half of the sixteenth century because of the influx of silver from America, while the rest of Western Europe had been immersed in an economic crisis since the end of the fifteenth century.[68] But the influence of Barcelona's Board of Exchange

---

65. Archivo Histórico of Tarragona, municipal agreements; Francesc Cortiella, "El municipio de Tarragona desde 1400 a 1475" (doctoral thesis, University of Barcelona 1978) 468–73.

66. Joaquín Pla y Cargol, *Gerona Histórica* (3rd ed. Gerona 1947) 90.

67. *Constitutions* (n. 21 above) 351: *Cortes* of Barcelona, 1564, chapter 11.

68. Ramón Carande Thobar, *Carlos V y sus banqueros* (3 vols. Madrid 1943–67; abridged ed. 2 vols. Barcelona 1977) 1: *La vida económica de España en una fase de su hegemonía, 1516–1556.*

soon reached southern Italy: Spaniards helped to found city banks in Palermo in 1552 and soon after in Naples—the two important international trade centers of the area.

The history of banking in Aragon, Catalonia, and the Balearic Islands is for the most part little more than a blank page, especially in the periods we have been dealing with. Many more aspects than I have even mentioned await serious investigation: the social and economic consequences of bankers' dealings with the various classes (the bourgeoisie's acquisition of land, for example),[69] treatises on usury and their influence on the development of credit, royal monetary policy and its effects, changes in currency values, industrialization (especially the wool industry) from the early fourteenth century on—and the list could of course be extended. The sources are quite dispersed, but I hope to have shown here that enough material has been preserved for that history to be eventually written.

69. No study has been made in Spain similar to the one by Alessandra Sisto, *Banchieri-feudatari subalpini nei secoli XII–XIV* (Turin 1963). This would require, first, studies of the families of the nobility and high bourgeoisie of Barcelona. Dr. Carmen Batlle has begun work on this subject.

BIBLIOGRAPHY

Part 1 lists guides to archival sources, and general studies of economics and banking in Spain. Part 2 includes specialized studies of various cities and topics.

PART 1

Cabana, Francesc. *La banca a Catalunya*. Prologue by Joan Sardà i Dexeus. Barcelona: Edicions 62, 1966. 269 pp.

Censo-guia de Archivos Españoles. Madrid: Ministerio de Educación y Ciencia, 1972. 2 vols. viii + 1,064 pp.

Irregular as far as information is concerned but useful as a primary reference source, the *Censo-guia* is a collective work by members of the Corps of Archivists and Librarians; their work of cataloguing is usually announced in the *Boletín de la Dirección General de Archivos y Bibliotecas*. Madrid, since 1951.

Estapé Rodríguez, Fabián. "Taula del Cambi." In *Diccionario de Historia de España*. Madrid: Editorial Revista del Occidente, 1952. 2 vols. 2.1242–44.

Feliu i Monfort, Gaspar. *Bibliografía de historia económica de Cataluña, 1950–1970*. Barcelona: Caja de Ahorros Provincial de la Diputación de Barcelona, 1971. 166 pp.
Includes some documentary material.

Giralt y Raventós, Emilio. "Fuentes y bibliographia." In Antonio de Capmany y de Montpalau, *Memorias históricas sobre la marina, comercio y artes de la antigua ciudad de Barcelona*. Barcelona: Edit. Teide, 1961–63. 2 vols. 2.1095–1196.
Includes detailed list of unpublished sources for economic history preserved in archives in Barcelona (pp. 1111–16 and 1129–46), though this list is not exhaustive. May be updated through the bibliographical review *Indice Histórico Español* (Barcelona, 3 issues yearly, since 1953), especially in the most recent issues.

Martin Alonso, Aurelio, and Cirera, Agustín Blasco. *La Banca a través de los tiempos*. Prologue by Pedro Gual Villalbí. Barcelona: Ed. Subirana, 1926. xix + 217 pp.

Mateu y Llopis, Felipe. "Archivos eclesiásticos." In *Diccionario de Historia Eclesiástica de España*. Madrid: C.S.I.C., 1972–74. 4 vols.

———. "Los catálogos de las bibliotecas y archivos eclesiásticos de España." *Hispania Sacra* 1 (1948) 207–28.

Noonan, John T. "Operazioni bancarie" and "Prestito professionale e istituzionale." In *L'etica economica medievale*, edited by Ovidio Capitani. Bologna: Il Mulino, 1974. Pp. 131–57 and 189–208.

Rahola y Trémols, Federico. *Los antiguos banqueros de Cataluña y la "Taula de Cambi."* In *Banco Municipal de Barcelona*. Barcelona: Fip. El Anuario, 1912. 52 pp.

Ruiz Martín, Felipe. "La banca en España hasta 1782." In *El Banco de España. Una Historia Económica*. Madrid: Servicio de Estudios del Banco de España, 1970. Pp. 3–196.
The best general survey.

Voltes Bou, Pedro. *Historia de la economia española hasta 1800*. Madrid: Editora Nacional, 1972.

PART 2

Ayats, J. V.; Udina, F.; and Alemany, S. *La "Taula" de cambio de Barcelona (1401–1714)*. Barcelona: Banco Español de Crédito, 1947. 157 pp.

Belenguer Cebrià, Ernest. *València en la crisi del segle XV*. Barcelona: Edicions 62, 1976. 383 pp.

Describes the period of the Catholic Monarchs without offering new material on the aspect under study, but does mention documentation from the archives of the kingdom of Valencia and the municipal archives.

Benito Ruano, Eloy. *La Banca Toscana y la Orden de Santiago durante el siglo XIII.* Valladolid: Facultad de Filosofía y Letras, 1961. 120 pp.

Carrère, Claude. *Barcelone: centre économique à l'époque des difficultés, 1380–1462.* Paris: Université de Toulouse, 1967. 2 vols. 994 pp.

Carreres Zacarés, Salvador. "La Taula de Valencia en el siglo XVI." *Boletín de la Sociedad Castellonense de Cultura* 25 (1949) 708–35.

Font y Solsona, José. "La 'Taula de Canvi' de Barcelona en el período 1401–1609." *El Trabajo Nacional* (Madrid), no. 1609 (1953) 11–12.

Forey, Alan J. *The Templars in the Corona de Aragón.* London: Oxford University Press, 1973. xii + 498 pp.
See especially pp. 344–55.

Marqués y Carbó, Luis. *Una historica institución municipal de carácter económico: la Tabla de Cambio y comunes depósitos de la ciudad de Gerona.* Madrid: Instituto de Estudios de Administración Local, 1952. 118 pp.

Melis, Federigo. *Aspetti della vita economica medievale.* Studi nell' Archivio Datini de Prato. Siena and Florence: Monte dei Paschi de Siena, 1962. 729 pp.
See especially pp. 18–25 and 237–79, for affiliates of the Datini in Spain.

Peris y Fuentes, Manuel. "Orígenes de la Taula de Valencia." *III Congreso de Historia de la Corona de Aragón.* Valencia 1923–28. 2 vols. 1.503–18.

Pons Pastor, Antoni. "La banca mallorquina en temps de Ferràn el Catòlic: Els seus precedents." *V° Congreso de Historia de la Corona de Aragón, Estudios* 4: *Instituciones económicas, sociales y políticas de la época fernandina.* Saragossa 1962. 143–200.
Has ten basic texts for the period from 1314 to 1507.

———. *Historia de Mallorca.* Palma de Mallorca: Panorama Balear/ Gráficas Miramar, 1963–70. 6 vols.
No new material on the subject of banking.

Santamaria Arández, Alvaro. *Aportación al estudio de la economía de Valencia durante el siglo XV.* Valencia: Institución Alfonso el Magnánimo, 1966. 231 pp.
See pp. 57–63 and 68–80 for loans and subsidies granted to the kings by the city.

Sayous, André Emile. *Els mètodes comercials a la Barcelona medieval.* Traducció, edició i estudi introductori per Arcadi García i Gaspar Feliu. Barcelona: Edit. Base, 1975. 194 pp.
Catalan translation of three articles, published in French between 1931 and 1936, on the commercial techniques used in Barcelona in the thirteenth to fifteenth centuries; includes an extensive and up-to-date bibliography, pp. 177–86.

————. "La technique des affaires, sa génèse. II: Une caisse de dépôts, La 'Table des changes' de Valence (1407 et 1418)." *Annales d'histoire économique et sociale* 6 (1934) 135–37.

Sevillano Colom, Francisco. "Las empresas nacionales de los Reyes Católicos y la aportación económica de la ciudad de Valencia," *Hispania* 14 (1954) 511–623.

Vilar Bonet, María. "Actividades financieras de la Orden del Temple en la Corona de Aragón," *VII° Congreso de Historia de la Corona de Aragón.* Barcelona 1962–64. 3 vols. 2.577–85.
For the twelfth and thirteenth centuries.

7 Bullionism and the Bill of Exchange in England, 1272–1663: A Study in Monetary Management and Popular Prejudice

John H. Munro

No scholar has done more to elucidate the functions, nature, and history of the medieval bill of exchange than Raymond de Roover. For de Roover, the great contribution of the bill of exchange was to provide a simple, effective loan contract that fully circumvented the ecclesiastical and civil bans on usury without any taint of fraud. It did so, he argued, by "cleverly concealing" the rate of interest within the exchange rates on bills.[1] Since canon and civil law defined usury

1. See the following by Raymond de Roover: "What is Dry Exchange? A Contribution to the Study of English Mercantilism," *Journal of Political Economy* 52 (1944) 250–66; "New Interpretations of the History of Banking," *Journal of World History* 2 (1954) 38–76; "Cambium ad Venetias: Contribution to the History of Foreign Exchange," *Studi in onore di Armando Sapori* (2 vols. Milan 1957) 1.629–48 (all reprinted in *Business, Banking, and Economic Thought in Late Medieval and Early Modern Europe: Selected Studies of Raymond de Roover,* ed. Julius Kirshner [Chicago and London 1974] 183–259); "Early Accounting Prob-

specifically and exclusively as a fixed, predetermined, certain return on a loan (*mutuum*), any uncertain return was considered to be a legitimate profit, a reward for risk.[2] The return on a bill of exchange was uncertain and therefore licit because the rate of exchange might rise or fall before the *recambium* or return bill was drawn. Any number or combination of factors could produce such fluctuations: a change in either country's mint par by debasement or reinforcement, a change in the official or market evaluations of gold and silver, changes in either country's trade and balance of payments, speculative buying and selling of bills in the money markets—or indeed changes in the market rate of interest.

De Roover nevertheless criticized the canonists for their "fallacious reasoning" in defending the bill: for not seeing, as many secular writers did, "that interest was being charged under the cloak of exchange," that "the market favored the lender," and that the banker "rarely lost." The very fact that the spread of exchange rates on bills between two cities varied with their usance, the length of time until the bill's maturity, was for him conclusive proof of an interest charge for the

lems of Foreign Exchange," *Accounting Review* 19 (1944) 381–407; "Le contrat de change depuis la fin du treizième siècle jusqu'au début du dix-septième," *Revue belge de philologie et d'histoire* 25 (1946–47) 111–28; *Money, Banking and Credit in Mediaeval Bruges* (Cambridge, Mass. 1948); *Gresham on Foreign Exchange: An Essay on Early English Mercantilism* (Cambridge, Mass. 1949); *L'évolution de la lettre de change, XIVe–XVIIIe siècles* (Paris 1953); *The Rise and Decline of the Medici Bank, 1397–1494* (Cambridge, Mass. 1963); "Le marché monétaire au moyen age et au début des temps modernes: Problèmes et méthodes," *Revue historique* 244 (1970) 5–40.

2. John T. Noonan, *The Scholastic Analysis of Usury* (Cambridge, Mass. 1957) 38–81, 89–99, 133–53, 175–95; T. P. McLaughlin, "The Teaching of the Canonists on Usury (XII, XIII and XIV Centuries)," *Mediaeval Studies* 1 (1939) 81–147; 2 (1940) 1–22; Raymond de Roover, "Scholastic Economics," *Quarterly Journal of Economics* 69 (1955) 161–90; and his "The Scholastic Attitude Toward Trade and Entrepreneurship," *Explorations in Entrepreneurial History* 2nd ser. 1 (1963) 76–87 (both reprinted in *Business, Banking, and Economic Thought* [n. 1 above] 306–45).

"sale of time," an oft-cited canonical criterion for usury. The return on a bill of exchange was, therefore, interest plus handling charges plus a speculative gain or loss.

De Roover was undoubtedly correct in contending that the usury ban was almost universally applied and that it had a profound influence upon medieval investment and banking. At the very least, interest-bearing contracts could not be enforced at law. For the bill of exchange and credit instruments in general, the usury ban effectively precluded open discounting and thus prevented them from becoming fully negotiable devices until more modern times.[3]

One may, however, still challenge de Roover's thesis that the usury ban was the cardinal force in making the bill of exchange such a popular and widespread investment contract. In the first place, lenders had simpler and equally effective means of evading the usury ban. In particular, they could include the interest charges in the amount of principal stated in the contract (and thus deduct interest in advance). They could also charge *poena* or penalty for "late" payment, prearranged. Whether any feelings of guilt about such elements of fraud dissuaded many from engaging in these subterfuges is certainly a moot question.[4]

Secondly, de Roover is not entirely fair to the canonists, who were quick and astute enough to condemn as usurious *cambio fittizio*—fictitious or, popularly, "dry" exchange. These were straight loan contracts, involving no foreign transactions, in which *cambium* and *recambium* were drawn simultaneously with predetermined exchange rates.[5] In discussing true mercantile bills, the canonists correctly contended, I believe, that the return was profit and not usury. What de Roover calls interest might better be termed the banker's op-

3. See the sources cited in n. 1 above and n. 125 below.
4. See Michael M. Postan, "Private Financial Instruments in Medieval England," *Vierteljahrschrift für Sozial- und Wirtschaftsgeschichte* 23 (1930), reprinted in his *Medieval Trade and Finance* (Cambridge 1973) 29–31; Noonan (n. 2 above) 100–32, 249–68.
5. See de Roover, "What is Dry Exchange?" and "Cambium ad Venetias" (n. 1 above); Noonan (n. 2 above) 175–92.

portunity cost: a return equivalent to the yield on other, fore-gone investment opportunities of similar risk and duration. The merchant buying a bill might, for example, have chosen instead to invest his funds in a *commenda-* or *collegantia*-type of limited liability trade contract. From these he could expect to earn profits that no one would contend were usurious; but they were not fundamentally different from the yield on bills.[6] Even if the "cards were stacked" in favor of the deliverer—who would not otherwise furnish funds to buy bills—the average rate of return did not have to be zero to be regarded as profit rather than interest. The fact remains, as de Roover's own evidence from the Datini and Medici archives shows, that some bills were not redeemed, that losses did occur, and that the yields varied with continuously oscillating exchange rates.[7] This is not a mere legalistic quibble, for the very uncertainty of returns on bills undoubtedly discouraged some conserva-tive investors from purchasing such bills. On the other hand, the limitation of liability that bills of exchange provided the purchaser made them a more attractive investment than a profit- and loss-sharing *compagnia* contract. That may have been as important a consideration for the investor-lender as avoiding the usury ban.

Thirdly, many bills of exchange transactions indicate that lending or borrowing was often of lesser concern than trans-ferring funds between countries, or making various interna-tional payments without having to ship precious metals. As de Roover's examples from the Datini archives show, even trilateral bills of exchange, to settle country A's deficits with B by drawing on credits in C, required only local currency payments in the three countries involved (often *in banco*, by

6. Noonan (n. 2 above) 133–53, 175–92, 249–68; *Medieval Trade in the Mediterranean World: Illustrative Documents,* ed. Robert S. Lopez and Irving W. Raymond (New York 1955) 157–235; Abraham L. Udo-vitch, "At the Origins of the Western *Commenda*: Islam, Israel, Byzan-tium?" *Speculum* 37 (1962) 198–207.

7. De Roover: *Medieval Bruges* 62–63, 353; *Gresham* 144–46; *Medici* 115–21; "Cambium ad Venetias" 243–50 (all in n. 1 above); and his *The Bruges Money Market Around 1400* (Brussels 1968).

bank-account transfers).[8] The attractions of the bill of exchange as a transfer instrument were far greater in the Middle Ages than now, first of all because the transport of precious metals was exposed to much greater risks of shipwreck, piracy, and brigandage. Even if safe delivery could be assured, transportation costs, relative to other prices, were then far higher. Finally, except for those few gold coins that enjoyed international acceptance, most of the metals would have had to be minted on arrival. Thus the merchant had more costs to pay in seignorage taxes, mintage charges, and exchange fees. Consequently, the "specie points" were much more widely separated than today. Only when foreign exchange rates fell well below or rose high above mint par, to cover all these costs, was it more economical to export or import bullion than to use bills of exchange.[9] Normally the exchange rates would rise or fall in this fashion to produce bullion movements only when a country had an overall surplus or deficit in its balance of payments.

Of all the risks facing the bullion exporter possibly the greatest was official brigandage: the confiscation of his metals by frontier officials on departure. Perhaps an adviser to Elizabeth I was unhistorical in declaring (ca. 1570) that "marchauntes naturall exchaunge . . . was first diuised and used by the trewe dealinge marchauntes immediately after that princes did inhibit the cariadge of gould and silver out of their Realmes."[10] But certainly the almost universally imposed ban on bullion exports deserves as much credit as the

8. De Roover: *Lettre de change* 64–65; *Medieval Bruges* 65–66; "New Interpretations" 206–07 (all in n. 1 above); and his "La balance commerciale entre les Pays-Bas et l'Italie au quinzième siècle," *Revue belge de philologie et d'histoire* 37 (1959) 374–86. Flanders then usually had a trade surplus with Spain but a deficit with Italy.

9. De Roover, *Gresham* 77–83, 138–40, 150–54 and *Lettre de change* 57–58 (both in n. 1 above). See also John H. Munro, *Wool, Cloth, and Gold: The Struggle for Bullion in Anglo-Burgundian Trade, 1340–1478* (Brussels and Toronto 1973) 29–31.

10. *Tudor Economic Documents*, ed. Richard H. Tawney and Eileen E. Power (3 vols. London and New York 1924) 3.362, no. iii.5 (Taverner to Elizabeth I's government, ca. 1570).

usury ban for fostering the use of the bill of exchange, from the early fourteenth to seventeenth centuries. One may contend, however, that some rulers applied the export ban to bullion alone, not to legal tender coins. That is quite true, but their coins were rarely accepted as anything but bullion in another country. Even the widely accepted Italian florins and ducats were generally undervalued abroad, since rulers naturally gave preference to their own coins in setting official rates.[11] Exports of specie would therefore lose the premium or *agio* that coins normally commanded over bullion in domestic payments by virtue of their greater portability and convenience. That agio, normally equivalent to the cost of seignorage and mintage, thus afforded the ruler some protection against the export of his coins.[12] Finally, while it is also true that no export ban on precious metals could ever be fully enforced, the risk of confiscation and fines remained for the merchant a cost that made bills of exchange more attractive.

Can any rational justification be found for late medieval bullionism—those policies designed both to induce an influx of precious metals and to prevent their efflux? Was bullionism merely a "phobia"? Did pre-Enlightenment Europe suffer from the delusion that money—gold and silver—was in itself wealth or the sole form of wealth? Certainly some such identification is evident, for example, in the Tudor tracts "A Treatise Concerninge the Staple" and "Howe to Reforme the Realme" by Clement Armstrong (ca. 1530):[13]

The holl welthe of the reame is for all our riche commodites to gete owt of all other reamys therfore redy money; and after the money is brought into the holl reame, so shall all

11. See the monetary ordinances of the Burgundian Low Countries cited in Munro (n. 9 above) 46, 101–02, 150, 169, 198–99; and also Denis Richet, "Le cours officiel des monnaies étrangères circulant en France au XVIe siècle," *Revue historique* 225 (1961) 359–96.

12. De Roover, *Gresham* (n. 1 above) 77–83; Munro (n. 9 above) 25–30.

13. *Tudor Economic Documents* (n. 10 above) 3.105, 124.

peple in the reame be made riche therwith. And after it is in
the reame, better it were to pay 6d. for any thyng made in
the reame than to pay but 4d. for a thyng made owt of the
reame, for that 6d. is owres so spent in the reame and the 4d.
spent owt of the reame is lost and not ours.

Condemning the loss of money spent on "wynes and silkes,
[the] ones every yere piste agenste the walles and [the other]
torne to ragges," he concludes that it is "better to have plentie
of gold and silver in the realm than plentie of merchauntes
and merchandizes." His hostility to the bill of exchange will
be cited later. Similar if more poetic sentiments can be found
a full century earlier in the famous *Libelle of Englyshe
Polycye* (1436), which spewed venom at Italian merchants
especially. By importing "thynges of complacence, . . . nifles,
trifles, that litell have availed,"

> . . . they bere the golde oute of thys londe
> And souke the thryfte awey oute of oure honde;
> As the waffore [wasp] soukethe honye fro the bee,
> So mynúceth [diminishes] oure commodite.[14]

In that same era (1435) even the commercially sophisticated
Flemish—so dependent upon foreign trade, so liberal generally in their monetary policies—evinced considerable passion
in denouncing a Hanseatic request for permission to take with
them any gold or silver that they themselves had brought to
Flanders or had earned from their trade there: "for it would
be the ruination of the land of Flanders and its entire commerce; and we hope that the aforesaid [Hanse] delegates
would not desire that."[15] European documents of the fourteenth and fifteenth centuries are filled with similar state-

14. *The Libelle of Englyshe Polycye: A Poem on the Use of Sea-
Power, 1436*, ed. Sir George F. Warner (Oxford 1926) 21–22. See also
G. A. Holmes, "The 'Libel of English Policy,'" *English Historical Review*
76 (1961) 193–216.
15. *Hanserecesse von 1431–1476*, ed. Goswin von der Ropp (7 vols.
Leipzig 1876–92) 1.332–33, no. 398:4 (3 June 1435). See also nos. 357, 397.

ments that the export of precious metals would lead to a country's impoverishment.[16]

In economies without fully developed credit institutions, central banks, and fiat moneys, however, concern about a country's coinage supply was hardly irrational. Furthermore, many historians contend that late medieval Europe experienced a veritable *famine monétaire*, chiefly from a well-documented slump in silver mining but perhaps also from chronic trade deficits with Asia that produced a drainage of precious metals. For some scholars, that monetary contraction was a major cause of that era's "great depression"; for others, it was at least a secondary factor aggravating the depression from the later fourteenth century.[17] Some historians, on the other hand, deny the existence of any serious monetary

16. See Eli F. Heckscher, *Mercantilism*, trans. Mendel Shapiro, rev. ed. E. F. Söderlund (2 vols. London and New York 1955) 2.175–216; Jacob Viner, "Power versus Plenty as Objectives of Foreign Policy in the Seventeenth and Eighteenth Centuries," *World Politics* 1 (1948–49) 1–29, reprinted in *Revisions in Mercantilism*, ed. Donald C. Coleman (London 1969) 61–91; Jacob Viner, *Studies in the Theory of International Trade* (London 1955) 1–57.

17. See, in particular, W. C. Robinson, "Money, Population and Economic Change in Late-Medieval Europe," *Economic History Review* 2nd ser. 12 (1959) 63–76; Johan Schreiner, "Wages and Prices in the Later Middle Ages," *Scandinavian Economic History Review* 2 (1954) 61–73; Robert S. Lopez and Harry A. Miskimin, "The Economic Depression of the Renaissance," *Economic History Review* 2nd ser. 14 (1962) 408–26; Harry A. Miskimin, "Monetary Movements and Market Structure: Forces for Contraction in Fourteenth- and Fifteenth-Century England," *Journal of Economic History* 24 (1964) 470–90; idem, *The Economy of Early Renaissance Europe, 1300–1460* (Englewood Cliffs 1969) 25–31, 132–58; N. J. Mayhew, "Numismatic Evidence and Falling Prices in the Fourteenth Century," *Economic History Review* 2nd ser. 27 (1974) 1–15. On monetary problems in general, see especially William A. Shaw, *The History of Currency, 1252–1894* (London and New York 1896) 1–60; Marc Bloch, *Esquisse d'une histoire monétaire de l'Europe* (Paris 1954) 35–77; Henri Laurent, "Crise monétaire et difficultés économiques: En Flandre, aux XIVe et XVe siècles," *Annales d'histoire économique et sociale* 5 (1933) 156–60; F. Graus, "La crise monétaire du 14e siècle," *Revue belge de philologie et d'histoire* 29 (1951) 445–54; Sir Albert E. Feavearyear, *The Pound Sterling: A History of English Money*, 2nd ed. rev. E. Victor Morgan (Oxford 1963) 10–15; Carlo Cipolla, "Currency

problems in this era; many others reject the entire thesis of a late medieval depression. Although I myself have long defended the depression thesis, I had adhered essentially to the Postan school, which emphasizes demographic decline, the various disruptions of the European economy by plague and warfare, and other "real" factors as the primary causes of that depression.

According to the Postan school, and its most recent, most able proponent John Hatcher, the accumulated silver stocks were so large by 1300 that no contraction in mining could possibly have reduced the money supply to match the great fall in Europe's population, by a third or more.[18] "Men were dying," writes David Herlihy, "but coins were not."[19] The very serious inflations that swept most of Europe from the late 1340s to the late 1370s certainly indicate that per capita spending had risen rapidly; or, conversely, in terms of the Fisher Identity $(MV = PT)$, that T had obviously contracted much more than had M and V.[20] From the late 1370s,

Depreciation in Medieval Europe," *Economic History Review* 2nd ser. 15 (1963) 413–22; Andrew M. Watson, "Back to Gold—and Silver," *Economic History Review* 2nd ser. 20 (1967) 1–34; John U. Nef, "Mining and Metallurgy in Medieval Civilisation," *Cambridge Economic History of Europe*, ed. Michael M. Postan et al., 2 (Cambridge 1952) 430–93; Etienne Fournial, *Histoire monétaire de l'occident médiéval* (Paris 1970).

18. Michael M. Postan, "Some Economic Evidence of Declining Population in the Later Middle Ages," *Economic History Review*, 2nd ser. 2 (1950) 221–46, reprinted in his *Essays on Medieval Agriculture and General Problems of the Medieval Economy* (Cambridge 1973) 186–213; idem, "Moyen âge: Rapport," *IXᵉ Congrès international des sciences historiques* (2 vols. Paris 1950) 1: *Rapports* 225–41, revised and republished as "The Economic Foundations of Medieval Society," in his *Essays on Medieval Agriculture* (1973) 3–27; idem, "Medieval Agrarian Society in Its Prime: England," *Cambridge Economic History* 1 (2nd ed. 1966) 560–70; idem, *The Medieval Economy and Society: An Economic History of Britain, 1100–1500* (London and Berkeley 1972) 27–40, 224–46; John Hatcher, *Plague, Population, and the English Economy, 1348–1530* (London 1977) 31–62; Munro (n. 9 above) 2–3, 14–25.

19. David Herlihy, *Medieval and Renaissance Pistoia: The Social History of an Italian Town, 1200–1430* (New Haven 1967) 125.

20. Ibid. 122–47; E. H. Phelps Brown and S. V. Hopkins, "Seven Centuries of the Prices of Consumables," *Essays in Economic History*, ed.

to be sure, prices did fall, in some places sharply. But I had attributed that deflation to severe hoarding and reductions in coinage velocity, in response to the economic and social crises, rather than to any reduction in M. I am no longer willing, however, to defend the position that changes in M were inconsequential for the late medieval European economy. For recently C. C. Patterson and N. J. Mayhew have published impressive articles demonstrating that a country's coinage can diminish drastically unless it is frequently and substantially replenished with fresh mintings.[21] Coins do die. Furthermore, my own recent investigations of mint outputs and prices in England (1235–1500) and the Low Countries (1334–1500), summarized in tables 1 and 2, also lend support to Harry Miskimin's famous but often challenged thesis that, relative to the transactions demand for money, northern Europe's coinage supplies seriously contracted during the late Middle Ages.[22]

How then, and to where, did a country like medieval England lose its precious metals? At the outset one must dis-

---

Eleanora M. Carus-Wilson (3 vols. London 1954–62) 2.183, 193–94; Harry A. Miskimin, *Money, Prices, and Foreign Exchange in Fourteenth-Century France* (New Haven 1963) 53–71; Earl J. Hamilton, *Money, Prices, and Wages in Valencia, Aragon, and Navarre, 1351–1500* (Cambridge, Mass. 1936) appendixes; Léopold Génicot, "Crisis: From the Middle Ages to Modern Times," *Cambridge Economic History* 1 (2nd ed. 1966) 677–94.

21. C. C. Patterson, "Silver Stocks and Losses in Ancient and Medieval Times," *Economic History Review* 2nd ser. 25 (1972) 205–35; Mayhew (n. 17 above). See also Marion M. Archibald, "Wastage from Currency: Long-Cross and the Recoinage of 1279," *Edwardian Monetary Affairs, 1279–1344*, ed. N. J. Mayhew (Oxford 1977) 167–86.

22. In *Economy of Early Renaissance Europe* (n. 17 above) 132–58, Miskimin has argued that chronic trade deficits drained precious metals from northwestern Europe to the Mediterranean basin and from there to Asia. For a contrary view, that England's balance of payments remained positive in the late Middle Ages (possibly with a diminishing surplus), see Terence H. Lloyd, "Overseas Trade and the English Money Supply in the Fourteenth Century," *Edwardian Monetary Affairs* (n. 21 above) 96–124. I myself am not so confident that accurate estimates of balance of payments may be made from medieval English or other customs accounts.

tinguish clearly between (1) the disappearance of coins and bullion from the country's money supply, and (2) a loss of metal from the coins themselves, for the consequences might differ. One should also consider whether the losses of metal were temporary or permanent. The most obvious and possibly the most important reason for the first type of loss was a deficit in the balance of payments. That might have been caused by one or more of the following: a trade deficit, military expenditures abroad, loans and subsidies to foreign allies, remittances of ecclesiastical taxes and revenues. If this type of loss was often temporary and reversible, obviously losses from shipwrecks, burials, and unrecovered hoards were permanent. The second type of loss was caused chiefly by wear and tear in normal circulation, and by fraudulent clipping and "sweating" of coins. The latter was only a temporary loss in that the clippings or metal rubbings would usually reappear as re-minted coins in that country's or another's circulation. Loss from wear and tear was, of course, permanent and may have amounted to as much as 1% per annum. Mayhew, adopting a much more conservative loss rate (0.2%), estimated that in fourteenth century England "seven tons of silver vanished into thin air through wear alone every decade."[23]

Even though the coins themselves would disappear much more slowly than that, such a deterioration of the coinage could have very serious consequences for minting and the money supply. It could bring mint production to a halt and encourage the export of precious metals through the operation of Gresham's Law. Thus, so long as large numbers of underweight or fraudulent coins circulated at their decreed

23. Mayhew (n. 17 above) 3: from 1279 to 1334 a hypothetical million pounds of freshly minted pence would have contained 352.389 tons of fine silver. A loss of 2% over ten years would thus have amounted to 7.048 tons. He has evidently employed an estimate of weight loss of 0.2% per annum given in Sir John Craig, *The Mint: A History of the London Mint from A.D. 287 to 1948* (Cambridge 1953) xvi, 60. If so, that would amount to 1.83% in the first decade, not 2.0%; and to 3.32% in the second decade, not 4.0%; etc. Patterson (n. 21 above, 220–21), however, offers a much higher estimate of per annum loss: 1.0%.

TABLE 1. Decennial Averages of English Mint Outputs in Kilograms of Fine Metal and Current Pounds Sterling, 1250–1259 to 1530–1539

Decade	Silver Coinage Output in Kilograms (Fine metal)	Gold Coinage Output in Kilograms (Fine metal)	Total Value of Coinage Output in £ sterling	Index of Value of Coinage Output (1275–99 = 100)
1250–59	21,156.5		65,909.0	161.3
1260–69	12,116.6		37,746.8	92.4
1270–79	6,532.5		20,380.9	49.9
1280–89	26,182.7		81,904.0	200.4
1290–99	2,088.2		6,532.0	16.0
1300–09	29,300.8		91,658.0	224.3
1310–19	9,275.8		29,016.3	71.0
1320–29	1,802.1		5,637.2	13.8
1330–39	341.1		1,176.6	2.9
1340–49[1]	3,370.9	397.2	27,709.8	67.8
1350–59	10,991.9	1,759.3	117,505.9	287.5
1360–69	1,071.1	2,121.9	95,098.1	232.7
1370–79	354.7	606.0	27,347.4	66.9
1380–89	257.0	313.9	14,450.4	35.4
1390–99	233.9	539.8	24,042.5	58.8
1400–09	48.6	149.1	6,579.7	16.1
1410–19[2]	870.0	1,404.8	70,894.2	173.5
1420–29	4,136.0	1,610.4	95,868.7	234.6
1430–39	5,360.8	200.7	34,401.6	84.2
1440–49	250.7	79.2	4,930.5	12.1
1450–59	1,360.5	54.1	8,879.4	21.7
1460–69	4,389.9	854.1	78,778.6	192.8
1470–79	1,905.4	515.7	44,198.9	108.1
1480–89	926.4	207.9	18,731.9	45.8
1490–99[3]	2,034.2	291.8	30,545.0	74.7
1500–09	4,306.0	948.9	85,962.8	210.3
1510–19	945.7	778.7	55,549.3	135.9
1520–29[4]	5,111.1	447.4	63,741.3	156.0
1530–39[5]	6,886.4	398.8	74,018.9	181.1

Table 1.—*Continued*

[1] The decennial mean of the gold coinage is the amount struck from 20 January 1344, when gold minting commenced, to 29 September 1349, thus 5.69 years, divided by 10.

[2] The mint accounts are missing from Michaelmas 1408 to 29 November 1411, when a debasement and general recoinage commenced. The coinage for the missing years has been estimated by averaging the preceding three years.

[3] Average of 1495–99 only; accounts for 1490–94 are missing.

[4] Average of 1520–23 and 1527–29 only (7 years).

[5] Average of 1530, 1534, and 1537–39 only (5 years).

SOURCES: C. E. Blunt and J. D. Brand, "Mint Output of Henry III," *British Numismatic Journal* 39 (1970) 61–66; C. G. Crump and C. Johnson, "Tables of Bullion Coined under Edward I, II, and III," *Numismatic Chronicle* 4th ser. 13 (1913) 200–45; G. C. Brooke and E. Stokes, "Tables of Bullion Coined from 1377 to 1550," *Numismatic Chronicle* 5th ser. 9 (1929) 27–69; Frederick A. Walters, "The Stamford Find and Supplementary Notes on the Coinage of Henry VI," *Numismatic Chronicle* 4th ser. 11 (1911) 171–72 (for York in 1423–24; Calais in 1436, 1439–40); Public Record Office, L.T.R. Exchequer E.364/59, 61–63, 65–66, 69, 72; K. R. Exchequer E.101/192–93 (Calais 1422–40); *Calendar of the Patent Rolls, 1422–1429* (Norwich 1901) 337–38, 502; *Calendar of the Patent Rolls, 1429–1436* (London 1907) 256–57, 259 (Calais 1422–40); Terence H. Lloyd, *The English Wool Trade in the Middle Ages* (Cambridge 1977) 241 (Table 15: Calais, 1384–1404). The London statistics for 1432–33, 1510–11, and 1537–39 have been corrected from information in Sir John Craig, *The Mint: A History of the London Mint from A.D. 287 to 1948* (Cambridge 1953) 408, 412–14.

TABLE 2. A Comparison of Long-Term Averages of the English and Flemish-Burgundian Mint Outputs, 1235–1499

Period of the Per Annum Mean	Value in Current Pounds Sterling	Value in Constant Pounds Sterling*	Pure Silver Struck in Kilograms	Pure Gold Struck in Kilograms
ENGLAND				
A. 1270–1369	47,661.88	53,467.21	9,095.69	427.83 [1,645.51][1]
B. 1370–1469	36,617.30	31,580.61	1,726.19	581.20
B as % of A	76.8	59.1	19.0	135.8 [35.3][1]
C. 1235–1299	44,998.63	55,708.28	14,424.92	—
D. 1300–1399	43,364.22	46,610.40	5,699.92	573.80 [1,024.65][2]
E. 1400–1499	39,845.89	31,800.17	2,133.18	549.64
C as % of D	103.8	119.5	253.1	—
E as % of D	91.9	68.2	37.4	95.8 [53.6][2]
FLANDERS– BURGUNDIAN LOW COUNTRIES				
A. 1335–1369		86,561.14	6,262.60	1,455.07
B. 1370–1469		33,654.51	3,440.32	475.14
B as % of A		38.9	54.9	32.7
C. 1335–1399		67,767.38	5,247.32	1,108.12
D. 1400–1499		28,514.42	4,077.49	297.83
D as % of C		42.1	77.7	26.9

* Constant pounds sterling = values of English coinage, 1351–1411
1 kg fine gold = £42.8676; 1 kg fine silver = £3.8619.

[1] Average of 1344–69 (26 years).
[2] Average of 1344–99 (56 years).

TABLE 2.—*Continued*

SOURCES: *Recherches sur les monnaies des comtes de Flandre,* ed. Victor
Gaillard (2 vols. Ghent 1852–56) 2: *Sous les règnes de Louis de Crécy et de
Louis de Mäle;* Hans van Werveke, *De muntslag in Vlaanderen onder
Lodewijk van Male,* Mededelingen van de koninklijke Vlaamse Academie
voor Wetenschappen, Letteren en Schone Kunsten van België; Klasse der
Letteren 11 no. 5 (Brussels 1949) appendix II (20–21); archival sources
cited in John H. Munro, *Wool, Cloth and Gold: The Struggle for Bullion
in Anglo-Burgundian Trade, 1340–1478* (Brussels and Toronto 1973) 187–
97; and in Peter Spufford, *Monetary Problems and Policies in the Burgundian Netherlands, 1433–1496* (Leiden 1970) 176–93; and the mint
accounts published in the appendices of Pieter O. van der Chijs, *De
munten der voormalige hertogdommen Brabant en Limburg* (Haarlem
1851); Pieter O. van der Chijs, *De Munten der voormalige graafschappen
Holland en Zeeland* (Haarlem 1858); and Algemeen Rijksarchief (België),
Rekenkamer nos. 18,121–28 (Bruges); 18,204–08 (Namur); 17,880–82 (Antwerp [not listed in the above]. For the English mints, see the sources
cited in table 1 above.

values—as halfpence, pence, groats (4d.)—merchants would
eventually respond to the metal loss by discounting the entire
coinage, good and bad coins alike. They would thus bid up
the market price of bullion in money-of-account terms and
thereby reduce or eliminate the premium on coinage. Unless
the premium was high enough to cover the costs of minting,
merchants obviously would not willingly supply bullion to
the domestic mint, but would take it, and heavy good coins,
to foreign mints; or they would utilize good coins and plate in
foreign trade, reserving the worn, inferior coins for domestic
commerce, further reducing the standard. Unless the prince
could compel merchants to furnish bullion or foreign coins,
he could reactivate his mints only by a debasement that would
match the current inferior standard and so restore the premium on coinage.[24]

24. Feavearyear (n. 17 above) 10–15; Munro (n. 9 above) 25–30. For
an analysis of such discounting and consequent price increases, see Mavis
Mate, "Monetary Policies in England, 1272–1307," *British Numismatic
Journal* 41 (1972) 37–45.

Thus a type 2 coinage loss could generate a type 1 loss: in particular the export of precious metals to foreign mints striking debased coins, often counterfeits of another country's good coins. The attractions of counterfeiting, a private vice that became in some princes' fiscal arsenal a public virtue, are obvious. In return for their bullion, merchants received from the counterfeiting mint a greater number of imitation coins than of the good coins offered by the honest mint. The risks of detection were fairly small, because the very inaccuracy of medieval minting techniques, as well as normal wear and tear, meant that a fair proportion of honest coins would also be underweight. When some weight variations were normal, merchants perforce had to accept coins by tale or face value. The more standard types of coinage debasement may be best understood as a counterfeiting of the ruler's own previous coinage that similarly augmented the coin's premium over bullion. For again, the mint offered merchants more coins of the same face value, in money-of-account terms, but with reduced precious metal contents. So long as the merchants supplying the bullion spent the debased coins quickly enough, before the almost inevitable inflation ensued from the augmented money supply, they stood to gain.[25]

The prince who engaged in counterfeiting or debasement of course also profited. The late medieval Flemish and Burgundian mint accounts demonstrate that debasements normally produced very substantial seignorage revenues: not just in money-of-account terms but in the amounts of fine metal sequestered as a tax from the incoming bullion. Such mint profits must be considered a prime motivation for "aggressive" debasements. In an age of steadily mounting fiscal pressures but relatively fixed feudal incomes, seignorage constituted one of the few independent and elastic revenue sources at a

25. See John H. Munro, "An Aspect of Medieval Public Finance: The Profits of Counterfeiting in the Fifteenth-Century Low Countries," and Pierre Cockshaw, "De quelques imitations de monnaies au XVe siècle," both in *Revue belge de numismatique* 118 (1972) 127–48 and 149–63; Munro (n. 9 above) 25–34, 47–53, 70–72, 75–83, 87–88, 187–214; Bloch (n. 17 above) 40–70.

prince's command.[26] For the prince, therefore, such mint policies and bullionism in general often had perfectly rational fiscal ends, however injurious they might be to the community at large in the long run.

But not all mint and bullionist policies were so profit-inspired and rapaciously aggressive. Princes were naturally concerned to protect the integrity of their mints, their coinage, and their country's "stock of treasure." Their honor and sovereignty were at stake, as well as their purse. Thus many mint alterations were legitimately defensive responses to foreign debasements or to any physical deterioration of the coinage. Certainly an influx of foreign debased or counterfeit coins depreciated the current standard of circulation more rapidly than did wear and tear, and thus encouraged an outflow of precious metals, usually to the offending mints. That manifestation of Gresham's Law is plaintively described in thousands of medieval monetary ordinances, frequently as the justification for the debasement.[27]

There remains one element of medieval mint policies that has particular significance for England: bimetallic ratios, or the relative prices offered for gold and silver bullion. The reintroduction of gold coinage in Western Europe in 1252, by Genoa and Florence, was a mixed blessing. On the one hand, it provided Europe with a much more suitable medium

26. Munro (n. 9 above) 52, 83, 198–211. See also Hans van Werveke, "Currency Manipulation in the Middle Ages: The Case of Louis de Mäle, Count of Flanders," *Transactions of the Royal Historical Society* 4th ser. 31 (1949) 115–27; and Peter Spufford, *Monetary Problems and Policies in the Burgundian Netherlands, 1433–1496* (Leiden 1970) 130–46.

27. See the documents and ordinances cited in Munro (n. 9 above) 33, 87, 101, 150, 157, 161, 169, 170; Munro (n. 25 above) 137–48; and also the ordinances cited in Appendixes A, B, and E below). A contemporary expression of Gresham's Law can be found in the later editions of *De Moneta* by Nicholas Oresme (1320–84); but the particular passages are a subsequent addition, possibly by Flemish mint officials: *The De Moneta of Nicholas Oresme, and English Mint Documents*, ed. Charles Johnson (London and New York 1956) xii, 32–33. See also Henri Laurent, *La loi de Gresham au moyen âge: essai sur la circulation monétaire entre la Flandre et le Brabant à la fin du XIVe siècle* (Brussels 1933).

for international trade that was cheaper to ship, relative to its purchasing power, and more trustworthy generally than silver coinages. Since the high value of gold coins made them unsuitable for most domestic trade, and since merchants in international trade were more likely to test coins, gold was much less subject to debasement. But gold was acquired at the expense of silver: if not purchased with silver, received in lieu of silver. A. M. Watson has indeed argued convincingly that Western Europe's adoption of gold coinages with high exchange values produced large outflows of silver, particularly in the later fourteenth and fifteenth centuries, to the Islamic world and Asia, which placed correspondingly higher values on that metal.[28] Since most European domestic economies were based upon silver, with moneys-of-account pricing systems tied directly to the current silver penny, their gold coinages may have become agents of deflation and contraction, unless counteracted by silver debasements.[29]

Late medieval complaints about the "scarcity of white money," therefore, must be considered in terms of coinage deterioration, foreign mint competition, and the country's own mint policies, especially concerning gold. In England, an effective gold coinage was not established until the noble of July 1344.[30] From that time the crown consistently maintained

28. Watson (n. 17 above). See also Robert S. Lopez, "Back to Gold, 1252," *Economic History Review* 2nd ser. 9 (1956) 219–40; and the very perceptive comments in Mate (n. 24 above) 34–35. The alteration of mint ratios (gold bullion price to silver coin, silver bullion price to gold coin values) to attract one or the other metal is too complicated to discuss here, except to note that the alteration had to be large enough to surmount the costs of seignorage, brassage, exchange, and transport. See Munro (n. 9 above) 29–32.

29. I have elaborated this further in "Bullion Movements and Monetary Contraction in Late-Medieval England and the Low Countries, 1235–1500," *International Conference on Pre-Modern Monetary History 1200–1750* (University of Wisconsin 28 August–2 September 1978), whose proceedings are to be published shortly. See also Shaw (n. 17 above) 1–60.

30. Henry III's gold penny of 1257 was ultimately a failure, as was Edward III's gold florin of December 1343. The gold noble, from July 1344, was worth 6s. 8d. or half a mark sterling. Feavearyear (n. 17 above) 24–32; Craig (n. 23 above) 36, 59–75.

mint ratios favoring gold over silver. With no silver debasements from 1351 to 1411, and not another until 1464, silver output declined sharply while gold output values remained generally much higher until the late fifteenth century. Flanders, England's chief trading partner, also pursued pro-gold policies with similar results until 1384, when the count reversed the mint ratio to favor silver. From then until 1425, when the mint ratio was altered to favor gold once more, the Flemish (and Burgundian) mints coined correspondingly more silver than the English; from 1425 to the next mint ratio alteration in 1466, correspondingly more gold.[31]

For medieval England, this analysis provides only a partial explanation of her bullionist policies, which were the most severe of any in Western Europe. English bullionism, and its role in shaping public attitudes toward credit, can be understood properly only if the case histories of the following six monetary policies are considered together: (1) bans on the importation of foreign coins; (2) bans on the export of bullion and coin; (3) parliamentary opposition to coinage debasement, forcing the crown to pursue "sound money" policies; (4) laws requiring exporters to supply bullion to the mints; (5) "employment" laws obligating importers to export English goods of equivalent value; and (6) attempts to control foreign exchange transactions and to limit the use of credit. Only broad, general analyses can be given here; but all the official ordinances (1275–1663) for each of these categories are listed in the Appendixes.

Early bans on coin imports and the export of plate and specie

As Appendixes A and B suggest, the predominant reason for the earlier bans on bullion exports was to support prohibitions against the import and circulation of counterfeit, debased, and

31. Munro (n. 9 above) 74–89, 100–03, 149–50, 168–71, 187–210; Munro, (n. 29 above) table 9. For prices, see Herman van der Wee, *The Growth of the Antwerp Market and the European Economy (Fourteenth to Sixteenth Centuries)* (3 vols. The Hague 1963) 1.173–331, 3 (graphs).

clipped coin: to check the operations of Gresham's Law. But the very first (extant) ban, issued on 7 December 1278, was prompted more by domestic causes of a deteriorating coinage standard. There had been no general recoinage since 1247, and clipping had recently become rampant. Edward I's decree, specifically prohibiting the export of "silver plate, clipped, and broken coins [to foreign mints]," was then followed in 1279 by a successful recoinage that necessitated only a minor reduction in weight (0.41%).[32] The newly restored "sterlings," however, now became an especially tempting target for continental counterfeiters. Sterlings had long been imitated in northern Europe because their unique reputation for both fineness (92.5% silver) and historic stability let them circulate as an international medium, before gold coinages became prevalent in northern Europe. Some imitations were faithful to the sterling; but from the early 1280s various princes in the Low Countries struck decidedly debased counterfeits that came to be known as pollards and crockards.[33] Edward I launched his first attack on counterfeits in the *Statutum de Moneta Magnum* of 1284: it prohibited the importation and circulation of all continental coins; and, for those apprehended with "counterfeited or strange coins," it prescribed "grievous forfeiture." On 21 June 1291 he reissued that prohibition in the *Statutum de Moneta Parvum* with more ex-

32. *Foedera, conventiones, litterae, et . . . acta publica, 1066–1383*, ed. Thomas Rymer et al. (Record Commission edition, 4 vols. London 1816–69) 1.ii.564; *Calendar of Close Rolls 1272–1279* (hereafter *CCR*) (London 1900) 518. For the recoinage and subsequent problems, see the excellent complementary articles by Mate (n. 24 above) 41–54, 75–79, and Michael Prestwich, "Edward I's Monetary Policies and Their Consequences," *Economic History Review* 2nd ser. 22 (1969) 406–07; *Mint Documents* (n. 27 above) xxii–xxx.

33. Jules Chautard, *Imitations des monnaies au type esterlin frappées en Europe pendant le XIIIe et le XIVe siècle* (Nancy 1871); S. E. Rigold, "The Trail of the Easterlings," *British Numismatic Journal* 26 (1949–51) 31–55; N. J. Mayhew and D. R. Walker, "Crockards and Pollards: Imitation and the Problem of Fineness in a Silver Coinage," *Edwardian Monetary Affairs* (n. 21 above) 125–46.

plicit penalties: confiscation of the metals on the first offense; of accompanying goods on the second; and of all goods, chattels, and "their bodies" on the third, presumably final, offense.[34]

Such draconian penalties, however, did not prevent an apparent inundation of crockards and pollards during the 1290s, at the time of Edward I's French war and Flemish alliance. In 1295, moreover, Philip IV ended almost a century of French monetary stability and inaugurated two centuries of periodic but often drastic coinage alterations that in turn provoked and responded to veritable *guerres monétaires* across Europe. The Low Countries retaliated against Philip's debasements in kind, especially by issuing more inferior crockards.[35] As table 1 shows, English mint outputs plummeted during the 1290s. Finally, in May 1299, Edward I responded by having Parliament enact the famous *Statutum de Falsa Moneta*. Reiterating the ban on all foreign coin imports, especially counterfeit sterlings, the act also prohibited the export of all silver coin, plate, and bullion. Unlike the ad hoc ban of 1278 (which had not included good coin), this one was intended to be permanent. It also prescribed far more severe penalties: forfeiture of life and goods.[36] But the only effective if short-term remedy was to demonetize and then forcibly recoin the counterfeits. Such a reminting was successfully achieved between Easter 1300 and late 1302; that was followed by re-

34. *Statutes of the Realm* (hereafter *SR*) (11 vols. London 1810–28) 1.219–21. On 20 October 1283, Edward I had ordered his searchers to seize any clipped or false coin brought into the kingdom. *Calendar of Patent Rolls 1281–1292* (hereafter *CPR*) (London 1893) 86. See Mate (n. 24 above) 54–61; Prestwich (n. 32 above) 408–09.

35. See Adrien Blanchet and A. Dieudonné, *Manuel de numismatique française* (4 vols. Paris 1912–36) 2.203–34; A. Grunzweig, "Les incidences internationales des mutations monétaires de Philippe le Bel," *Le moyen âge* 59 (1953) 117–72; Hans van Werveke, "Munt en politiek: de Frans-Vlaamse verhoudigen voor en na 1300," *Miscellanea Mediaevalia* (Ghent 1968) 209–26; Rigold (n. 33 above); Prestwich (n. 32 above) 409–12; Mate (n. 24 above) 57–66.

36. *SR* (n. 34 above) 1.131–35 (27 Ed I).

markably high mint outputs at London and Canterbury until 1309.[37]

As table 1 also indicates, coinage outputs then fell sharply. By the early 1330s the fall had become a disastrous slump that marks the nadir of medieval English minting. Counterfeiting and various debasements in France and the Low Countries undoubtedly contributed to this slump, for the crown issued numerous proclamations (listed in Appendixes A and B) commanding strict enforcement of the bans against both foreign coin imports and the export of precious metals. Frequently the two bans were combined into one ordinance aimed specifically at counterfeits, as in the Statute of York of 1335. Not surprisingly, complaints about the scarcity of money became more frequent in the parliaments of the 1330s.[38]

Debasements of the coinage

In the same year as the Statute of York, Edward III responded more decisively with the first significant debasement of the coinage since the chaotic reign of Stephen (1135–54), reducing the silver fineness and weight by 13.1%.[39] Although forced by

37. *Foedera* (n. 32 above) 1.ii.919 (26 March 1300); Mate (n. 24 above) 63–79; Prestwich (n. 32 above) 411–16; C. G. Crump and C. Johnson, "Tables of Bullion Coined Under Edward I, II, and III," *Numismatic Chronicle* 4th ser. 13 (1913) 208–15 (London), 228–32 (Canterbury). See also table 1 above; and Mavis Mate, "High Prices in Early Fourteenth-Century England: Causes and Consequences," *Economic History Review* 2nd ser. 28 (1975) 1–16.

38. See table 1, and Appendixes A and B below; Crump and Johnson (n. 37 above) 214–17, 232–33; *Rotuli Parliamentorum* (hereafter *Rot Parl*) (6 vols. London 1767–77) 2.62: no. 14 (1331), 377: no. 15 (1334); *Foedera* (n. 32 above) 2.ii.814 (3 April 1331); *SR* 1.273–74 (9 Ed III stat 2 c. 1–11 [1335]); R. Cazelles, "Quelques réflexions à própos des mutations de la monnaie royale française (1295–1360)," *Le moyen âge* 72 (1966) 83–105, 251–78; Joseph Ghyssens, "Le monnayage d'argent en Flandre, Hainaut et Brabant au début de la guerre de Cent Ans," *Revue belge de numismatique* 120 (1974) 109–91; Michael Prestwich, "Currency and the Economy of Early Fourteenth Century England," *Edwardian Monetary Affairs* (n. 21 above) 45–58.

39. Crump and Johnson (n. 37 above) 216–17; Prestwich (n. 32 above) 410; Prestwich (n. 38 above) 45–46.

Parliament to restore at least the old sterling fineness in January 1344, Edward reduced the penny's weight four more times, for an overall loss of 19% by June 1351.[40] If the initial debasement was certainly defensive, the subsequent ones were more likely aggressive measures related to the fiscal demands of his French war. These debasements, as a form of disguised taxation, provoked strong public hostility, as debasements certainly did elsewhere in medieval Europe. England was unique, however, in having a parliament that could express such opposition effectively. In January 1352, by the Statute of Purveyors, Parliament exacted the king's promise never again to "impair" the current gold and silver coinages in weight or fineness, but to restore them to their "ancient state."[41] Several succeeding parliaments exhorted Edward III to restore the coinage as promised, but had to be content with royal renunciations of debasements.[42] When another debasement was finally undertaken sixty years later (1411–12), after serious coinage deterioration and foreign counterfeits called galley-halfpence had certainly contributed to a "graunde Escarcete" of money, the crown first had to obtain Parliament's consent.[43] The next two debasements (1464, 1526) were also more than a half century apart, and were probably justifiable for the same reasons.[44] No other West European nation even approached such conservatism in its mint policies.

40. *Rot Parl* 2.138: no. 15; *SR* 1.299 (17 Ed III c. 1 [December 1343]); Crump and Johnson (n. 37 above) 216–21.

41. *Rot Parl* 2.240: no. 32; *SR* 1.322 (25 Ed III stat 5 c. 13). Earlier, in March 1348, a Commons petition had requested that "la bone Monoye ne soit en nule manere chaunge," *Rot Parl* 2.201: no. 6. For complaints of monetary scarcity and of counterfeits in circulation, see also ibid. 2.160: nos. 15–16 (1346), 167: no. 19 (1347); *SR* 1.320 (25 Ed III stat 5 c. 2 [1352]); Edward Ames, "The Sterling Crisis of 1337–1339," *Journal of Economic History* 25 (1965) 496–522; Feavearyear (n. 17 above) 15–20.

42. *Rot Parl* 2.253: no. 37 (1353), 260: no. 33 (1354), 276: no. 12 (1363); 3.64: no. 39 (1379).

43. *Rot Parl* 3.658–59: no. 28. See also ibid. 3.470: no. 61 (1401); *SR* 2.122 (1401), 163 (1410), 168 (1411), 191 (1415), 195 (1416).

44. Munro (n. 9 above) 161–62; Feavearyear (n. 17 above) 37–45, 48–49; Craig (n. 23 above) 72–75. In debasing the coinage in 1464, however, Edward IV appears to have had strong fiscal motives as well.

192 John H. Munro

Bans on the export of all forms of precious metals

Having thus lost ready access to debasement as a weapon to protect their mints and coinages, what recourse did English kings have? Obviously they sought to enforce more stringently their bans on exports of precious metals. Appendix B shows an interesting historical progression of such bans. The first (1278) applied to silver bullion alone; the second added silver coin, domestic and foreign. Gold in plate or as bullion was periodically included in export bans from 1307, and permanently from 1344, when English gold coins were first struck.[45] For the next twenty years English gold nobles could be freely exported; evidently the crown viewed this new gold coinage as a supplementary medium whose use in foreign trade might thus keep silver within England. A surprisingly liberal monetary ordinance was included in the Statute of the Staple of September 1353: foreign merchants were permitted to reexport good foreign coin; and all merchants, to export current English gold and silver coins. But that concession was a temporary expedient necessitated by Edward III's scheme to let only foreign merchants export wools, so that he might tax exports at the higher alien rate.[46] This monetary liberalism came to an abrupt end ten years later when, in 1363, Edward organized a group of English merchants as the Calais Staple Company to control the wool trade. Thereafter, from 20 January 1364 to 1 August 1663, the export of gold and silver in any form was strictly forbidden except, as in the past (Appendix B), by royal licenses, which were generally restricted to the military and aristocracy.

Laws requiring wool exporters to supply bullion to the mints

Bans on the export of precious metals were not, of course, seen as a sufficient remedy for England's monetary problems;

45. See n. 30 above.
46. *Rot Parl* 2.249: no. 18; *SR* 1.338 (27 Ed III stat 2 c. 14). On the Staple policy, see Terence H. Lloyd, *The English Wool Trade in the Middle Ages* (Cambridge 1977) 204–12.

and the crown then resorted to various measures imposed on the export and import trades to conserve and augment the bullion supply. The export trade was the first to suffer, in March 1340, when Parliament responded to complaints about the "great dearth of money" by requiring merchants to supply the mint with two marks (26s. 8d.) in silver plate for each woolsack exported.[47] The crown had to admit defeat in 1348 when merchants complained in Parliament that the count of Flanders, Louis de Mäle, had made compliance impossible by rigorously enforcing his own ban on bullion exports.[48] Nevertheless, as Appendix C shows, English monarchs resurrected variations of this bullionist policy ten more times before finally renouncing it in the 1470s. With one exception (1379), these ordinances required only the wool trade to supply bullion because it was by far the major export trade, until the mid-fifteenth century, and because it had an apparently captive market, chiefly in the Low Countries. Although the Low Countries rightly considered themselves victimized, they had certainly provoked most of the ordinances themselves by their coinage debasements, especially counterfeiting.

The connections between such debasements, English bullionism, and a consequent hostility to credit can best be seen in the ordinance imposed at the Calais Staple in March 1364, a year after its establishment. The crown, justifiably concerned "que les monoies que feurent receux pur leines . . . estoient si febles que les dites leines et marchandises ne poent estre venduz au pris convenable," required that only English coin be received for wool sales, and thus set up a mint at Calais. Merchants evaded this regulation, however, by credit transactions—"par voi d'apprest sanz rien paiere d'or ou d'argent." Moreover, they continued to export good English

47. *Rot Parl* 2.105: no. 14 (petition of October 1339 requesting that 40s. in silver plate be supplied for each sack exported); *SR* 1.289 (14 Ed III stat 1 c. 21), 291 (14 Ed III stat 2 c. 4); *Rot Parl* 2.137–38: no. 16 (1343).

48. *Rot Parl* 2.202: no. 15 (referring to the reissue of the ordinance by the crown in January 1348). Cf. Munro (n. 9 above) 35–37; Lloyd (n. 46 above) 183–84, 196–97.

coin to the offending foreign mints. Expressing dire fears that consequently "notre dit roialme serra destitut deinz breve des monoies," the crown then demanded that merchants buying wool bring 5s. weight (3 oz.) fine gold for each sack to the mint.[49] No further mention is made of this onerous bullion regulation, but the Calais mint itself was very successful in coining gold until the early 1380s.[50] Then, from October 1388, the Flemish sought to lure English gold by counterfeiting the prized English noble.[51] Richard II responded first by banning the Flemish noble and then in 1391–92, and more forcefully in 1397–99, by requiring merchants to bring one ounce in foreign gold—bullion or Flemish nobles—to the mint for each woolsack exported. The bullion laws themselves provoked so much hostile opposition from both English and Flemish merchants that they were allowed to lapse.[52] But the crown did finally eliminate the counterfeits, reputedly a quarter of the English gold circulation, by ordering a general recoinage of all suspect nobles in January 1401. The Flemish mint ceased issuing its nobles in June 1402;[53] and for the next twenty years the Low Countries posed no serious monetary threat to England.

From 1425 on, the Burgundian Low Countries, responding to French and German debasements, again engaged in a series

49. *Foedera* (n. 32 above) 3.ii.725 (1 March 1364). For other payment regulations at Calais, see ibid. 3.ii.699 (10 May 1363), 724 (22 February 1364), 727 (16 March 1364), 773 (26 July 1365). See also Louis Deschamps de Pas, "Etude sur les monnaies de Calais," *Revue belge de numismatique* 39 (1883) 185–86; A. Stanley Walker, "The Calais Mint, 1347–1470," *British Numismatic Journal* 2nd ser. 6 (1931–32) 107–08.

50. Crump and Johnson (n. 37 above) 234–35, 242–45; Lloyd (n. 46 above) 241.

51. Munro (n. 9 above) 46–58.

52. *CCR 1385–1389* (London 1921) 647 (12 February 1389: ban on Flemish nobles); *CCR 1392–1396* (London 1925) 110 (28 December 1392: ban on Flemish nobles); *Rot Parl* 3.285: no. 7 (bullion law of November 1391); 340: no. 19 (Ordenance de la Bullion of January 1397); 369–70: no. 80 (late 1397); 429: no. 86 (October 1399). See Munro (n. 9 above) 53–57; Lloyd (n. 46 above) 243–47.

53. *Rot Parl* 3.470: no. 61 (1400); *SR* 2.122 (2 Hen IV c. 6); Munro (n. 9 above) 243–47; Lloyd (n. 46 above) 245.

of drastic mint manipulations, with further counterfeiting of the gold noble as well, which produced the very epitome of English bullionist retaliation: the Calais Staple Bullion Ordinances of 1429.[54] That legislation required the Staplers to raise wool prices; to exact the "hool paiement" in ready money, to be received as English coin; and to bring one third of the sales price in bullion to the Calais mint.[55] These requirements brutally disrupted the traditional credit system upon which the wool trade and the Low Countries' drapery industries had long depended. In buying wools, drapers from the Low Countries had normally paid one third down in cash and provided two bills or letters obligatory for the remainder, payable in six and twelve months following at one of the Low Countries' fairs. Only when the drapers had sold their textiles, usually at these fairs, could they afford to redeem their bills with the Staplers.

When the Staplers, and also the Merchants Adventurers in the cloth trade, collected these bills, they did not send the money home in specie. Instead they remitted their funds by buying bills of exchange drawn upon London by the Mercers: that is, they advanced Flemish money to the Mercers, who bought goods at these fairs, shipped them to England, and then used the sterling proceeds to redeem their bills. In England, the Staplers themselves similarly bought wool from the growers by this tripartite credit system, sometimes selling foreign bills to the Mercers to obtain the cash for their down payments.[56] Obviously this interlocking credit system with

54. For the background to this, see Eileen E. Power, "The Wool Trade in the Fifteenth Century," *Studies in English Trade in the Fifteenth Century,* ed. Eileen E. Power and Michael M. Postan (London 1933) 82–90; Munro (n. 9 above) 82–126; Lloyd (n. 46 above) 257–62.

55. *Rot Parl* 4.359: no. 60; *SR* 2.254–55 (8 Hen VI c. 18).

56. For analyses of fifteenth century credit operations, see H. L. Gray, "English Foreign Trade from 1446 to 1482," and Eileen E. Power, "Wool Trade in the Fifteenth Century" (n. 54 above) 16–18, 54–58, 62–70; Eileen E. Power, "The English Wool Trade in the Reign of Edward IV," *Cambridge Historical Journal* 2 (1926–28) 24–35; Michael M. Postan, "Private Financial Instruments" (n. 4 above) and his "Credit in Medieval Trade," *Economic History Review* 1st ser. 1 (1928) 234–56;

bills of exchange would thwart the crown's whole bullionist policy. To ensure that no such transactions took place, the 1429 statute obligated the Staplers to sign declarations that "no Merchaunt seller, sal not leen agayn to no Merchant, no manere money of hym receyved, noyr of Wolle ne [Wolle] Felle."[57] The result was a bitter Anglo-Burgundian conflict, and bitter strife within the Staple itself, that raged sporadically until the 1470s, as the English crown reasserted, revised, and withdrew these laws, later reissuing modified versions, all summarized in Appendix C. Since I have analyzed this bullionist conflict extensively elsewhere, suffice it to say that both sides lost the war.[58] Irreparable damage was done to both the English wool trade and the draperies of the Low Countries, except for those that switched to Spanish wools. The English crown had veritably killed the goose that laid the golden eggs, at least for royal finance.[59]

Employment Laws

Although the crown required *importers* to deliver bullion to the mint only once, in 1379–80,[60] from the late fourteenth century it subjected the import trades to complementary bullionist measures known as the Employment Acts. They

---

M. R. Thielemans, *Bourgogne et Angleterre: Relations politiques et économiques entre les Pays-Bas bourguignons et l'Angleterre, 1435–1467* (Brussels 1966) 356–61; *The Cely Papers . . . 1475–1488*, ed. Henry E. Malden, Camden Third Series 1 (London 1900) introduction.

57. *Rot Parl* 4.359: no. 60. Very likely this ordinance refers as much to the Staplers' buying bills of exchange from the Mercers-Adventurers in the Low Countries as it does to their extending sales credit to the Flemish and Dutch wool buyers at Calais. See Munro (n. 9 above) 86.

58. Munro (n. 9 above) chaps. 3–6; idem, "An Economic Aspect of the Collapse of the Anglo-Burgundian Alliance, 1428–1442," *English Historical Review* 85 (1970) 225–44.

59. Although the English cloth trade undoubtedly benefited greatly from the damage inflicted upon the English wool trade and the Low Countries' draperies, the English crown itself did not gain because the rate of duty on cloth exports was so low: about 2% vs. about 35% for wool.

60. *Rot Parl* 2.66: no. 54; *CCR 1377–1381* (London 1914) 193.

were designed, in essence, to prevent a supposed outflow of precious metals by forcing importers to export their net earnings in English goods alone. The initial statute of November 1390 was quite modest in its aims: only alien importers were affected, and they were obligated to "employ" just half of their net receipts on English merchandise.[61] The same act removed the Staple to English home ports and revived Edward III's alien wool cartel, with the obvious intent of having such merchants "employ" their proceeds on wool exports. But strong domestic opposition forced Richard II to restore the English wool trade and the Calais Staple in 1392.[62] That left as a viable export for aliens just woolen cloth, then still quite secondary to wool.

Furthermore, the 1390 statute seemed to legitimize the export of the other half of the import receipts in precious metals. Indeed, when Henry IV reiterated the ban on precious metal exports in January 1401, his statute permitted aliens complying with the Employment Law to export on license the rest of their earnings in coin.[63] That evidently produced vigorous protests in both this and the following parliament, of September 1402. The latter enacted a far more severe Employment Law requiring all importing merchants, domestic and foreign, to employ the full value of their imports upon English export goods, "without carrying any Gold or Silver in Coin, Plate, or Mass."[64] The following Parliament of January 1404 confirmed this statute and enacted enforcement mechanisms obligating alien importers to furnish surety for equivalent exports to the royal Customers, to sell all imports and to employ the receipts within three months, and to register with English "hosts," who were to record all such transactions

---

61. *Rot Parl* 3.278: no. 6; *SR* 2.76 (14 Ric II c. 1); see also *CCR 1389–1392* (London 1922) 184 (ban on the export of precious metals of June 1390).

62. *Rot Parl* 3.285: no. 7 (also containing the 1391 bullion law); *SR* 2.76 (14 Ric II c. 5); De Roover, *Gresham* (n. 1 above) 38–42, 45–46; Lloyd (n. 46 above) 243.

63. *Rot Parl* 3.468: no. 53; *SR* 2.122 (2 Hen IV c. 5).

64. *Rot Parl* 3.468: no. 53; 510: nos. 104–05 (1402); *SR* 2.138 (4 Hen IV c. 16).

and ensure compliance with the law.[65] These Employment and Hosting Laws were reenacted, with some refinements and new penalties summarized in Appendix D, over the following eighty years. The final statute, of November 1487, affirming a penalty of one year's imprisonment, was made "perpetual."[66]

Royal and public hostility to bills of exchange transactions

Even if these statutes were but rarely enforced, they are nevertheless significant as manifestations of a bullionist mentality that helps to explain both royal and public hostility to the bill of exchange. Indeed, from first to last, these statutes contained similar "employment" provisions for bills of exchange transactions, restrictions that the crown took much more seriously than the rest of the legislation. Such hostility to the bill of exchange has puzzled some historians, since the bill was designed to obviate bullion exports.[67] But, as the history of the Staple bullion laws has demonstrated, the crown was well aware that in this respect the bill of exchange was a two-edged sword that hampered its policies to secure foreign bullion. This very reason is cited in the first extant proclamation concerning the bill of exchange, issued by Edward I on 14 October 1283. He thus forbade anyone "to make exchange of the King's money in parts beyond [the] sea by receiving there money or silver on condition that they by themselves, their friends or fellows, shall pay in England the sum of such money or the price of such silver, whereby the money or silver

65. *Rot Parl* 3.543: no. 80 (1404); *SR* 2.145–46 (5 Hen IV c. 9). For petitions demanding enforcement of the hosting laws, see *Rot Parl* 3.661–62: no. 35 (1411); 4.104: no. 29 (1416); 126–27: no. 21 (1420); 276: no. 17 (1425); 328–29: no. 31 (1427); 402: no. 32 (1432); 453–54: no. 62 (1443); 5.24–25: no. 38b (1439); 155: no. 4 (1449). Only the 1439 hosting law (*SR* 2.303–05, 18 Hen VI c. 4) seems to have been enforced, and then just in the 1440s. See Public Record Office (London), K. R. Exchequer Accounts Various E. 101/128/30–31 (March 1440–April 1444); Alwyn A. Ruddock, "Alien Hosting in Southampton in the Fifteenth Century," *Economic History Review* 1st ser. 16 (1946) 30–37.

66. *SR* 2.517–18 (3 Hen VII c. 9).

67. See de Roover, *Gresham* (n. 1 above) 41.

that ought to come to the realm may not come as it was wont to do."[68] Certainly by this time, indeed by at least the 1260s, Italian banking firms had brought the bill of exchange to England, especially in their role as papal tax collectors.[69]

A second reason for royal opposition to bills of exchange transactions is that they were regarded as infringements of the royal prerogative to establish exchange rates, asserted at least as early as 1100.[70] Exchange rates—foreign coin or bullion for domestic coin, gold for silver—were clearly seen to have an effect upon the mint's ability to attract bullion. Private money changers were also suspected of purchasing bullion or heavy coins above the official rates and of exporting those metals instead of delivering them to the king's mint or Exchange. Thus, in June 1351, Edward III complained in an edict that "because our gold and silver coins are so much stronger and lower priced than coins of other kingdoms, merchants have been taking our said coins to foreign mints for their own gain, so that little coin remains in our kingdom." He blamed foreign counterfeiters especially for causing this export of metals. Therefore he proclaimed that "no exchange nor sale of any manner of gold or silver money shall be made anywhere except by those to whom we assign [the Exchange] to be held in our name."[71] The following January 1352

68. *CCR 1279–1288* (London 1902) 244.

69. Richard W. Kaeuper, *Bankers to the Crown: The Riccardi of Lucca and Edward I* (Princeton 1973) 3–6, 20–24, 27–48. The device then used may still have been the *instrumentum ex causa cambii* rather than the fully developed bill of exchange: a notarized promise to pay rather than an informal command. But in de Roover's view, "this distinction, being purely formal, is more superficial than real." See his "New Interpretations" 203, *Medieval Bruges* 49–51, *Lettre de change* 29–31 (all in n. 1 above).

70. Craig (n. 23 above) 29. See also *Foedera* (n. 32 above) 1.i.207 (28 September 1232).

71. *Foedera* (n. 32 above) 3.i.223–24 (21 June 1351: "que nul eschaunge ne vente de nule manere de monoie, d'or ne d'argent, soit fait en citee . . . forsque par celui ou par ceux, que nous a ceo assigneroms a tenir en nostre noun, ou par lour deputees, es lieux ou ils serront ordenez par nous.").

Parliament enacted 25 Edwardi III stat. 5 c. 12, which forbade anyone but the King's Exchanger to exchange money for profit.[72] This was the first of two key statutes cited until the seventeenth century in asserting royal control over all foreign exchange transactions.

A third reason for general hostility to bills of exchange was the belief that they were used to cloak surreptitious exports of precious metals, especially ecclesiastical taxes and revenues. As early as 1307 Parliament forbade religious houses to send money to their superiors or to Rome by exchange: "sub nomine redditus, tallagi, aposti, seu impositionis cujuscumque alias nomine escambii, vendicionis, mutui, vel alterius contractus quocumque."[73] Possibly the major role of the bill of exchange in fourteenth century English finance was to remit ecclesiastical payments of various kinds abroad. A deep and growing resentment at the amounts of such remittances, especially revenues from benefices, was thus bound to arouse public hostility against bills of exchange transactions.[74] The

72. *SR* 1.322; *Rot Parl* 2.241: no. 38. See also *CCR 1354–1360* (London 1908) 222 (June 1355). Mavis Mate, in commenting on an earlier version of this paper, suggested that the original intent of this legislation may merely have been to protect those merchants to whom the crown had farmed the Exchange. But subsequent parliaments did not place such an interpretation upon the 1352 statute.

73. *Rot Parl* 1.217 (Carlisle Parliament of March 1307). This parliamentary ordinance was undoubtedly instigated by a decree of Pope Clement V, dated 1 February 1306, that required holders of new ecclesiastical benefices in England to remit the "first fruits," the first year's net income, to the papal treasury—the famous papal annates that subsequently, in the 1530s, played a significant role in the Henrician Reformation (William E. Lunt, *Financial Relations of the Papacy with England to 1327* [Cambridge, Mass. 1939] 487–90). But the 1307 ordinance was evidently also partly in response to a Commons petition of 1305 demanding that the Cistercians be prevented from sending any money abroad (*Rot Parl* 1.178: no. 11). The prohibition was soon relaxed. In April 1307, Parliament permitted papal agents to send "reasonable amounts" of money to Rome "per viam cambii" on condition that they first obtain royal licenses to do so (ibid. 1.222b). See also n. 106 below.

74. See G. A. Holmes, "Florentine Merchants in England 1346–1436," *Economic History Review* 2nd ser. 13 (1960) 193–98, 203–08. See also *Rot Parl* 4.626: no. 27 (1410).

Italians, of course, managed all these transactions, secular and ecclesiastical; and the nature of their commercial activities, their role as papal agents, and their obvious wealth and power invited envious suspicions. They were observed to import much costly merchandise, to collect papal taxes in large sums of cash, but to export fewer and fewer English goods, especially as their share of the wool trade fell sharply after the 1350s.[75] When Italian merchants explained that they remitted their earnings not in specie but "by making money over by exchange," by buying bills of exchange from other merchants, they were often misunderstood and generally disbelieved.

A strong parliamentary movement to suppress the bill of exchange developed during the 1370s, when exports were depressed and the mint outputs had fallen to very low levels.[76] In the aggressive Good Parliament of 1376, during Edward III's final year, a petitioner demanded that no one be permitted to send money abroad "par lettre de Lumbard" and that no Lombard be allowed "to make such letters" on pain of forfeiture and imprisonment.[77] Richard II in effect granted this petition when renewing the ban on the export of precious

75. Lloyd (n. 46 above) 99–224; Munro (n. 9 above) 37–39; Holmes (n. 74 above) 198–204; Eleanora M. Carus-Wilson and Olive Coleman, *England's Export Trade, 1275–1547* (Oxford 1963) 43–57. By the late 1360s, alien wool exports had fallen to 29% of the total; by 1400, to less than 10%.

76. Craig (n. 23 above) 411–12 (app. 1); Carus-Wilson and Coleman (n. 75 above) 49–51, 78–81; Eleanora M. Carus-Wilson, "Trends in the Export of English Woollens in the Fourteenth Century," *Economic History Review* 2nd ser. 3 (1950), reprinted in her *Medieval Merchant Venturers* (London 1954) 252–55; George A. Holmes, *The Estates of the Higher Nobility in Fourteenth-Century England* (Cambridge 1957) 115–20. See table 1 above.

77. *Rot Parl* 2.338: no. 103 (April 1376). See a previous petition, of January 1365, against the export of money "en autri Court hors du Realme par instrumentz . . . en asseurtee de paiement faire as creansours," ibid. 2.286: no. 16. In the Good Parliament (1376), another petitioner complained about Florentines and Lombards who, in buying wools, "preignent les dites marchandies a creance." Ibid. 2.350: no. 160.

metals in October 1377.[78] With Richard's full support, the
parliament of January 1380 strengthened the long-standing
ban on aliens' holding ecclesiastical benefices by forbidding
anyone acting as agent or attorney for such benefices to send
money abroad "par lettre d'eschange," merchandise, treasure,
or otherwise without the king's special license.[79]

The following year a committee of mint officials presented
reports to explain why "no gold or silver comes into England"
but was instead exported. While all were agreed that foreign,
especially Flemish, debasements were a major reason, several
also blamed an excess of imports over exports and "Exchanges
made to the Court of Rome" and elsewhere. As remedies they
all opposed any alteration of the English coinage "for the
universal damage it would cause." Instead they recommended
in particular: (1) that "each merchant importing merchandise
into the kingdom be required to export domestic goods of
the same value"; (2) that no exchanges to the Court of Rome
be allowed; (3) that "no exchanges nor other payments by
letter be made outside of Flanders for payment in England on
account of any merchandise."[80] This committee was thus
responsible for enunciating a balance of trade theory whose
principles would subsequently be enacted in the Employment
Laws. The committee was also responsible for the enactment
of 5 Ricardi II stat. 1 c. 2 later that year, in November 1381.
This was the other law upon which the crown based its
authority to regulate bills of exchange until 1661.[81]

78. *Rot Parl* 3.22–23: no. 91 (October 1377). See Appendixes B and
E below.
79. *SR* 2.14–15 (3 Ric II c. 3); *Rot Parl* 3.82–83: no. 37 (January
1380).
80. *Rot Parl* 3.126–27: nos. 1–2. In 1379 a Commons petitioner had
complained that "pur defaute de bone ordinance, nul or, n'argent n'en
vient en Engleterre, mais de ce q'est en Engleterre grande partie ad
este, et de jour en autre est, emporté hors de la terre." But he agreed
with Mint officials "qe la Monoie ne soit chaungé en aucun poynt."
Ibid. 3.64: no. 39. See Feavearyear (n. 17 above) 33–36.
81. *SR* 2.17–18; *Rot Parl* 3.119–21: no. 107. The petition inspiring
the statute had made no provision for prelates and peers; that exemption
was the crown's amendment.

In its first provision the statute forbade the export of all precious metals except for military payments, "by Exchanges made in England or elsewhere to be received abroad." But the second provision exempted prelates and peers of the realm on condition "that, of the same Payments only, they make Exchanges in England by good and sufficient Merchants to pay beyond the Sea, and first special Leave and Licence [be] had of the King, as well for the Exchangers as for the Person which ought to make the Payments, containing expressly the Sum which shall be so exchanged." To obtain such special licenses, merchants were to swear "that they shall not send beyond the See any Manner of Gold or Silver under the Colour of the same Exchange." The very next year a group of English and Italian merchants presented a joint petition in the Commons pleading for repeal of this statute "because wools and other English merchandise are not being sold as they used to be, nor can they be without exchange between merchant and merchant, as practiced in all the good cities of the world." Richard II advised the merchants to request special exemptions from the Chancellor.[82] The records subsequently show several licenses for bills of exchange granted to various Italian merchants; and also several cancellations of licenses.[83]

While the statute itself remained unamended, the subsequent enactment of the 1390 Employment Laws included a compromise that both legitimized the mercantile bill of exchange and more firmly regulated its use: to ensure that exports at least matched imports and that alien importers did not export specie. Thus, while only half of alien import receipts had to be "employed" (until 1402), the *full* value of any sum they remitted abroad had to be spent on English export merchandise within three months of making that ex-

82. *Rot Parl* 3.138: no. 36.

83. *CCR 1389–1392* (n. 61 above) 106, 341; *CCR 1392–1396* (n. 52 above) 518–48; *CCR 1399–1402* (London 1927) 199; *CCR 1405–1409* (London 1931) 395; *CCR 1409–1413* (London 1932) 439–45; Rogers Ruding, *Annals of the Coinage of Great Britain and Its Dependencies* (3rd ed. 3 vols. London 1840) 2.142; Holmes (n. 74 above) 195–96, 204, 207.

change, which still required a royal license.[84] One modern economist has applauded this statute for its wisdom in requiring merchants to produce export earnings that would counterbalance the purchase of foreign currency in bills, and thus avoid a specie outflow.[85] But it was hardly necessary to make the same aliens who remitted funds make the exports themselves. Furthermore, the use of such bills of exchange would produce a specie ouflow only if: (1) the purchases of bills drawn on places abroad were not matched in value by bills drawn on London, so that foreign exchange rates were rising against sterling (pence per florin); that would be the case when England was experiencing a balance of payments deficit; (2) the foreign exchange rate rose above the specie export point. In any event, it is doubtful that the framers of this statute really understood the relationships between bills, exchange rates, and specie movements.

Certainly such laws and controls did nothing to abate public suspicions, frequently voiced in Parliament, that importers were using these bills to disguise bullion exports. Italian pleas for repeal because "Merchandise ne purra estre faite sanz Eschaunge entre Merchant et Merchant" only served to invite new controls.[86] In 1402 Parliament required merchants to provide surety for the "employment" of all funds exchanged abroad;[87] and in 1410, another statute stipulated that estreats of "briefs d'Eschange" were to be deposited with the Exchequer every fifteen days.[88] The only concession that the aliens won was an amendment, enacted in 1421, to extend

84. *Rot Parl* 3.278: no. 7; *SR* 2.76 (14 Ric II c. 2).

85. Paul Einzig, *The History of Foreign Exchange* (2nd ed. London and New York 1970) 95–96.

86. See *Rot Parl* 3.553: no. 38 (1404).

87. *Rot Parl* 3.510: nos. 105, 107 (Michaelmas 1402); *CCR 1399–1402* (n. 83 above) 596 (September 1402). See also a petition in the 1407 parliament complaining about the use of bills to remit money to Rome; it requested that all ecclesiastical elections should be free: *Rot Parl* 3.621: no. 56. This was a period of very low mint output and one that experienced a flurry of monetary legislation (1397–1411). See Craig (n. 23 above) 412; and table 1 above, Appendixes A–E below.

88. *Rot Parl* 3.626: no. 27; *SR* 2.165 (11 Hen IV c. 8).

the time within which "employment" of funds had to be made: from three to nine months after the bill was drawn.[89]

Bans and restrictions upon the use of credit in foreign trade

The major feature of fifteenth century commercial legislation was a general assault upon the use of credit in foreign trade, including bills of exchange. The most striking example was, of course, the Calais Staple bullion laws of 1429, reenacted for the last time, in modified form, in 1463.[90] When Edward IV finally renounced this policy and reorganized the Staple by the Act of Retainer in February 1473, he granted the Staplers special exemption from other exchange restrictions as well. The statute noted that since wools were sold for foreign moneys, "which hath no cours within this Reame," the Staplers could not receive payment "withoute eschaunge made in the Landes beyond the See, which eschaunge, if they any make, shuld be unto theym by dyvers other Statutes to excessively grevous and penall."[91] The Staplers' right to make such exchange transactions abroad "contrarie to thoo Estatutes" was reconfirmed by Parliament in 1487, 1503, and 1515. It was never challenged thereafter.[92]

89. *Rot Parl* 4.155–56: no. 24; *SR* 2.210–11 (9 Hen V stat 2 c. 9). The aliens (evidently Italians) also pointed out that "pur defaute de tielx chaungeours" they would indeed have to export specie "& tielx Merchandises . . . ne fuissent achatiez par tielx Merchants chaungeours, a graunde damage du Roi." The next year, when they boldly requested that the period of grace be extended to one year, the crown curtly refused them. *Rot Parl* 4.178: no. 37 (1422).

90. *Rot Parl* 5.503: no. 18; *SR* 2.393–94 (3 Ed IV c. 1 [April 1463]). The Staplers were to take "redy payment and contentation for the same Wolle, Wolfell, . . . wherof the half part be in lawfull money of Englond, Plate or Bullion of Sylver or Gold." See Munro (n. 9 above) 155–79; Lloyd (n. 46 above) 278–81. *Pace* Lloyd, who argues that no credit at all was permitted, I interpret "contentation" from many contemporary documents to mean agreement to pay, i.e. credit sales.

91. *Rot Parl* 6.60: no. 59. For the crown's final renunciation of the policy, by the Anglo-Burgundian treaty of 12 July 1478, see *Foedera*, ed. Thomas Rymer et al. (2nd ed. 20 vols. London 1726–35) 12.77–86.

92. *Rot Parl* 6.395–97: no. 14; 525: no. 3. See Lloyd (n. 46 above) 279–81; Munro (n. 9 above) 176–78.

Thus the wool trade had not been alone in suffering such credit restrictions. In fact, the same bullionist parliament of September 1429 had forbidden any English merchant to sell any kind of merchandise to any foreign merchants on credit, "but oonely for redy money, or Merchandis' for Merchandis'."[93] In the next parliament, however, held in January 1431, some merchants loudly complained that this ordinance had prevented them from selling woolen cloths abroad. Parliament therefore reluctantly permitted cloths to be sold "upon Loan of Payment, to be made in Money or in Merchandise, from Six Months to Six Months next"—in two bills over one year. But the credit ban was reaffirmed for the sales of all other merchandise to aliens.[94]

The reasons given for the 1429 credit ban are very illuminating about public attitudes toward alien merchants. The petitioner complained that foreigners used credit to exploit the English, "consideryng, that thorowe the grete apprestes that has been made [t]hem in this Roiaume, thai have ful gretely encreased and avaunced [t]her Merchandises, and broght doune to noght the pris of the commodite of this Roiaume, makyng [t]hem riche and us pouere, that is shame and abusion."[95] Such attitudes were very common in the 1430s, an era of economic dislocation and depression.[96] Other condemnations of credit combine bullionist fears, a devout loathing of usury, and envious hatred especially of the Italians, whose international banking networks undoubtedly gave them enormous commercial advantages. Thus a petition in the July 1433 parliament charged that alien "broccours" were making "many bargeins and chevysaunces of usurie, grevous, horrible, and dishonest," and that they generally "sende [t]her money

93. *Rot Parl* 4.360–61: no. 66; *SR* 2.257 (8 Hen VI c. 24).

94. *Rot Parl* 4.377: no. 31; *SR* 2.263–64 (9 Hen VI c. 2).

95. *Rot Parl* 4.361: no. 66.

96. See Munro (n. 9 above) 106–26; Holmes (n. 74 above) 197–202; Ralph Flenley, "London and Foreign Merchants in the Reign of Henry VI," *English Historical Review* 25 (1910) 644–47; Carus-Wilson and Coleman (n. 75 above) 58–61, 93–96.

overe the See by soche eschaunges . . . betwene merchaunt and merchaunt," without exporting any English goods.[97] The Italians were singled out for especially abusive attack in the 1437 parliament and in the famous *Libelle of Englyshe Polycye*, written the previous year.[98] The latter accused the Italians of buying English wool on long-term credit, selling the wool in Venice or Bruges for ready money, and then lending that money to English merchants, giving "it oute by eschaunge to be paide ageyne . . . here in Englonde." If the bill is paid "at the receyvyng and sighte of a letter," the English merchant loses 12d. on the pound; if the usance is one month, he loses 24d. Thus the Italians "gayne ageyn in exchaunge makyng, full lyke usurie," "bere there golde sone overe the see into Flaundres ageyne" when the bills are collected, and live comfortably there while letting the English wool dealers wait for their money.

The next assault upon the bill of exchange came in the 1480s, a period of international economic disruptions and considerable inflation.[99] In response to renewed charges that the Italians were "empoverysyng" the realm, Richard III's one parliament of January 1484 forbade them "to make any money over the See by exchange."[100] Although Henry VII granted the Italians' petition to repeal this statute in November 1485, shortly after his victory at Bosworth, he too sought to restrict their credit dealings in the "Acte Agaynst Exchaunge and Rechaunge without the Kynges Lycence" of November 1487.[101] Another statute of the same parliament outlawed "drye exchaunge" and other "dampnable bargaynes groundyt in

97. *Rot Parl* 4.449: no. 51; 453–54: no. 62.

98. *Rot Parl* 4.509: no. 37 (". . . thurgh whiche apprestes thai have been and yet beth daily gretly enriched, thair Merchaundis' double avanced"); *Libelle* (n. 14 above) xxvi–xxviii, 21–24. See also Power, "Wool Trade in the Fifteenth Century" (n. 54 above) 64–65.

99. Phelps Brown and Hopkins (n. 20 above) 183, 194; van der Wee (n. 31 above) 2.89–112; 3. graphs 2–4, 6–7, 16–17, 44–50.

100. *Rot Parl* 6.263: no. 27; *SR* 2.489–93 (1 Ric III c. 9).

101. *Rot Parl* 6.289–90: no. 20; *SR* 2.507–08 (1 Hen VII c. 10); 2.515 (3 Hen VII c. 7).

usurye."[102] Genuine "merchant's exchange" escaped this fate; but a statute of the 1489 parliament, in renewing for twenty years the ban on the export of precious metals, also forbade anyone to "paye or delyver wyttyngly be way of exchaunge" any precious metals to any aliens for any merchandise, on pain of double forfeiture.[103] That provision does not seem to have been enforced; and there were no further restrictions on exchanges in the following forty years of general prosperity and monetary stability. Indeed, toward the end of that period, in May 1522, the crown for the first time formally authorized the circulation of certain foreign gold coins.[104]

Abortive foreign exchange controls, 1531–1663

Although the exchange laws evidently lay dormant for four decades, popular attitudes certainly do not seem to have changed in Tudor times. Thus Clement Armstrong, writing in the 1530s, lamented the revocation of the Calais bullion laws, asserting that since then

the staplers . . . covenauntid with the adventurers in London [the Merchants Adventurers and Mercers] to delyver ther money, that rose of ther wolle sales, to theym by exchaunge. So begane the staplers and the adventurers for ther own singler profite to make ther exchaunge to geders in kepyng owt of the reame all such money as yerly shuld be brought into the reame for our riche comodites. . . . Which money the adventurers of London, receyvyng it at the marte of the

102. *SR* 2.514 (3 Hen VII c. 6). See also *Tudor Economic Documents* (n. 10 above) 3.363 (ca. 1570); de Roover, *Gresham* (n. 1 above) 181; and n. 5 above.

103. *SR* 2.546 (4 Hen VII c. 23 [January 1489]).

104. *A Bibliography of Royal Proclamations of the Tudor and Stuart Sovereigns, 1485–1714*, ed. Robert Steele (4 vols. London 1910) 1.9: nos. 82, 88 (May and November 1522): legal circulation and official rates for Italian ducats and florins, French écus, and then Imperial caroli. See also ibid. 1.12: no. 105 (November 1526); 20: no. 1792 (March 1539); and *SR* 3.949 (34–35 Hen VIII c. 27 [January 1543]); 1030–31 (37 Hen VIII c. 25 [November 1545]).

staplers [in the Low Countries], bestowith it ther upon all straunge merchaundise and bryngith it over into England, wher before that tyme the staplers for ther wolle broughte ther money into England.[105]

A renewal of accusations that aliens did not "employ" their import receipts upon exports but "delivered the money to merchants in exchange" led Henry VIII, in July 1531, to issue a proclamation resurrecting 5 Ricardi II stat. 1 c. 2.[106] That licensing of exchange contracts proved so vexing that the Merchants Adventurers asked the mayor of London, Richard Gresham, to intercede on their behalf. In July 1538, he duly informed the king that his new regulations were causing the cloth trade great harm, "for the merchaunts can no more be wythoute exchaunges an[d] rechaunges, than the shyppes in the see to be why[th]oute wattyr." He also argued "th[at these] exchaunges and rechaunges doo moche to the stey of [the said] golde in Englaunde, wych wolld ellse be conveyde [over]."[107] Whether convinced or not, Henry VIII restored full freedom of "exchaunges and rechaunges by marchaunts" on 6 August 1538.[108]

Despite the wisdom of Gresham's arguments, the govern-

---

105. *Tudor Economic Documents* (n. 10 above) 3.94 ("Treatise Concerninge the Staple").

106. *Royal Proclamations* (n. 104 above) 1.14: no. 127; Ruding (n. 83 above) 1.307 (with a date of 29 September 1530). In July 1530 the council had advised Henry VIII "that all the statuttes sholde be inserchyd" to find a solution for the increasing "conveyaunce of coyne out of the realme." Georg Schanz, *Englische Handelspolitik gegen Ende des Mittelalters* (2 vols. Leipzig 1881) 2. *Urkunden* 631–32: no. 155. Obviously the exchange laws had long lain dormant. In January 1532, Parliament banned the payment of annates to Rome to prevent the "impoverisshement" of the realm: *SR* 3.385–88 (23 Hen VIII c. 20).

107. Schanz (n. 106 above) 2.632–33: no. 156. See also 2.635: no. 158 (Chancellor Thomas Audley's letter of ca. 1538).

108. Schanz (n. 106 above) 2.634: no. 157 (30 July); *Royal Proclamations* (n. 104 above) 1.19: nos. 172 (30 July), 173 (6 August). See analyses of this policy in de Roover, *Gresham* (n. 1 above) 182–83 and Richard H. Tawney, "Introduction" to Thomas Wilson, *A Discourse Upon Usury* [1572] (New York 1925) 143–44.

ment, especially under Elizabeth I, increasingly entertained
the belief that foreign bankers in the Low Countries were
acting in concert to drive down the exchange rate on sterling
(Flemish groots per pound sterling) in order to cause an
outflow of precious metals to Antwerp.[109] To be sure, a royal
commission on the exchanges set up in response to the cloth
trade crisis of 1564 correctly explained that such a trade
deficit would produce the fall in exchanges and specie outflow. Nevertheless, the report also maintained that "the
Rysynge and Fallynge of the Exchange by Cunynge handlyng
dothe spessyally Consyste in the Conspyrasye of the greate
Bankers [in Antwerp]" in the absence of such crises. It thus
recommended inter alia that the crown establish some banking
agency to regulate exchange rates.[110] But not until another
commercial crisis in the mid-1570s produced another report
reciting the same conspiracy theory to explain the exodus of
specie did Elizabeth experiment with such a policy to "peg
the pound."[111] In September 1576 she appointed her chief
minister William Cecil (Lord Burghley) Royal Exchanger;
and, citing "abuses of merchants and brokers upon bargains
of exchange," she forbade any bills of exchange transactions
that were not licensed and endorsed by one of three deputy
exchangers. They, in turn, were forbidden to authorize any

109. Thus, in January 1551, William Lane advised the crown that
the "fall off the exchange . . . ys the only cawse that all we the merchants . . . Robbe ynglonde and cary a waye all the golde in the land
in to forin Remes." *Tudor Economic Documents* (n. 10 above) 2.182–84.
In June 1551, Warwick (later duke of Northumberland) forbade "eschaunge and reeschaunge" in the hope of preventing specie outflows;
but he had to withdraw this proclamation in March 1552, after vigorous
merchant protests. *Royal Proclamations* (n. 104 above) 1.42: no. 398;
SR 3.154 (5–6 Ed VI c. 19); Ruding (n. 83 above) 1.320; de Roover,
Gresham (n. 1 above) 183; Tawney (n. 108 above) 145–46.

110. *Tudor Economic Documents* (n. 10 above) 3.346–59: no. iii.4
(quotation on 352). See de Roover, *Gresham* (n. 1 above) 184–93; Tawney
(n. 108 above) 147–48.

111. De Roover, *Gresham* (n. 1 above) 193–94. See also Taverner's
recommendations to the crown (ca. 1570–75) in *Tudor Economic Documents* (n. 10 above) 3.359–63; no. iii.5.

bills by unknown merchants or any bills in which "the moneys of this Realme [are] deliuered vnder the iust values of their standerd." Finally, the deliverer and taker were to be taxed 1½d. in the pound on both *cambium* and *recambium*.[112] A storm of protest from English and Italian merchants ensued. Politely but firmly, the Italians rejected charges of manipulating the exchange rates, explaining "that the abondaunce of the deliverers or of the takers make thexchaunge rise or fall [in Antwerp]." Again they denied exporting their receipts in specie, patiently reiterating that "we deliver it by exchaunge unto your Englishe merchaunts, that may better traffique outwardelye" than they could. It is doubtful that, after several centuries of antialien prejudice, many Englishmen would admit that the Italian import and banking trades helped finance the English export trades. Finally, the Italians argued that the tax on bills of exchange was likely to bring about the very thing that the new system was designed to prevent: the export of specie to make payments abroad.[113] That may have been the most convincing argument. The licensing scheme was evidently allowed to expire by July 1577.[114]

Apart from various royal proclamations to reassert the old statutes on exchanges, summarized in Appendix E, the final serious attempt to assert the royal prerogative in exchange was Charles I's appointment of Henry Earl of Holland as

112. *Tudor Economic Documents* (n. 10 above) 2.167–69: no. iii.15; *Royal Proclamations* (n. 104 above) 1.76: nos. 706–07; Ruding (n. 83 above) 2.148. See analyses in de Roover, *Gresham* (n. 1 above) 193–94, 210–18; Tawney (n. 108 above) 149–53.

113. Schanz (n. 106 above) 2.642–46: no. 163 (Italian merchants' petition), 646–47: no. 164 (English merchants' petition); *Tudor Economic Documents* (n. 10 above) 2.169–73: no. iii.16.

114. According to de Roover, the Exchanger's accounts terminate on 11 July 1577: *Gresham* (n. 1 above) 217–18. For subsequent attempts to license the exchanges until the 1620s, for further royal commissions on exchanges (1586, 1600, 1621–22), and for the Misselden–Malynes debate on this issue, see de Roover, *Gresham* (n. 1 above) 193–210; Tawney (n. 108 above) 153–54; Heckscher (n. 16 above) 2.243–52; and Appendix E below.

Royal Exchanger, in May 1627, with exclusive powers over the exchange of money and precious metals. This measure was actually directed not against bills of exchange but against the activities of the London goldsmiths, who, as money changers and bullion dealers, were accused of exporting precious metals.[115] The following June a House of Commons committee condemned Charles's measure for its "inconvenience." As Tawney remarks, "the Royal Exchanger seems after 1628 to vanish from history."[116] Nevertheless, in June 1661 Charles II issued a proclamation for the enforcement of those two old statutes of Edward III and Richard II that had been so often used to license bills of exchange.[117]

An end to assertions of royal prerogative in exchange dealing necessarily had to await the crown's final rejection of medieval bullionism. The end came just two years later in statute 15 Caroli II c. 7. Clearly reflecting Thomas Mun's now famous concept of the "overall balance" in foreign trade, the preamble affirmed that "several considerable and advantageous trades cannot be conveniently driven and carried on without the species of money or bullion." Therefore, from 1 August 1663, the export of "all sortes of Forreigne Coyne or Bullion of Gold or Silver" was declared lawful.[118] Mun argued that, by exporting silver for the purchase of goods in the Baltic and Asia, England gained far more treasure in return from the sale of such goods in Western Europe.[119] Whether or not England did then enjoy an overall "favorable balance," the bill of exchange also played an important role in these trades.

115. *Royal Proclamations* (n. 104 above) 1.178: no. 1512; Ruding (n. 83 above) 1.383–84, 2.149–51.

116. Tawney (n. 108 above) 154; Ruding (n. 83 above) 2.151–52; *Journals of the House of Commons, 1547–1714* (117 vols. London 1803–63) 1.917–18.

117. *Royal Proclamations* (n. 104 above) 1.398: no. 3309; Ruding (n. 83 above) 2.3.

118. *SR* 5.451 ("An Act for the Encouragement of Trade").

119. Thomas Mun, *England's Treasure by Forraign Trade* (London 1664, rpt. Oxford 1959) chap. 4: "The Exportation of our Moneys in Trade of Merchandize is a means to encrease our Treasure." Written in the 1620s, it was published only posthumously.

By economizing on scarce, inelastic supplies of precious metals, the bill of exchange thereby directed the metals to their most profitable use, in trading with lands without banking facilities and with little demand for European merchandise. But conversely, the greater historical significance of the bill of exchange had been to conserve that generally scarce silver coinage for domestic commerce, while rapidly mobilizing capital and transferring it to whom and to where it was most needed in international trade.

Finally, if few would dispute the great importance of the bill of exchange in European economic development over the past six centuries, some may well question the significance of English economic policies and social attitudes concerning credit. Indeed, the bullionist mentality of late medieval England may appear to be nothing more than a reflection of commercial and financial backwardness.[120] But the undoubted fact that the English then were less advanced economically than the Italians or the Flemish is hardly a satisfactory explanation of their bullionist policies. English bullionism was unique only in that Parliament was so successful, usually, in forcing the crown to maintain sound money. The cost of that policy, and of the pro-gold policy, was the operation of Gresham's Law, which necessarily made the crown more zealous to conserve the nation's precious metals. If other princes were less jealous of their coinages, because they could more freely resort to debasement to reactivate their mints, almost all nevertheless imposed severe restrictions on the influx of bad coin and the efflux of bullion. Nor did public attitudes toward credit and precious metals differ substantially in other countries from English views. The one significant difference in practice is that

120. See de Roover, *Gresham* (n. 1 above) 117–19 ("The backwardness of England in trade, finance, and business organization before Elizabeth is not sufficiently emphasized"). He further portrays the English as chiefly borrowers. The evidence presented here, however, suggests that the English very frequently extended credit to the Flemish and Italians. English bullionism de Roover considers just a "phobia." See also *Lettre de change* (n. 1 above) 58–59.

public prejudice in England so often coincided with the crown's monetary management.

Late medieval England, moreover, despite its status as an "under-developed" nation, was far from being primitive or backward in the development of credit instruments. As Postan, Power, Gray, Holden, and van der Wee have conclusively demonstrated, credit was the very soul of medieval English commerce. One only has to read the published Cely papers to be convinced of that.[121] Even if Italians dominated foreign exchange banking, Englishmen in all branches of foreign and regional trade used a wide variety of credit instruments, including especially the letter obligatory and the bill of exchange. Furthermore, the latter instruments had been customarily made payable to bearer from at least the 1270s; and by the later fourteenth century, letters obligatory were freely assignable, so that merchants customarily paid debts by "setting over" their own financial claims to others.[122] As Postan comments, "a financial instrument which could pass hands so many times, and apparently without any formalities or additional documents, almost deserves the name of 'currency.'"[123] These credit instruments were not yet fully negotiable, not discountable. But in 1437 the London Mayor's

121. Postan (n. 4 above) 40–64 and "Credit" (n. 56 above) 5–27; Power, "Wool Trade in the Fifteenth Century" (n. 54 above) 54–70 and "Wool Trade in the Reign of Edward IV" (n. 56 above) 24–35; Gray (n. 56 above) 16–18; van der Wee (n. 31 above) 2.337–53; idem, "Anvers et les innovations de la technique financière aux XVIe et XVIIe siècles," *Annales: Economies, Sociétés, Civilisations* 22 (1967) 1067–89 and "Monetary, Credit, and Banking Systems, II. The World of Trade and Finance," *Cambridge Economic History of Europe* 5 (Cambridge 1977) 306–57; James Holden, *The History of Negotiable Instruments in English Law* (London 1955) 4–84; *The Cely Papers* (n. 56 above).

122. Postan (n. 4 above) 40–64; Holden (n. 121 above) 4–10, 21. The letter obligatory, like the older *instrumentum ex causa cambii*, was a two- or three-party promise to pay rather than a four-party command to pay. De Roover does "not hesitate to classify these instruments as genuine bills of exchange," *Gresham* (n. 1 above) 117. See also n. 69 above.

123. Postan (n. 4 above) 49.

Court issued a landmark decision (*Burton* v. *Davy*) that recognized the transferability of a formal bill of exchange and the
bearer's legal claim to full payment, crucial steps to negotiability.[124] In Catholic countries, as noted in the introduction, the
usury bans evidently prevented full negotiability with discounting until the eighteenth century. De Roover also argues
that transfers by endorsement were rare on the Continent before the mid-seventeenth century. He does not, however, deny
the English evidence presented by Postan and others. Indeed,
he even credits the London goldsmiths of the early seventeenth
century with developing true negotiability through the discounting of "inland" or domestic bills and promissory notes.[125]

Herman van der Wee, on the other hand, has found
evidence that English letters obligatory were being discounted
at the Antwerp fairs as early as 1536. If that was exceptional
then, letters obligatory and bills of exchange, many of them
issued or held by English merchants, came to be frequently
discounted at the Antwerp fairs from the 1560s, with the full
protection of the courts for the bearer in assigning such
debts.[126] Might not the impediments of English bullionism
have provided the necessary incentives to make bills and
letters obligatory the much more effective payment instruments that they became by the sixteenth century? For a
country that was to become the homeland of the modern Industrial Revolution, that is surely not an irrelevant question.

124. Holden (n. 121 above) 23–27.
125. See (all in n. 1 above) *Lettre de change* 83–146; "Le marché
monétaire" 27–36; "New Interpretations" 190, 219–20, 230–36; *Medici*
137–40; *Gresham* 117–22; *Bruges* 350. On assignability, see also Abbott
Payson Usher, *The Early History of Deposit Banking in Mediterranean
Europe* (New York 1943) 94–109; van der Wee, "Monetary . . . Systems"
(n. 121 above) 322–32.
126. Van der Wee (n. 31 above) 337–53; "Anvers" (n. 121 above)
1067–89; and "Monetary . . . Systems" (n. 121 above) 322–32, 347–50.
See also Jacob Strieder, *Aus Antwerpener Notariatsarchiven: Quellen
zur deutschen Wirtschaftsgeschichte des 16. Jahrhunderts* (Stuttgart 1930).

Appendix A.

Prohibitions against the Importation and Circulation of Counterfeit and Debased Coins and/or Foreign Coins in General

Letters and symbols (sources and notes follow this table)

C = Counterfeit coins

D = Debased and clipped coins

All = All foreign coins (see note 2)

x = Forbidden coin

n.s. = Good foreign coins not specified, since the ordinance is concerned with just counterfeit coins; see note 2 below

* = Ordinance also containing a ban on the export of precious metals

FM = Forfeiture of moneys seized

FMG = Forfeiture of money and goods

FMGL = Forfeiture of moneys, goods, and "life" (prison or execution)

Date	Ordinance or Statute	Form of Coins Prohibited			Penalties	Source
		C	D	All		
Apr 1275	3 Ed I c. 15 Statute of Westminster	x			As for felony	SR 1.30
Oct 1283	Proclamation	x	x		FM	CPR 1281–92, 86
Sep 1284	Statutum de Moneta Magnum	x	x	x[1]	FMGL (?)	SR 1.219
Jan 1289	Proclamation	x	x	x	FMGL	CCR 1288–96, 9

(continued on following page)

Appendix A.—continued

Date	Ordinance or Statute		Form of Coins Prohibited			Penalties	Source
			C	D	All		
Jun 1291	Statutum de Moneta Parvum		x	x	x	1st: FM 2nd: FMG 3rd: FMGL	SR 1.220
May 1299	Statutum de Falsa Moneta	*	x	x	x[2,3]	FMGL	SR 1.131–35
Mar 1300	Proclamation	*	x	x	x[4]	FMGL	Foed 1.ii.919 CCR 1296–1302, 385–86, 390
Aug 1310	Proclamation		x	x	x	FM	CCR 1307–13, 329
Jan 1317	Proclamation		x	x	n.s.	As in 1291	CCR 1313–18, 448 Foed 2.i.311
Feb 1319	Proclamation		x	x	n.s.	FM	Foed 2.i.386
Jan 1324	Proclamation	*	x	x	n.s.	FMGL	Foed 2.i.544 CCR 1323–27, 156
Apr 1331	Proclamation	*	x	x	n.s.	FMGL	Foed 2.ii.814 CFR 1327–37, 251–52
1335	9 Ed III stat 2, c. 2, 4, 9 (Statute of York)	*	x	x	x[2]	FM	SR 1.273–74

(continued on following page)

Appendix A.—*continued*

Date	Ordinance or Statute		Form of Coins Prohibited			Penalties	Source
			C	D	All		
Nov 1342	Proclamation	*	x	x	x^2	FMGL	*CCR 1341–43*, 685–86
Apr 1343	17 Ed III c. 1	*	x	x	n.s.[5]	FMGL	*SR* 1.299 *Rot Parl* 2.137–38
Jul 1344	Proclamation	*	x	x		FMGL	*Foed* 3.i.16–17 *CCR 1343–46*, 351
Oct 1346	Proclamation	*			x	FMGL	*CCR 1346–49*, 150
Jun 1351	Proclamation	*	x	x	x.	FMGL	*Foed* 3.i.223
Jan 1352	25 Ed III stat 5 c. 2		x	x	n.s.	FMGL (penalty for treason)	*SR* 1.320
Sep 1353	27 Ed III stat 2 c. 14	*	x	x	$x^{2,6}$	FM	*SR* 1.338 *Rot Parl* 2.249
Mar 1355	Proclamation		x	x	n.s.[7]	FM	*Foed* 3.i.297
Dec 1367	Proclamation			x	x[7]	FM	*Foed* 3.ii.838
Jun 1371	Parl. decree			x	n.s.[7]	FM	*Rot Parl* 2.308
Jun 1371	Proclamation			x	x	FM	*Foed* 3.ii.919
Feb 1389	Proclamation	*	x		n.s.[8]	FMGL	*CCR 1385–89*, 647
Dec 1392	Proclamation		x		n.s.[8]	FM and prison	*CCR 1392–96*, 110

(continued on following page)

Appendix A.—*continued*

Date	Ordinance or Statute		Form of Coins Prohibited			Penalties	Source
			C	D	All		
Jan 1394	17 Ric II c. 1	*	x	x	x[7]	FM	*SR* 2.87; *Rot Parl* 3.320
Jan 1401	2 Hen IV c. 6	*	x	x	x[7,8]	FM	*SR* 2.122; *Rot Parl* 3.470
Jan 1410	11 Hen IV c. 5	*	x	x	x[7,9]	FM	*SR* 2.163
Nov 1411	13 Hen IV c. 6		x	x	x[7,9]	FM	*SR* 2.168
Nov 1415	3 Hen V c. 1		x	x	x[7,9]	FM; felony	*SR* 2.191
Apr 1417	Proclamation		x	x	n.s.[8]	FM	*CCR 1413–19*, 427
Dec 1421	9 Hen V stat 2 c. 1	*	x	x	x	FM	*SR* 2.209
Aug 1423	2 Hen VI c. 9	*	x	x	n.s.[10]	FMG; felony	*SR* 2.221
Jan 1478	17 Ed IV c. 1	*	x	x	x	FM; felony	*SR* 2.452–53; *Rot Parl* 6.184
Jan 1504	19 Hen VII c. 5		x	x	n.s.[11]	FM	*SR* 2.650–51; *Rot Parl* 6.542
Sep 1560	Proclamation	*	x	x		For felony	*TSP* 1.56, no. 530
May 1627	Proclamation	*	x	x		Star Chamber	*TSP* 1.178, no. 1512

(continued on following page)

Appendix A.—continued

NOTES:

[1] Circulation of Scottish and Irish coins permitted.

[2] Counterfeit and debased or clipped coins to be forfeit; good foreign coins to be delivered to the Royal Exchangers and exchanged for English sterling.

[3] Limited circulation permitted for pollards and crockards; but not for wools, woolfells, leather, lead, or tin sales.

[4] Crockards and pollards demonetized and called in for recoinage from Easter 1300.

[5] If Flemish mint coins as good as sterling, they may circulate.

[6] Foreign merchants may reexport good foreign coins and are not compelled to accept sterling.

[7] Scottish coins banned in particular as fraudulent.

[8] Flemish coins banned in particular as fraudulent.

[9] Galley-halfpence banned in particular as fraudulent.

[10] French coins banned in particular as fraudulent.

[11] No one to import Irish coin above 6s. 8d. in value; but "coyne of other landys nowe curraunt in this Realme for grotes" or for 4d. and those current for 2d. are legal tender.

SOURCES:

SR	= *Statutes of the Realm* (11 vols. London 1810–28)
Rot Parl	= *Rotuli Parliamentorum* (6 vols. London 1767–77)
Foed	= *Foedera, conventiones, literae, et . . . acta publica, 1066–1383*, ed. Thomas Rymer et al. (Record Commission Edition, 4 vols. London 1816–69)
CCR	= *Calendar of the Close Rolls*
CFR	= *Calendar of the Fine Rolls*
TSP	= Robert Steele, ed., *A Bibliography of Royal Proclamations of the Tudor and Stuart Sovereigns* (4 vols. London 1910)
Annals	= Rogers Ruding, *The Annals of the Coinage of Great Britain and Its Dependencies* (3rd. ed. 3 vols. London 1840)

Appendix B.

Prohibitions against the Export of Precious Metals without a Royal License

Letters and symbols

SC	= English silver coins	**FM**	= Forfeiture of moneys seized
SB	= Silver bullion, plate, foreign silver coin	**FMGL**	= Forfeiture of moneys, goods, and life (prison or execution)
GC	= English gold coin (nobles)		
GB	= Gold bullion, plate, foreign gold coin	x	= Metal whose export is banned
a	= No English gold coins minted	*	= Ordinance also contains a ban on the importation of foreign coins
b	= Current English gold nobles may be exported, but no other gold coin (except d)	e	= Export ban contained in an Employment Law
c	= Current English silver coins may be exported	f	= Aliens may export half of import receipts after employing other half
d	= Aliens may reexport good foreign gold and silver coin	g	= Confirms prior statute(s)

Date	Ordinance or Statute	Form of Metal Specified				Penalties; Special Provision	Source
		SC	SB	GC	GB		
Dec 1278	Proclamation		x	a		FM	*Foed* 1.ii.564 *CCR 1272–79*, 518
May 1299	Statutum de Falsa Moneta	* x	x	a		FMGL	*SR* 1.131–35

(continued on following page)

Appendix B.—*continued*

Date	Ordinance or Statute		Form of Metal Specified				Penalties; Special Provision	Source
			SC	SB	GC	GB		
Apr 1300	Proclamation	*	x	x	a		FMGL	CCR 1296–1302, 390
Jan 1307, Nov 1307	Proclamation		x	x	a	x	FMGL	Foed 1.ii.1007 CCR 1302–07, 522 CCR 1307–13, 44
Jan 1324	Proclamation	*	x	x	a		FMGL	Foed 2.i.544 CCR 1323–27, 156
Feb 1326	Proclamation		x	x	a	x	FM	Foed. 2.i.619
May 1331	Proclamation	*	x	x	a	x	FM	CFR 1327–37, 251–52
Feb 1333	Proclamation		x	x	a		FM	CFR 1327–37, 347
1335	9 Ed III stat 2 c. 1, 3	*	x	x	a	x	FM	SR 1.273
May 1338	Proclamation		x	x	a	x	FM	CCR 1337–39, 414
Nov 1342	Proclamation	*	x	x	a	x	FM	CCR 1341–43, 685–86
Apr 1343	17 Ed III c. 1	*	x	x	a		FM	SR 1.299 Rot Parl 2.137–38
Feb 1344, Jul 1344	Proclamation	*	x	x	b	x	FMGL	CCR 1343–46, 351 Foed 3.i.16–17
Jul 1345	Parl. decree		x	x	b	x	FM	Rot Parl 2.452 CCR 1343–46, 586–87

(continued on following page)

Appendix B.—continued

Date	Ordinance or Statute		Form of Metal Specified				Penalties; Special Provision	Source
			SC	SB	GC	GB		
Oct 1346	Proclamation	*	x	x	b	x	FMGL	*CCR 1343–46*, 150
Jun 1351	Proclamation	*	x	x	b	x	FMGL	*Foed* 3.i.223
Sep 1353	27 Ed III stat 2, c. 14	*	x^c	x^d	b	x^d	FM	*SR* 1.338 / *Rot Parl* 2.249
Jan 1364	38 Ed III stat 1 c. 2		x	x	x	x	FM	*SR* 1.383 / *Foed* 3.ii.728
Oct 1377	Parl. decree		x	x	x	x	FM	*Rot Parl* 3.22
Nov 1381	5 Ric II stat 1 c. 2		x	x	x	x	FMGL	*SR* 2.17–18 / *Rot Parl* 3.119–20
Sep 1388	Proclamation		x	x	x	x	FM	*CCR 1385–89*, 614
Feb 1389	Proclamation	*	x	x	x	x	FMGL	*CCR 1385–89*, 647
Jun 1390	Proclamation		x	x	x	x	FM	*CCR 1389–92*, 184
Jan 1394	17 Ric II c. 1	*	x	x	x	x	FM	*SR* 2.87 / *Rot Parl* 3.320
Jan 1401	2 Hen IV c. 5	*	x	x	x	x	FM^e, f	*SR* 2.122 / *Rot Parl* 3.468
Sep 1402	4 Hen IV c. 16		x	x	x	x	FM^e	*SR* 2.142 / *Rot Parl* 3.509

(continued on following page)

Appendix B.—continued

Date	Ordinance or Statute		Form of Metal Specified				Penalties; Special Provision	Source
			SC	SB	GC	GB		
Jan 1404	5 Hen IV c. 9		x	x	x	x	FM$^{e,\,g}$	SR 2.145–46 Rot Parl 3.543
Oct 1407	9 Hen IV c. 8		x	x	x	x	FM	SR 2.161 Rot Parl 3.621
Jan 1410	11 Hen IV c. 5	*	x	x	x	x	FM^{g}	SR 2.163
Nov 1410	Proclamation		x	x	x	x	FM	CCR 1409–13, 180
Dec 1420	Parl. decree		x	x	x	x	FM^{g}	Rot Parl 4.126–27
Dec 1421	9 Hen V stat 2 c. 1	*	x	x	x	x	FM^{g}	SR 2.209
Oct 1423	2 Hen VI c. 6	*	x	x	x	x	FM	SR 2.219 Rot Parl 4.252
Jun 1448	Proclamation		x	x	x	x	FM	CCR 1447–54, 10
Feb 1449	27 Hen VI c. 3		x	x	x	x	FM$^{e,\,g}$	SR 2.349–50 Rot Parl 5.155
Jan 1478	17 Ed IV c. 1	*	x	x	x	x	Pain of felony	SR 2.453–59 Rot Parl 6.184
Jan 1489	4 Hen VII c. 23		x	x	x	x	Double FM	SR 2.546 Rot Parl 6.437
Jan 1510	1 Hen VIII c. 13		x	x	x	x	Double FM^{g}	SR 3.7

Appendix B, continued

Date	Ordinance or Statute	Form of Metal Specified				Penalties; Special Provision	Source
		SC	SB	GC	GB		
Aug 1531	3 Hen VIII c. 1	x	x	x	x	Double FM^g	SR 3.23
Feb 1512	Proclamation	x	x	x	x	Double FM	TSP 1.14, no. 127
Mar 1553	7 Ed VI c. 6	x	x	x	x	Double FM^g	SR 4.i.170
Sep 1560	Proclamation	* x	x	x	x	Pain of felony	TSP 1.56, no. 530–31; Annals 1.334–36
Mar 1600	Proclamation	x	x	x	x	Double FM^g	TSP 1.103, no. 907; Annals 1.353
May 1611	Proclamation	x	x	x	x	Double FM^g	TSP 1.131, no. 1111
Mar 1615	Proclamation	x	x	x	x	Double FM^g	TSP 1.136, no. 1157; Annals 1.371
Jun 1622	Proclamation	x	x	x	x	Star Chamber	TSP 1.157, no. 1332; Annals 1.377
May 1627	Proclamation	* x	x	x	x	Star Chamber	TSP 1.178, no. 1512; Annals 1.178; 2.150
Jun 1661	Proclamation	x	x	x	x	Double FM	TSP 1.398, no. 3309; Annals 2.3
May 1663	15 Car II c. 7	x	x	x		Double FM	SR 5.451, sec. 9

Appendix C.

Laws or Decrees Requiring Specified Amounts of Bullion to be Delivered to the Mint for Wools or Other Goods Exported, 1340–1463

Code: n.s. = not specified; N.T. = no specified term; indefinite

Date	Ordinance or Statute	Amount of Bullion to be Delivered to the Mint per Woolsack Exported	Duration to; or Number of Years	Source
Mar 1340	14 Ed III stat 1 c. 21	Two marks (26s. 8d.) in silver plate	27 May 1341	*SR* 1.289
1340	14 Ed III stat 2 c. 4	Two marks in silver plate	n.s.	*SR* 1.291
1343	Parl. decree	Two marks in silver plate	n.s.	*Rot Parl* 2.138: no. 16
Jan 1348	Proclamation	Two marks in silver plate	n.s.	*Rot. Parl* 2.202: no. 15
Mar 1364	Proclamation	5s. (3 oz.) of fine gold	n.s.	*Foed* 3.ii.725
Apr 1379	Parl. decree	[Silver bullion worth 5% of goods exported or imported]	To the next parl.	*Rot Parl* 2.66: no. 54 *CCR 1377–81*, 193
Nov 1391	Parl. decree	One ounce of gold bullion	24 June 1392	*Rot Parl* 3.285: no. 7

(continued on following page)

Appendix C.—*continued*

Date	Ordinance or Statute	Amount of Bullion to be Delivered to the Mint per Woolsack Exported	Duration to; or Number of Years	Source
Jan 1397	Parl. decree	One ounce of gold bullion	N.T.	*Rot Parl* 3.340: no. 19 *CCR 1396–99*, 37–38
Dec 1420	8 Hen V c. 2	One ounce of gold bullion by aliens not frequenting the Calais Staple	N.T.	*SR* 2.203 *Rot Parl* 4.125: no. 15
Sep 1429	8 Hen VI c. 18	One third of the price in bullion; the rest in English coin	3 years	*SR* 2.254–55 *Rot Parl* 4.359: no. 60
Aug 1433	11 Hen VI c. 13	Reenactment of 8 Hen VI c. 18	3 years or longer	*SR* 2.287 *Rot Parl* 4.454: no. 63
Oct 1435	14 Hen VI c. 2	Reconfirmation of 11 Hen VI c. 18	N.T.	*SR* 2.289–90 *Rot Parl* 4.490: no. 19
Jan 1442	20 Hen VI c. 12	One third of the sales price in silver bullion	7 years	*SR* 2.324–25 *Rot Parl* 5.64: no. 38
Apr 1463	3 Ed IV c. 1	Half of the sales in bullion, plate, or English coin	3 years	*SR* 2.393–94 *Rot Parl* 5.503: no. 18

Appendix D.

Employment and Hosting Laws: For Imports and Bills of Exchange, 1390–1487

Code: % = Percentage of import receipts or of amount in bills of exchange to be "employed" on English goods for export

Date	Ordinance	%	Special Provisions	Source
Nov 1390	14 Ric II c. 1	50	For alien imports only	*SR* 2.76 *Rot Parl* 3.278
Nov 1390	14 Ric II c. 2	100	For all exchanges made abroad	*SR* 2.76 *Rot Parl* 3.278
Jan 1401	2 Hen IV c. 5	50	Aliens complying with the Employment Law may export other half in specie	*SR* 2.122 *Rot Parl* 3.468
Sep 1402	4 Hen IV c. 15	100	For all imports, by both denizens and aliens; no export of precious metals	*SR* 2.138 *Rot Parl* 3.502
Jan 1404	5 Hen IV c. 9	100	Confirmation of 4 Hen IV c. 15. Aliens to register with English "hosts"	*SR* 2.145–46 *Rot Parl* 3.543
Nov 1411	Parl. decree	100	Hosting provisions of 5 Hen IV c. 9 to be enforced	*Rot Parl* 3.661

(continued on following page)

Appendix D.—*continued*

Date	Ordinance	%	Special Provisions	Source
Oct 1416	Parl. decree	100	Hosting provisions of 5 Hen IV c. 9 to be enforced	*Rot Parl* 4.104
Dec 1420	Parl. decree	100	Hosting provisions of 5 Hen IV c. 9 to be enforced	*Rot Parl* 4.126
Dec 1421	9 Hen V stat 2 c. 1, 9	100	5 Hen IV c. 9 confirmed; aliens given 9 months from date of bill of exchange to "employ" funds on English goods	*SR* 2.209, 210–11
Apr 1425	Parl. decree	100	Aliens to be "hosted" within 15 days of arrival and to sell goods and employ receipts within 40 days	*Rot Parl* 4.276: no. 17
Nov 1439	18 Hen VI c. 4	100	Hosting provisions to be enforced for all aliens but the Hanse; aliens to have 8 months to sell their goods and employ their receipts. For 8 years	*SR* 2.303–05 *Rot Parl* 5.24–25: no. 38b
Jun 1448	Proclamation	100	5 Hen IV c. 9 (1404) to be enforced; aliens to provide surety	*CCR 1447–54*, 10

(*continued on following page*)

Appendix D.—*continued*

Date	Ordinance	%	Special Provisions	Source
Feb 1449	27 Hen VI c. 3	100	4 Hen IV c. 15 (1402) to be enforced; new powers for Searchers	*SR* 2.349–50 *Rot Parl* 5.155: no. 4
Jan 1465	4 Ed IV c. 6	100	Confirmation of 5 Hen IV c. 9. Aliens to employ import proceeds within 3 months, but surety provisions are relaxed	*SR* 2.413–14
Jan 1478	17 Ed IV c. 1	100	5 Hen IV c. 9 confirmed; but penalty increased to one year's imprisonment	*SR* 2.458–59 *Rot Parl* 6.186: no. 27
Jan 1484	1 Ric III c. 9	100	Aliens to sell goods and employ proceeds within 8 months, but are not to send funds abroad by bills of exchange on pain of FMG	*SR* 2.489–93 *Rot Parl* 6.263: no. 27
Nov 1485	1 Hen VII c. 10	100	Repeal of provisions of 1 Ric III c. 9 against Italian merchants	*SR* 2.507–08 *Rot Parl* 6.289–90
Nov 1487	3 Hen VII c. 9	100	Employment provisions in 17 Ed IV c. 1 confirmed and made perpetual	*SR* 2.517–18 *Rot Parl* 6.403

Appendix E.

Ordinances Banning Private Exchange or Regulating Foreign Exchange

Date	Ordinance	Provisions	Source
1222	Proclamation	No one to make exchange except at the Royal Exchanges of London and Canterbury	*Annals* 2.138–39
Sep 1232	Proclamation	No one to exchange new coins for old or make exchanges but at the King's Exchanger	*Foed* 1.i.207
Oct 1283	Proclamation	Ban on all letters of exchange made abroad for payment in England	*CCR 1279–88*, 244
Mar 1307	Parl. decree	Religious houses not to send money abroad to their superiors by exchange or any other such contracts	*Rot Parl* 1.217
Apr 1307	Parl. decree	Papal agents not to send money to Rome in specie or by exchange without royal licenses	*Rot Parl* 1.222
1312	Parl. decree	Manner and places of exchange (coinage) to be determined by the King-in-Parliament	*Rot Parl* 1.285: no. 30

(continued on following page)

Appendix E.—*continued*

Date	Ordinance	Provisions	Source
Nov 1329	Proclamation	No moneyer or changer to leave the kingdom without license	*Foed* 2.ii.774
1335	9 Ed III stat 2 c. 7	Tables of Exchange to be set up at London and Dover	*SR* 1.274
Apr 1343	17 Ed III c. 1	"None to make Exchanges with them that shall pass the Sea, of Gold, for their good sterling to the Value"	*SR* 1.299 *Rot Parl* 2.138
Jun 1351	Proclamation	"que nul eschaunge ne vente de nule manere de monoie d'or ne d'argent soit fait"	*Foed* 3.i.223–24
Jan 1352	25 Ed III stat 5 c. 12	No one to hold or to profit from Exchanges but the King's Exchanger	*SR* 1.322 *Rot Parl* 2.241: no. 38
Jun 1355	Proclamation	No one to hold private exchange on forfeiture of life & limb	*CCR 1354–60,* 222
Jul 1365	Proclamation	"Ne quis cambium de moneta . . . nisi ex causa mercaturae faciat": at the Calais Staple	*Foed* 3.ii.773

(continued on following page)

Appendix E.—*continued*

Date	Ordinance	Provisions	Source
Oct 1377	Parl. decree	"qe par null paiement ne par eschaunge en or, argent, plate . . . riens plus ne soit tret" by aliens. In ban on precious metal exports	*Rot Parl* 3.22: no. 91
Jan 1380	3 Ric II c. 3	Alien ecclesiastics to be prevented from sending money, treasure, etc., abroad "par lettre d'eschange . . ."	*Rot Parl* 3.83: no. 37 *SR* 2.15
Nov 1381	5 Ric II stat 1 c. 2	No one but prelates and peers to send money or bullion abroad by "Exchanges to be made" or otherwise; latter by licenses	*SR* 2.17–18 *Rot Parl* 3.119–20: no. 107
Nov 1389	Proclamation	As in 5 Ric II stat 1 c. 2	*TSP* 1.clxx
Jan 1390	Proclamation	Richard II revokes patents that had permitted payment abroad by letters of exchange	*CCR 1389–92*, 106
Nov 1390	14 Ric II c. 2	For any sum remitted by letter of exchange the merchant must buy English goods to full value within 3 months	*SR* 2.76 *Rot Parl* 3.278: no. 7

(*continued on following page*)

Appendix E.—*continued*

Date	Ordinance	Provisions	Source
May 1391	Proclamation	"No man shall make any exchange of the King's money to foreign parts without his special license"	*CCR 1389–92,* 341
Sep 1400	Proclamation	"No one shall make any change within the realm . . . in order to receive gold or silver in foreign parts, by reason thereof, without a royal license"	*CCR 1399–1402,* 199
Sep 1402	Parl. decree	Confirmation of 14 Ric II c. 2. Merchants to provide security for "employment" of sums exchanged abroad by license	*Rot Parl* 3.510: no. 105 *CCR 1399–1402,* 596
Jun 1408	Proclamation	No one to "make any exchanges [to foreign parts] by virtue of any letters patent or writs of the king"	*CCR 1405–09,* 395
Jan 1410	11 Hen IV c. 8	14 Ric II c. 2 to be enforced. Estreats of "briefs d'Eschange" to be deposited at the Exchequer every 15 days	*SR* 2.165 *Rot Parl* 3.626: no. 27

(continued on following page)

Appendix E.—*continued*

Date	Ordinance	Provisions	Source
Dec 1421	9 Hen V stat 2 c. 1, 9	Confirms all prior statutes, but permits merchants 9 months to buy English goods to value of the sum exchanged abroad	*SR* 2.209, 210–11
Jan 1422	Proclamation	25 Ed III stat 5 c. 12 (1352) to be enforced	*CCR 1419–22*, 221
Sep 1429	8 Hen VI c. 18	No sales credit to be allowed in Staple wool sales	*SR* 2.255–56 *Rot Parl* 5.359
Sep 1429	8 Hen VI c. 24	No sales credit to be allowed for any goods to aliens	*SR* 2.257 *Rot Parl* 5.360–61: no. 66
Jan 1431	9 Hen VI c. 2	8 Hen VI c. 24 amended to allow credit for "six months to six months" in the cloth trade; but credit ban confirmed for all other commodities	*SR* 2.263–64 *Rot Parl* 4.377: no. 31
Feb 1473	Parl. decree	Use of bills of exchange at the Calais Staple explicitly permitted for 16 years	*Rot Parl* 6.60: no. 59

(continued on following page)

Appendix E.—*continued*

Date	Ordinance	Provisions	Source
Jan 1484	1 Ric III c. 9	Italians to "employ" all import proceeds on English goods and forbidden "to make [any suche Moneye] over the See by Exchaunge" on pain of FMG	*SR* 2.489–93 *Rot Parl* 6.263: no. 27
Nov 1485	1 Hen VII c. 10	Repeal of 1 Ric III c. 9: of provisions against bills and Italian merchants	*SR* 2.507–08 *Rot Parl* 6.289–90
Nov 1487	Parl. decree	Permission to use bills of exchange at Calais Staple extended for 16 years from April 1488	*Rot Parl* 6.395–97: no. 14
Nov 1487	3 Hen VII c. 6	Prohibition of "drye exchaunge" and "newe chevessaunce"	*SR* 2.514 *Rot Parl* 6.403: no. 29
Nov 1487	3 Hen VII c. 7	Prohibition of "exchaunge and rechaunge without the Kynges lycence." Confirmation of 25 Ed III stat 5 c. 12 and 5 Ric II stat 1 c. 2	*SR* 2.515 *Rot Parl* 6.403: no. 28
Jan 1489	4 Hen VII c. 23	No one to "pay or deliver wittingly by way of eschaunge or otherwise" any precious metals to aliens	*SR* 2.546 *Rot Parl* 6.437: no. 52

(continued on following page)

Appendix E.—*continued*

Date	Ordinance	Provisions	Source
1503	Parl. decree	Permission to use bills of exchange at Calais Staple extended for 16 years from April 1504	*Rot Parl* 6.525: no. 3
Jul 1531 (Sep 1530?)	Proclamation	No one to make exchanges contrary to 5 Ric II stat 1 c. 2 on pain of FMGL	*TSP* 1.14, no. 127 *Annals* 1.307, 2.147 *EHP* 2.631–32, no. 155
Jul 1538	Proclamation	Right of merchants "to make their exchaunge and rechaunges" restored to 1 Nov 1538	*TSP* 1.19, no. 172 *EHP* 2.634, no. 157
Aug 1538	Proclamation	Decree "freely licencinge Exchaunges and Rechaunges by Marchaunts" indefinitely	*TSP* 1.19, no. 173
1546	Proclamation	3 Hen VII c. 7 and 25 Ed III stat 5 c. 12 to be enforced	*Annals* 2.148
Jun 1551	Proclamation	3 Hen VII c. 7 to be strictly enforced; "eschaunge and reeschaunge" prohibited	*TSP* 1.42, no. 398
Jan 1552	5–6 Ed VI c. 19	25 Ed III stat 5 c. 12 to be enforced, with 1 year's imprisonment for violations	*SR* 3.154

(*continued on following page*)

Appendix E.—*continued*

Date	Ordinance	Provisions	Source
Mar 1552	Proclamation	Proclamation of 10 June 1552 prohibiting bills of exchange is annulled	*Discourse*, p. 146
1558	Proclamation	Prohibition of carrying money abroad by way of exchange	*Annals* 2.148
Sep 1576	Proclamation	Existing statutes and laws "upon bargains of exchange" to be enforced. Bills of exchange not valid unless endorsed by a deputy-Exchanger. Exchangers not to endorse bills in which money is "deliuered vnder the iust values of their standerd"	*TSP* 1.76, nos. 706–07 *Annals* 2.148 *TED* 2.167–69: no. iii.15
Mar 1601	Proclamation	5–6 Ed VI c. 19, 5 Ric II stat 1 c. 2 and 25 Ed III stat 5 c. 12 to be strictly enforced	*TSP* 1.103, no. 907 *Annals* 1.353
Feb 1619	Proclamation	Official coinage rates to be respected; gold and silver not to be exchanged for profit	*TSP* 1.147, no. 1240

(continued on following page)

Appendix E.—*continued*

Date	Ordinance	Provisions	Source
May 1627	Proclamation	Royal Exchanger to have sole control over exchanges from 29 Sep 1627. Goldsmiths condemned for culling & exporting coins	*TSP* 1.178, no. 1512 *Annals* 1.383–84
Jun 1661	Proclamation	5 Ed VI c. 19, 5 Ric II stat 1 c. 2 and 25 Ed III stat 5 c. 12 to be enforced	*TSP* 1.398, no. 3309 *Annals* 2.3
May 1663	15 Car II c. 7	Free export of foreign coins and of bullion to be lawful from 1 Aug 1663	*SR* 5.451, sec. 9

SOURCES:

EHP = Georg Schanz, *Englische Handelspolitik gegen Ende des Mittelalters* (2 vols. Leipzig 1881)
TED = *Tudor Economic Documents*, ed. Richard H. Tawney and Eileen E. Power (3 vols. London and New York 1924)
Discourse = Thomas Wilson, *Discourse upon Usury* [1572], ed. Richard H. Tawney (New York 1925)

8 Italian Creditors in Dubrovnik (Ragusa) and the Balkan Trade, Thirteenth through Fifteenth Centuries

Bariša Krekić

THE EASTERN SHORE OF THE ADRIATIC SEA attracted the attention of merchants from the Apennine peninsula long before the Venetians conquered Dalmatia for the first time in the year 1000. However, it was only after 1204 and the creation of the Venetian colonial empire in the East that this area became particularly important for Venice, as its main route for trade and communication with the Levant. Other Italians too, especially from southern Italy, maintained constant and intense contacts with the eastern Adriatic coast.

Exploitation of the natural resources in the area's hinterland soon followed. Mining started in Serbia in the mid-thirteenth century, in Bosnia early in the fourteenth. Silver, copper, iron, and lead now began flowing in large quantities from the Balkan hinterland toward the West. This flow went primarily through Dubrovnik, whose merchants captured the lion's share of Balkan mining profits from the very beginning, thanks to links they had established earlier.[1] The predominance of people from Dubrovnik, Ragusans, in the Balkan mineral trade was one source of the city's prosperity in the later Middle Ages. The other was naval trade, for Dubrovnik was able to profit from its excellent position on the main naval route from Venice toward the Levant and the Mediterranean world at large.

And so Dubrovnik, at the point of confluence between maritime and continental commerce, became the focus of varied economic operations, in which, apart from the Ragusans themselves, the main participants were Italians, mostly Venetians. As political overlord in Dubrovnik and Dalmatia from 1205 to 1358, Venice had a direct economic interest in the area.

From the mid-thirteenth century on, the rapidly expanding Ragusan economy needed ever larger capital for investment. Not surprisingly, credit operations became an important part of economic activity in the city. We can follow the development of this activity beginning with the 1280s, from the earliest preserved volumes of the important series *Debita notariae* (1282) and *Diversa cancellariae* (1282) in the Historical Archives in Dubrovnik. From the beginning of the fourteenth century on, we can add the *Diversa notariae* and *Aptagi*.

Between 1280 and 1400 a total of slightly over two million Venetian ducats was loaned in Dubrovnik. Of the creditors, the Ragusan patricians constituted about two thirds, foreigners close to a fifth; the rest were other local people. Of the total, foreigners loaned about 220,000 ducats, and of these 198,000

1. Mihailo J. Dinić, *Za istoriju rudarstva u srednjevekovnoj Srbiji i Bosni* (2 vols. Belgrade 1955–62); Desanka Kovačević, "Dans la Serbie et la Bosnie médiévales: Les mines d'or et d'argent," *Annales: Economies, Sociétés, Civilisations* 15 (1960) 248–58. On Dubrovnik at this time, see Bariša Krekić, *Dubrovnik in the 14th and 15th Centuries: A City between East and West* (Norman, Okla. 1972).

were loaned by Italians.[2] On the other hand, among borrowers in the same period only about 11% were foreigners: their debts amounted to almost 137,000 ducats. This means that foreigners' loans were more than a third larger than their debts. Among the foreign borrowers, the Italians accounted for less than 11%. With loans amounting to 198,000 ducats and debts to less than 15,000 ducats in this period, the Italians were primarily lenders, not borrowers, in Dubrovnik's financial transactions.

Their credit went primarily to local people, mainly patricians, who constituted about 90% of the borrowers. Among the foreigners, the largest percentage went to merchants from the Montenegrian, Dalmatian, and Albanian coast, followed by those from Bosnia and Serbia.[3] There is no doubt that much of the money loaned to local people and to the foreigners, by both Ragusan patricians and foreigners, was used to carry on trade with the Balkan hinterland. This conclusion is confirmed by numerous archival documents, from which I shall give just a few examples.

On 18 May 1335, the distinguished Venetian merchant and financier in Dubrovnik, Çaninus Giorgio, received 200 golden ducats from another prominent Venetian, Nicoletto Quirino. Çaninus promised to pay Nicoletto by mid-June an amount of Serbian *grossi de cruce* equivalent to the 200 ducats, or to give the corresponding value in silver.[4] In November of the same year, the Ragusan Marinus *quondam* Nicole de Stillo contracted a debt of 160 ducats with Çanino Quirino in Dubrovnik. Stillo was at the time very actively engaged in

2. These and subsequent calculations are based on data found in Ignacij Voje, *Kreditna trgovina u srednjovjekovnom Dubrovniku* (Sarajevo 1976) and on my own data from research in the Historical Archives in Dubrovnik (hereafter HAD).

3. For example, in 1331 the Venetians loaned to Ragusan patricians close to 10,000 ducats; almost 1,500 ducats to merchants from the Montenegrian coast; 600 ducats to non-noble persons from Dubrovnik; and 450 ducats to people from the Balkan hinterland.

4. HAD, *Diversa cancellariae*, vol. 12, fol. 96v.

trade with Serbia; for example, only two months earlier he had taken measures concerning the regulation of a debt of 276 ducats that the Serbian king, Stefan Dušan, owed him and his companion Jache de Crossi.[5]

In April 1336, the Venetian Stephanus Çiurano, procurator of a group of Venetian merchants, received from a Ragusan patrician "libras XXVIII, oncias VIII et exsagia IIII de argento fino cum auro . . . de Nouaberda." This silver mixed with gold, brought from the most important Balkan silver mine, was worth 240 ducats in Dubrovnik. It was to be sent to Venice and sold there by another Ragusan patrician— all of this in payment of a debt of 1,218 ducats that the Ragusan patrician had contracted with Çiurano in February 1336.[6]

In the same month of April, a Venetian merchant long resident in Dubrovnik, Franciscus Scarpaçius, received "ab illustri et serenissimo domino, domino rege Rascie et toto regnamine ipsius" and from several Serbian noblemen the complete settlement of debts that they owed him and one of his associates for purchases "pannorum de lana" and of other goods.[7] A similar statement of acquittal was issued in December 1338 by two Venetian merchants in Dubrovnik to "excellentissimo domino principi, domino Stephano, Dei gratia regi Rassie" and several noblemen from Kotor, Ulcinj, and Dubrovnik in the Serbian service, and to "omnibus baronibus et hominibus dicti regni," for all debts incurred up to that time with the two Venetians.[8]

Venetians obviously played an important role as creditors in fourteenth century Dubrovnik. Between 1331 and 1339 alone the Venetians there extended credit for 118,000 ducats, that is to say 50% of the total extended for that period, or 70% of that advanced by foreigners. Table 1 gives an annual

5. HAD, *Debita notariae,* vol. 2, fols. 60, 62.
6. Ibid., fol. 93.
7. Ibid., fol. 91; *Div. canc.,* vol. 12, fol. 218. Similar declaration in September 1337: *Debita,* vol. 2, fol. 183.
8. *Debita,* ibid., fol. 232.

breakdown of the total. The participation of some individual Venetian merchants in credit operations was truly outstanding. Thus Franciscus *speciarius*, a leading Venetian in Dubrovnik between 1331 and 1339, loaned close to 15,000 ducats, or 12.5% of the total credit given by Venetians in Dubrovnik during the period.

TABLE 1

1331	11,629 ducats		1336	10,664 ducats
1332	13,065 ducats		1337	2,647 ducats
1333	33,608 ducats		1338	2,937 ducats
1334	15,397 ducats		1339	492 ducats
1335	27,566 ducats			

The sharp drop between the first and second half of the decade is immediately noticeable. While the credit advanced by the Venetians between 1331 and 1335 amounted to over 101,000 ducats, that advanced between 1336 and 1339 hardly reached 17,000 ducats. The average annual amount of credit in the first five years was over 20,000 ducats, while it fell to less than 4,200 ducats in the following four years. This trend corresponds to a general decline in the amount of credit transactions in Dubrovnik at this time. It has been suggested that the change was caused by the crisis in the Florentine banking companies.[9] But the Florentine companies—of which more shortly—did not play a major role in the Ragusan economy and their collapse could not affect Dubrovnik so dramatically.[10] The reason for the decline in credit operations should be sought elsewhere. The Venetians—very much preoccupied with developing their trade with faraway Asian regions—may

9. Voje (n. 2 above) 200–01.
10. Bariša Krekić, "Four Florentine Commercial Companies in Dubrovnik (Ragusa) in the First Half of the Fourteenth Century," *The Medieval City,* ed. Harry A. Miskimin, David Herlihy, and Abraham L. Udovitch (New Haven and London 1977) 25–41.

simply have been temporarily losing interest in the nearby Ragusan and Balkan market.

Another interesting group of Italians in Dubrovnik in the first half of the fourteenth century were the representatives of the Florentine banking companies of Bardi, Peruzzi, Acciaiuoli, and Buonaccorsi. The Bardi are mentioned between 1318 and 1339/40, the Peruzzi from 1318 to 1334, the Acciaiuoli from 1318 to 1333, and the Buonaccorsi from 1333 to 1335. The Peruzzi had the largest number of agents, nine; the Bardi had five, the Acciaiuoli four, and the Buonaccorsi only one; but the loyalties of all these men shifted and were sometimes divided among several companies. With one exception, all the agents were Florentines, but the Florentine companies did use Ragusans in their operations, especially in transfers of money from Dubrovnik to Venice. Of twenty-nine such cases, twenty-six were handled by Ragusan patricians, one by a local merchant, and two by a Florentine who was a citizen of Dubrovnik. Some of these transfers were made by a *littera cambii*, which appeared in Dubrovnik in the 1320s but at that time was always used by foreigners or in transactions between foreigners and Ragusans. The littera cambii was first used among Ragusans themselves in 1368.[11]

Most of the money sent by Florentine companies from Dubrovnik to Venice was acquired not from credit investments in Dubrovnik but from the companies' commercial operations in southern Italy: Dubrovnik served merely as a transit point for its transfer to Venice and Florence. Some of it, however, did originate in Florentine operations in Dubrovnik itself, as well as in Kotor. Between 1323 and 1335 the Florentines transferred a total of 6,200 ducats from or through Dubrovnik to Venice.

The main role of the Florentine companies in Dubrovnik was to provide cereals from southern Italy, not credit.[12]

11. Voje (n. 2 above) 156–59.
12. Krekić (n. 10 above). See also Mirjana Popović, "Prilog ekonomskoj istoriji Dubrovnika," *Zbornik Filozofskog fakulteta u Beogradu* 5 (1960) 211–15.

Nevertheless, individual Florentines did play a major role as creditors. The most important among them was Bencius del Buono, father of the famous Italian novelist Franco Sacchetti. Bencius lived in Dubrovnik from 1318 until 1341.[13] His numerous and far-flung affairs involved trade and credit transactions not only in Dubrovnik but also in southern Italy, Serbia, Bosnia, the Montenegrian and Dalmatian coasts, Florence, Venice, and even Constantinople and Thessalonica. Credit operations were an important part of Bencius's business: between 1331 and 1339 he gave over 16,000 ducats in credit,[14] mostly to Ragusan patricians, and in some instances to the Ragusan government itself. Bencius del Buono was undoubtedly one of the most important and respected merchants in fourteenth century Dubrovnik, but the Florentines as a group cannot compare with the Venetians in Ragusan trade and credit activity.

In the first half of the fifteenth century a new group of Italians became prominent in the city's credit transactions. These were Tuscan merchants and artisans mainly from Prato and Florence. Their appearance is related to the beginnings of large-scale textile production in Dubrovnik in the second decade of the fifteenth century.[15] This new industry also attracted a substantial number of Spanish merchants, importers of wool, who certainly played a role in credit operations as well—but that aspect of their activity has yet to be studied in detail.[16]

Textile production became one of the most successful enterprises in the Ragusan economy, because it had a ready-

---

13. Ignacij Voje, "Bencio del Buono," *Istorijski časopis* 18 (1971) 189–99; Krekić (n. 10 above) 37.

14. Voje (n. 2 above) 206.

15. Dragan Roller, *Dubrovački zanati u XV i XVI stoljeću* (Zagreb 1951) 5–83. Dušanka Dinić-Knežević, "Petar Pantela, trgovac i suknar u Dubrovniku," *Godišnjak Filozofskog fakulteta u Novom Sadu* 13 (1970) 87–144.

16. Momčilo Spremić, *Dubrovnik i Aragonci (1442–1495)* (Belgrade 1971) 119–25.

made market in the Balkan hinterland, and its growth considerably influenced the credit market.[17] From a partial analysis of fifteenth century data, I concluded some time ago that the average loan declined in Dubrovnik between 1418 and 1479 (see table 2). In my opinion, this pattern reflects the paramount need for money in the initial development of textile manufacturing and its subsequent decline once production got under way.[18]

TABLE 2

1418	192 ducats	1458	112 ducats
1419	198 ducats	1459	89 ducats
1438	180 ducats	1478	65 ducats
1439	120 ducats	1479	63 ducats

An incomplete survey of the amounts of credit given in Dubrovnik between 1401 and 1440 gives a total of about 1,373,000 ducats. If one recalls that during the prior one hundred and twenty years the amount given in credit totaled a little over two million ducats, it becomes clear that the volume of credit for the period 1401–40 had doubled (and the data here are only for fifteen years out of forty!). This mirrors the general increase in economic activity, due primarily to the development of the textile production and to the continued growth of Balkan mining.

Tuscan participation in this activity was substantial: in only nine selected years between 1418 and 1459, the Tuscans gave a total of 73,900 ducats in loans.[19] This amounted to about 7.5% of the total credit advanced in Dubrovnik in those years. Clearly, the Tuscans had a significant share of the Ragusan

17. See Voje (n. 2 above) 259–332.
18. Bariša Krekić, "Quelques remarques sur la politique et l'économie de Dubrovnik (Raguse) au XVe siècle," *Mélanges en l'honneur de Fernand Braudel* (2 vols. Paris 1973) 1: *Histoire économique du monde méditerranéen 1450–1650*, 314.
19. The total is based on my own research in HAD.

credit market, the result of their prominent role in the organization of the textile industry.[20]

Certain Tuscans, like individual Venetians, played an outstanding role as merchants and creditors. Thus, Georgius *quondam* Georgii domini Guçii de Florentia, who lived in Dubrovnik at least from 1418 to 1428, gave a total of 14,000 ducats in credit in the four years 1418–21 alone, which amounted to more than a third of the Tuscan credits in the city. Upon his death in Dubrovnik in 1428, Georgius left 1,350 ducats invested in credit with various Ragusan and Italian merchants.[21] Many of these transactions were to finance textile production and Balkan hinterland trade.[22]

Another prominent Tuscan creditor in Dubrovnik was Martinus Chierini de Florentia, whose credit operations in 1458 and 1459 alone amounted to a total of slightly over 17,000 ducats (75% of Tuscan credits in the city at the time).[23] Chierini must have been a man of vast financial means; his activity continued in Dubrovnik after this time, but not enough is known about him yet to have a complete picture.

It should be pointed out that many credit transactions involved merchandise, not cash; that is, merchandise was often loaned directly or accepted as payment. This is particularly

20. Mirjana Popović, "La penetrazione dei mercanti Pratesi a Dubrovnik (Ragusa) nella prima metà del XV secolo," *Archivio storico italiano* 117 (1959) 503–21; Bariša Krekić, "I mercanti e produttori Toscani di panni di lana a Dubrovnik (Ragusa) nella prima metà del Quattrocento," *Produzione, commercio e consumo dei panni di lana* (Prato and Florence 1976) 707–14.

21. HAD, *Testamenta notariae*, vol. 11, fols. 178v–180.

22. To give just one example of the contact with the hinterland trade: in 1420 two men, Vlachusa Blasii and Matchus Stiepanouich, borrowed 420 ducats from one Georgius for three months. It was agreed "ut possimus pro dicto debito conveniri tam in Ragusio, quam in Bosna et specialiter in Nouaberda et per totam Sclauoniam et Rassiam," after which it was added more briefly, "et per totam Dalmatiam, in Apulea, in Marchia, Venetiis et ubique locorum. . . ." *Debita*, vol. 13, fol. 199.

23. These calculations are based on archival documents in my possession.

true of Balkan minerals, above all silver. It cannot be stressed enough how important Balkan mining, especially silver mining, had become for Dubrovnik's life and prosperity. Silver mining had attained unprecedented levels in the Balkan hinterland during the first half of the fifteenth century. Data concerning quantities are very limited and calculations vary widely. The great historian of Dubrovnik, Jorjo Tadić, on the basis of the books of a Ragusan commercial company in existence between 1427 and 1432, had calculated that 25 tons of Serbian and Bosnian silver were exported annually through Dubrovnik toward the West.[24] This very high estimate has recently been revised by Sima Ćirković, of the University of Belgrade. Using records of the Ragusan mint for the year 1422, he established that the production of silver in the Balkans for that particular year could not have been less than 5.67 tons. However, in view of the fact that the annual production of the famous Serbian mine of Novo Brdo reached, at its peak, about 9 tons, and the production of the biggest Bosnian mine, Srebrenica, attained about 5–6 tons, Ćirković puts the minimum output of silver in Serbia and Bosnia in the first half of the fifteenth century at an average of 12 tons a year.[25]

To get the proper proportions, one should keep in mind that the total European production at the time was very limited. Soetbeer calculated almost a century ago that a total of 47 tons of silver was produced annually in Central Europe in the late fifteenth and early sixteenth centuries.[26] His cal-

24. Jorjo Tadić, "Privreda Dubrovnika i srpske zemlje u prvoj polovini XV veka," *Zbornik Filosofskog fakulteta u Beogradu* 10/1 (1968) 531.
25. Sima Ćirković, "Dubrovačka kovnica i proizvodnja srebra u Srbiji i Bosni," *Istorijski glasnik* 1–2 (1976) 91–98. See also Mihailo J. Dinić, *Iz dubrovačkog arhiva* 2 (Belgrade 1963), and idem, "Dubrovačka kovnica u 1422 godini," *Istorijski glasnik* 1–2 (1976) 81–90. On Novo Brdo, see Vojislav Jovanović, "Novo Brdo—grad zaista srebrni i zlatni," *Obeležja* 2 (Priština 1971) 75–111.
26. Adolf Soetbeer, "Edelmetall-Produktion und Werthverhältniss zwischen Gold und Silber seit der Entdeckung Amerika's bis zur Gegenwart," in *Dr. A. Petermann's Mittheilungen aus Justus Perthes' Geographischer Anstalt* Erg. 13 no. 57 (Gotha 1879) 107.

culations were later revised upward by John U. Nef, who concluded that silver production "in Bohemia, Saxony and most of the mountainous districts peopled by the Germans, Slavs and Hungarians probably reached a low point during the Hussite wars" but grew impressively after 1450.[27] This scheme certainly cannot be applied to Balkan mining. For comparative purposes, however, it might be interesting to mention that, in Nef's opinion, "around 1450 there was probably not a single mining center yielding 10,000 marks of silver a year,"[28] that is to say, at the most 2.80 tons.[29] On the other hand, the production of Srebrenica in the first half of the fifteenth century has been estimated at 5–6 tons and that of Novo Brdo at the even higher level of about 9 tons. Thus, it is clear that Balkan mining was of great importance, even more so if we accept Nef's assumption of a decline of mining in Central Europe at the time.

Such an evaluation can be made not only from a local point of view—Ragusan, Serbian, or Bosnian—but also from a broader European, and especially Italian, viewpoint. It should not be forgotten that this was a time of crisis in the Venetian silver trade. A Venetian document from 1407 explains the situation:

Cum ab uno tempore citra argentum, quod totum solebat conduci Venetias, ceperit aliam viam, nec conducatur ut conducebatur per elapsum, et hoc est quia argentum non navigatur ad presens ad partes levantis, prout navigari solebat, quum tota Syria vult ducatos auri et non argentum, et propter hoc deficiunt emptores argenti in tali maneria, quod non habet precium aliquod rationabile.

---

27. John U. Nef, "Silver Production in Central Europe, 1450–1618," *Journal of Political Economy* 49 (1941) 583–85.

28. Ibid. 586.

29. Calculated in Viennese marks (280.668 grams) and not in Cologne marks (233.855 grams), which would yield only 2.33 tons. On outputs of English and Flemish-Burgundian mints, see John H. Munro, "Bullion Movements and Monetary Contraction in Late-Medieval England and the Low Countries, 1235–1500," to be published in the *Proceedings of the International Conference on Pre-Modern Monetary History 1200–1750*, University of Wisconsin.

And so the Venetian government introduced special measures "ut mercantia argenti revertat et fiat Venetiis, ut fieri solebat per elapsum."[30]

Consequently, it is not surprising that Balkan silver should play a major role in the Ragusan economy, including the credit market in Dubrovnik. Although—as stated before—it is impossible in many cases to discern from the archival documents whether a loan is made in cash, silver, or other goods, the important thing is that the value of the loan remained the same and its role unaltered.

As a side-note let me adumbrate the rate of devaluation of the Ragusan money between the end of the thirteenth and the end of the fifteenth century. Calculations in credit transactions were made mostly in Ragusan *hyperperi* or in Venetian ducats (I have, for reasons of convenience, converted all calculations into ducats). The Ragusan hyperperus was an ideal money of account, having the permanent value of twelve grossi.[31] By observing variations in the rate of exchange between ducats and grossi it is possible to calculate the devaluation rate of the Ragusan hyperperus. Table 3 illustrates this devaluation.[32]

Over a period of roughly 220 years, the Ragusan money lost about 70% of its value, or 0.31% annually—a remarkable record under the circumstances. It is interesting to note that the rate of devaluation was highest between 1350 and 1450. This can, in all probability, be attributed to the consequences

30. Šime Ljubić, *Listine o odnošajih izmedju Južnoga Slavenstva i Mletačke Republike* 5 (Zagreb 1875) 95–96.

31. On Ragusan coins and monetary system in general, see the unsurpassed work by Milan Rešetar, *Dubrovačka numizmatika* (2 vols. Sremski Karlovci 1924–25), especially 1.29–70.

32. This table is based on several sources: Rešetar (n. 31 above) 1.472–73; Vuk Vinaver, "Der venezianische Goldzechin in der Republik Ragusa," *Bollettino dell'Istituto di Storia della società e dello stato* 4 (1962) 119; Voje (n. 2 above) 224, 230, 237, 247, and table 9; and on numerous data from unpublished archival documents in my possession.

TABLE 3

One Venetian ducat in grossi:

late 13th–mid-14th cent. = 24 gr.

1351–1360 = 24–26 gr.		1421–1430 = 32–36 gr.
1361–1370 = 27–28 gr.		1431–1440 = 36–42 gr.
1371–1380 = 29–30 gr.		1441–1450 = 35–45 gr.
1381–1390 = 30–32 gr.		1451–1460 = 36–42 gr.
1391–1400 = 30 gr.		1461–1470 = 39–41 gr.
1401–1410 = 30–33 gr.		1471–1480 = 37 gr.
1411–1420 = 30–36 gr.		1481–1490 = 39–40 gr.
		1491–1500 = 40 gr.

of the Black Death, which struck Dubrovnik very hard,[33] and later to the disruption caused in the Balkan trade and economy by internal problems in the Balkan states and by the Ottoman invasion and conquest.[34] On the other hand, the relative stability of Ragusan money in the second half of the fifteenth century should probably be attributed to the recovery and stabilization of the Balkan market after the Ottomans consolidated their conquest and the situation was more or less normalized as the frontier moved northward. Also, the development of the textile industry in Dubrovnik was certainly an asset in strengthening the local currency.

Dubrovnik was an important market for credit operations, both for local people and for foreigners, in the late Middle Ages. Among the foreigners, the Italians held the leading position, and among the Italians the Venetians were most

33. See Risto Jeremić and Jorjo Tadić, *Prilozi za istoriju zdravstvene kulture starog Dubrovnika* (3 vols. Belgrade 1938–40) 1.66–68; M. D. Grmek, "Quarantäne in Dubrovnik," *Ciba Symposium* 7 (1959) 30–31; Dušanka Dinić, "Uticaj kuge od 1348. na privredu Dubrovnika," *Godišnjak Filozofskog fakulteta u Novom Sadu* 5 (1960) 11–33; Vladimir Bazala, *Pregled povijesti zdravstvene kulture Dubrovačke Republike* (Zagreb 1972) 30–32.

34. Ivan Božić, *Dubrovnik i Turska u XIV i XV veku* (Belgrade 1952).

important, followed by the Florentines and Tuscans in general. Money (or goods) invested in credit transactions were used chiefly for trade in the Balkan hinterland or, in the fifteenth century, for the organization of textile production in Dubrovnik. The Italians themselves rarely ventured into the Balkan hinterland; but because of the great importance of Balkan mining, especially silver output, their extension of credit to Ragusans, who did go there, was particularly valuable. We cannot say precisely what percentage of Italian credits was invested in which activity, nor what part of the Balkan trade was financed by Italian creditors; but we can say that the role of Italian capital in Dubrovnik's Balkan trade was substantial. Dubrovnik served as an essential link—in this case as in many others—between East and West for their benefit and its own profit and prosperity.

9 Bankers without Banks: Commerce, Banking, and Society in the Islamic World of the Middle Ages

IN HIS MASTERFUL INTERPRETIVE SURVEY of the history of banking in Western Europe from the Middle Ages until the mid-eighteenth century, Raymond de Roover observed, "there can be no banking where there are no banks."[1] This proposition may hold true for the development of banking in medieval Europe, but it certainly does not describe the medieval Islamic world. In the sporadic information on this subject from medieval Islamic literary or documentary sources, we encounter bankers and we encounter extensive and ramified banking activities, *but we do not encounter banks.* That is, we cannot identify any autonomous or semiautonomous institutions whose primary concern was dealing in money as a specialized, if not exclusive, pursuit. Banks do not make their appearance in the Islamic Middle East until comparatively

1. Raymond de Roover, "New Interpretations of the History of Banking," *Journal of World History* 2 (1954) 43.

recently, and, partially at least, as a result of economic and political contact with premodern Europe.[2]

Such constituent elements of banking as deposits, credit, loans, and bills of exchange were quite differently construed within the medieval Islamic setting, and their role and function in the development of banking differed markedly from what we observe during the dawn of Western European banking. A rapid overview of the major medieval Near Eastern financial practices associated with banking will provide a context and partial explanation of how and why banking could flourish without banks, as well as an illuminating comparison and contrast with parallel institutions in Western Europe.

Prohibition against Interest

A strict and pervasive religiously inspired prohibition against usurious transactions was a powerful cultural feature shared by the medieval Islamic world and the Christian West. The Arabic term for usury and interest is *ribā*. The prohibition against it is absolute and the theoretical elaborations of what constitutes a usurious transaction comprehend a variety of commercial and exchange operations. Literally, *ribā* is defined as "any unjustified increase of capital for which no compensation is given"[3] or "a monetary advantage without a countervalue which has been stipulated in favour of one of the two contracting parties in an exchange of two monetary values."[4] The practice of ribā is sharply denounced in a number of passages in the Qur'ān, as it is in all subsequent Islamic religious writings such as the prophetic traditions (*Ḥadith*) and in Islamic religious law (*sharīʿa, fiqh*). Indeed, discussions of the law of contract in medieval Islamic law are largely concerned with how to prevent any usurious element from contaminating economic and commercial exchange. Not only

2. Charles P. Issawi, ed., *The Economic History of the Middle East 1800–1914* (Chicago 1966) 10–11.

3. H. A. R. Gibb and J. H. Kramers, eds., *Shorter Encyclopaedia of Islam* (Leiden 1953) 471.

4. Joseph Schacht, *An Introduction to Islamic Law* (Oxford 1964) 145.

straightforward interest-bearing cash loans, but also a large number of other practices, such as speculative transactions and certain forms of delayed payment, are declared beyond the pale by Islamic law.[5]

Investigating the Islamic legal and religious literature condemning usury is, of course, an interesting and valuable exercise in intellectual history. For the economic and social historian, however, the relevant questions are: To what extent was the uncompromising Islamic prohibition against usury observed in actual practice? Did it inhibit the conduct of economic life, did it restrain or in other ways affect the process of commercial exchange? And how did it affect credit operations, money exchange, and other operations normally associated with banking?

The sparse and episodic nature of our source material makes any answer to these questions tentative and qualified. The frequent, copious, and vehement reiteration of the prohibition against usury in medieval Islamic religious writings has been interpreted by some scholars as indirect testimony to its equally frequent violation in practice. They have consequently concluded that the Islamic prohibition against usury had little impact on the conduct of affairs and constituted at most a minor inconvenience to merchants, bankers, and others. In one sense this conclusion is correct: the ban on usury apparently did not interfere with an active and flourishing commercial life. However, our evidence does not support the supplementary conclusion that interest-bearing loans and other overtly usurious practices were in common use. In those periods for which we have secure documentary evidence, we find, on the contrary, that such loans were an infrequent means of extending commercial credit, and most references to such loans do not occur in the context of banking or commerce.[6]

Islamic law provided several means by which the antiusury

5. The most concise and authoritative summary of the prohibition against usury in Islamic law is the article by Joseph Schacht in *Shorter Encyclopaedia of Islam* (n. 3 above) 471–73.

6. S. D. Goitein, *A Mediterranean Society* (2 vols. Berkeley 1967–71) 1.250–62.

prohibition could be circumvented. Various legal fictions, based primarily on the model of the "double-sale," were, if not enthusiastically endorsed by the religious lawyers, at least not declared invalid. Furthermore, the urban populations of the medieval Islamic world included commercially active Christian and Jewish minorities. While Christians and Jews may have been inhibited from conducting usurious practices within their own religious communities, no such constraints affected their economic contacts with each other or with commercial colleagues from the dominant Muslim communities. Thus there existed no insuperable barrier to using interest-bearing loans for commercial credit or to finance perennially cash-hungry governments. The fact that this option was not exercised had very little to do with the religious rejection of usury. Rather, numerous other commercial techniques were available which played the same role as interest-bearing loans and so made the significant use of loans unnecessary. These other techniques included a variety of partnership forms, *commendas*, credit arrangements, transfers of debt, and letters of credit, all of which were sanctioned by religious theory and hallowed by long practice. Most importantly, because these alternate forms of investment and credit were a socially more congenial and effective means of economic connection, they were preferred over loans.

While the formal legal and religious rejection of usurious practices was common to both the medieval Christian and Islamic worlds, its impact on economic life, and particularly on banking practices, was apparently somewhat different in each domain. In the Islamic it was minimal; in the Christian it shaped the development of financial practices and institutions and may even have been a major barrier to the development of exchange and commerce.

Deposit

A characteristic feature of the formation of banking capital since the dawn of European banking was the accumulation of interest-bearing deposits used in turn to provide loans at a high premium to merchants or princes. This notion of deposit is completely foreign to the Islamic Middle East. In Islamic law, deposit is a custodial contract by which the depositor hands over to the depositary property or money to be kept and returned intact at a later date. It involved no payment of a fee or any other compensation to either depositor or depositary. Its function in Islamic law, as well as in earlier Near Eastern legal traditions and practices, was restricted to that implied by its title, the deposit and safeguarding of money or goods when doing so served the purposes of their owner. The Near Eastern conception of deposit emphasized reliable safekeeping, and consequently the uses to which the depositary could put the deposited property were severely prescribed. Indeed, under most circumstances, if he put it to any use at all he might become liable to the depositor for any benefits he derived.[7]

This conception stands in sharp contrast to that prevalent in the medieval West, where the depositary not only kept the funds entrusted to him but also had the right to use them for a variety of commercial purposes. In consideration of this privilege, the deposit was returned to its owner with a premium. Deposit thus evolved into an important element in the growth of European banking, whereas in the Near East its role was quite modest, limited almost entirely to facilitating the payment of personal and commercial debts.

The Near Eastern notion and practice of deposit precluded the coalescence of two financial practices which in the history of Western banking proved a potent combination: the generation of capital by means of numerous deposits on the one hand, and moneylending and the provision of credit on the other. This combination of deposits and lending could not develop in the medieval Near East.

7. Subhi Mahmassani, "Transactions in the Sharīᶜa," in Majid Khadduri and H. J. Liebesny, eds., *Law in the Middle East* (Washington, D. C. 1955) 200–01; Schacht (n. 4 above) 157; O. Spies, "Das Depositum nach islamischen Recht," *Zeitschrift für vergleichende Rechtswissenschaft* 45 (1930) 241–300; idem, article *wadīᶜa*, *Encyclopaedia of Islam* (1st ed.) 4.1079–81.

Loans to kings and princes were a great opportunity and also, all too frequently, a fatal pitfall to the Italian banking houses of the thirteenth through fifteenth centuries. In the Islamic world, advances of cash to the public treasury and the ruling dynasties were handled quite differently. They took the form of tax-farming arrangements in which individuals possessing liquid capital—presumably generated from commercial profits—advanced cash to the government in return for the right to farm the taxes of a given region for a fixed period.[8] The nature of this credit mechanism was very different from that of a loan. It was essentially an advance payment of rent to a ruler in return for deferred collection from the inhabitants of rural areas. Usually quite lucrative for the tax farmer, subject to arbitrary and shortsighted abuses by both parties to the arrangement, it was a frequently unstable and high-risk enterprise. For the history of banking, the significant point is that the private funds provided to the perennially impecunious public treasuries of the medieval Islamic world were not loans and were not generated by accumulating and risking the deposits of many people, but came from individual commercial fortunes and were in the nature of a high-risk investment.

The Near Eastern conception of deposit had one further major consequence for the early history of banking in that region. Since no premium was paid on deposits, they could not be used as a form of productive investment. To a Near Eastern investor seeking a return on his capital many alternate possibilities were available. If he wanted no involvement beyond his financial participation, he could avail himself of various forms of partnership and *commenda* associations which could provide a return on his investment. In practice, however, there was nothing abstract or institutionalized about these investments: they involved either investing in a specific commercial venture, or entrusting capital to a specific person whose normal business activities were well known. Invest-

8. For example, see Walter J. Fischel, *Jews in the Economic and Political Life of Medieval Islam* (London 1937); also, C. Cahen in *Encyclopaedia of Islam* (2nd ed.) 1.1144 (s.v. *bayt al-māl*).

ments were rarely if ever impersonal in the way a deposit in the medieval West might be, without the investor knowing the eventual disposition of his capital. In the Near East, the investor knew who was going to work with his capital, he knew the quality of the merchant to whom he was entrusting his funds, and he had a fairly good idea of what was going to be done with them. Investment was always embedded in a network of personal-commercial relations.

Credit

The role of credit in medieval economic life has been a subject of some dispute among economic historians. Some, viewing the Middle Ages as a precredit era in which credit transactions (to the extent that they were employed) were restricted to consumption, have denied any significant relationship between credit and trade. The work of Postan and others has put this view to rest by demonstrating that by the thirteenth century in northern Europe, and at least a century earlier in southern Europe, credit had already assumed a major role in trade. For the medieval Near East, the records of the Cairo Geniza show that by the eleventh century, credit operations constituted an integral element of Mediterranean and Indian Ocean commerce; and on the basis of nondocumentary Muslim sources we can assert that as early as the late eighth century, credit arrangements of various types were an important feature of both trade and industry in the Near East.[9]

Credit fulfilled several important functions in medieval trade. It financed trade by providing capital or goods for those

9. For medieval Europe, see Michael M. Postan, "Credit in Medieval Trade," *Economic History Review* 1 (1927–28) 234–61, in which Postan convincingly demonstrates that, in the commercial sector, the European Middle Ages were very definitely not a "precredit era." There is no comparable study for the medieval Islamic world. For data amply confirming the widespread use of credit in Islamic commerce, see Goitein (n. 6 above) 1.229–62; Abraham L. Udovitch, *Partnership and Profit in Medieval Islam* (Princeton 1970) 77–86; Sobhi Labib, "Geld und Kredit, Studien zur Wirtschaftsgeschichte Aegyptens im Mittelalter," *Journal of the Economic and Social History of the Orient* 2 (1959) 225–46.

who did not have the means of engaging in trade; it provided an outlet for surplus capital to be utilized in a productive and profitable way; and it contributed to the expansion of trade by enabling merchants to do business in an age when the supply of coins was frequently inadequate. In international trade, credit arrangements could alleviate the problem of transporting large quantities of specie across perilous routes and, in combination with other contracts, they could serve as a means of sharing the risks of commercial ventures.

A variety of credit arrangements were known and practiced in the medieval Islamic world. Made necessary by the lively regional and international trade of the Near East, they constituted the components of banking activity.

Buying and selling on credit was an accepted and widespread commercial practice, whether a merchant was trading with his own capital or with that entrusted to him by an associate or investor. The eleventh century legal scholar Sarakhsī declares that "selling on credit is an absolute feature of trade,"[10] and another writer, referring to merchants, states that "it is their custom to sell for cash and credit."[11] Credit sales—deferred payments for goods bought and advance payments for future delivery—were not only considered fully legitimate forms of commercial conduct but were viewed as indispensable to successful and profitable trading. In his monumental legal compendium, Sarakhsī expresses this view explicitly and crisply: "We hold that selling for credit is part of the practice of merchants and that it is the most conducive means for the achievement of the investors' goal which is profit. In most cases, profit can only be achieved by selling for credit and not selling for cash."[12]

This statement, intended to apply to all types of trade, was especially relevant to international trade, as the same writer goes on to tell us: "trade can also be long-distant, and this

10. Sarakhsī, *Al-mabsūṭ* (30 vols. Cairo 1905–12) 22.38.
11. Kāsānī, *Badā'i' aṣ-ṣanā'i' fī tartīb ash-sharā'i'* (7 vols. Cairo 1910) 6.68.
12. *Mabsūṭ* (n. 10 above) 22.38.

latter type of trade cannot come about except by selling on credit."[13]

This statement not only makes clear *why* a greater profit was to be derived from credit transactions but also explains *how* traders could extend credit, sometimes for long periods of time, without straining or completely immobilizing their resources.

Islamic commercial law, besides outlining methods of dealing for credit, also makes provision for dealing *in* credit. Instruments of credit such as the *ḥawāla* and *suftaja* are prime examples of this category of credit. The ḥawāla was the payment of a debt through the transfer of a claim, and the suftaja a letter of credit or bill of exchange.[14] From as early as the eighth century, these two financial techniques made possible the transfer of large sums of money over considerable distances without the use of any specie. The suftaja always, and the ḥawāla usually, occurred as a written obligation, and were thus the first and most important forms of commercial credit papers in the medieval Near East.

Among the most interesting and original credit techniques emanating from the early Islamic period are certain forms of commercial association based primarily on credit and not on cash or goods. Examples are a commercial partnership designated as a "credit partnership," and a commenda in which the investment is based on debts or credit purchases.

The credit partnership is an arrangement in which the capital of the parties consists of neither cash nor merchandise but entirely of credit. Its essential features are summarized by Sarakhsī:

The credit partnership is also called the partnership of the penniless (*sharikat al-mafālīs*). It comes about when people form a partnership without any capital in order to buy on credit and then sell. It is designated by the name "partnership of good reputations," because the capital of

13. Ibid.
14. Schacht (n. 4 above) 148–49.

the partners consists of their status and good reputations;
for credit is extended only to him who has a good
reputation.[15]

These two designations for the credit partnership—"the
partnership of the penniless" and "the partnership of those
with status and good reputations"—reflect two of the major
functions of credit in trade. The first reflects a situation in
which traders without sufficient resources of their own seek
financing, the traders hiring the capital; the second reflects a
situation in which the capital seeks a profitable investment
outlet, the capital hiring the trader.

In discussing the operations of the credit partnership, the
medieval Islamic lawyers revealed a remarkably sophisticated
appreciation of the function of credit in economic and commercial life. To paraphrase one writer on the subject: the
purpose of commercial investments based on cash is the increase of capital; the purpose of a credit partnership is both
the increase and *the creation* of the capital itself, since credit
is a means for augmenting or creating capital.[16]

When we move from the theoretical level of the discussions
in Muslim legal works to day-to-day commercial practice depicted in the Geniza documents of the eleventh through
thirteenth centuries, we find virtually all of these earlier credit
techniques translated into practice. The documents also provide us with an intimate glimpse of the banking operations
generated by the use of credit in the Mediterranean trade of
Egypt and North Africa.[17] Without the extensive use of credit
and its attendant banking operations, the Mediterranean trade
of the medieval Near East would have been inconceivable.

Of the thousands of business letters, contracts, and miscel-

15. *Mabsūṭ* (n. 10 above) 12.152.
16. Kāsānī (n. 11 above) 6.58.
17. Most of the data upon which the following discussion is based
are to be found in Goitein (n. 6 above) 1.229–50. See also idem, "Bankers
Accounts from the Eleventh Century A.D.," *Journal of the Economic
and Social History of the Orient* 9 (1966) 26–68.

laneous commercial documents from Geniza, very few do not contain a reference to some form of a credit transaction. On the highest commercial level, sales, both wholesale and retail, were normally conducted on a credit basis—on the basis, that is, of deferred payment for a fixed period. The documents make clear that the buyer paid a premium for deferring payment. This was expressed either by granting a discount from the stated price in return for an immediate cash payment (discounts varied from 2% to 4%), or by quoting two prices: one for a cash transaction and a slightly higher one for a credit transaction. Although the great majority of merchants mentioned in these documents were Jews, it is nevertheless worth noting that the practice was sanctioned by at least one of the major early Islamic schools of law, and was not considered usurious. Its prevalence is emphatically confirmed by a *responsum* of Maimonides, the twelfth century Jewish philosopher and legal scholar, who states, "This is the accepted custom among people in trade, and without it most commerce would come to a standstill."[18]

In addition to widespread commercial credit sales, many petty transactions of daily domestic life were also executed on a credit basis. Written orders were sent to tradesmen, grocers, and other suppliers, and after a certain number had accumulated they were added up and returned and payment was made.

Money Changing and Merchant Banking

Considering the profusion of credit transactions, it is no surprise that we encounter in eleventh century Egypt and North Africa an elaborate system of banking and money exchange to accommodate the various needs and circumstances. The institutions which arose in response can, for the purpose of analysis, be divided into two major categories: money changing and merchant banking. Their functions frequently overlapped.

18. Maimonides, *Responsa*, ed. Jehoshua Blau (3 vols. Jerusalem 1957–61) 1.88–89.

Exchange, the central feature of the money market, was performed "manually" by money changers or merchants who dabbled in money changing, rather than through written instruments. The money market of the medieval Near East was not highly structured. It was not subject to any consistent and effective governmental or administrative controls or regulation. Intervention by the authorities was infrequent and of short duration. The exchange rate between various currencies was governed, in the first instance, by their intrinsic value and secondarily, by the demand at any given moment for a particular type of coin. This demand was in turn determined by the requirements of local or regional commerce. Merchant bankers were quite well informed on these matters and engaged in exchanges as a matter of course.

The operations of money changers were less complex than those of merchant bankers, and their profession relatively more specialized. The simultaneous circulation in the medieval Islamic world of a great variety of gold and silver coins whose value was subject to frequent fluctuations required knowledgeable persons to facilitate their interchangeability; the demand of international traders for specific coinages to finance their far-flung operations required a ready source for obtaining them; and the fact that coins were not only a means of exchange but also an object of trade required their reliable assaying and evaluation. All these functions were fulfilled by the money changers, who served as the nerve centers of financial exchange. The magnitude of their operations varied: some dealt in small sums and limited issues only, others had semiofficial status and oversaw exchanges amounting to thousands of dinars. Profits from these operations derived not only from shrewd currency speculation based on an intimate acquaintance with the money market, but also, and maybe primarily, from a fixed commission charged for each exchange transacted. Although we do not have sufficient data for a firm generalization, the commission was approximately 1% for sums of about 100 dinars, and slightly higher for smaller sums.

Money changing operations were by no means restricted to the money changers. Almost every merchant dabbled in them, and for many, especially those significantly involved in international trade, money changing was a large part of their activities. In addition to money changing, many middle-level and grand merchants engaged in a variety of protobanking activities.

The Geniza material published or studied thus far offers no example of an individual whose exclusive occupation was banking. No matter how extensive the banking operations of any single merchant, they invariably accompanied a correspondingly thriving trade in commodities. Thus, even more than in the medieval West, we can characterize them as merchant bankers, emphasizing the first element of this compound profession; that is, banking activities were closely related to private trading and commercial activities.

Among the chief banking functions was the exchange and transfer of specie to facilitate payments in both local and international commerce. This was accomplished by distributing coins in sealed purses with the exact values in money of account indicated on the outside. The seals on the purses were either those of a governmental or semiofficial exchange, or those of individual merchants. From business correspondence and from entries in account books we can infer that two separate figures were noted on the exterior of the sealed purses: the number of coins, and their weight and value. So, for example, we read of purses containing 308¼ gold coins with a value of 300 dinars, or 122 gold coins with a value of 119⅜ dinars. These packaged and labeled purses made settlement of accounts much more convenient, of course, by obviating the need to weigh, assay, and evaluate coins for every individual transaction. Significantly, most payments and transfers of funds were executed by the actual physical transfer of these purses. Book transfers, even when they involved the accounts of two customers of a single merchant banker, do not appear to have been a frequent practice, and the use of written instruments of credit, although common, was not nearly so important as the physical transfer of sealed purses.

Whereas it was customary for merchants and others to keep at least a portion of their money on deposit with merchant bankers, and whereas the merchant bankers themselves kept deposits of various sizes with several other merchant bankers, there is no evidence whatsoever that any interest or other type of premium was paid to depositors. The merchant bankers served, as Goitein has pointed out, as a clearinghouse for payments.[19] Indeed, the service itself may have constituted a premium for deposits, since we do not possess any evidence that the merchant bankers charged a fee for their payment service, which, as the Geniza papers show, required the investment of time and the maintenance of careful accounting records.

The advantages accruing to the merchant banker from these deposits were numerous. A supply, on hand, of varied currencies was a great help in his money changing activities; he could use the funds in his care to issue suftajas for which he received a substantial fee; and he could use them for investments of his own in commendas and partnerships, or to cover his current expenses until returns from his other investments—which often involved a substantial time lag—were realized.

Written Instruments of Credit

Written instruments of credit were of several types—some already anticipated in the earlier theoretical legal works, though occasionally in modified form, and others apparently innovations. The ḥawāla, or transfer of debt, functioned pretty much in the manner outlined in the lawbooks and is encountered frequently in the Geniza documents as a substitute for cash payment. The suftaja, a bill of exchange or letter of credit which in the West entailed the initial payment of one type of currency in return for the payment of another type of currency in a different location, consistently appears in the Geniza as involving the repayment of exactly the same type of money paid to the issuing banker. Suftajas were issued by and drawn upon well-known bankers, and a high fee was charged for their issue. They were as good as money; the bearer could

19. Goitein (n. 6 above) 1.231.

expect to redeem his suftaja for cash immediately upon arrival at his destination, since a daily penalty was assigned for any delay in payment. There is no indication that these suftajas were transferable or negotiable. Only the person to whom they were made out could cash them, and only in the place where they were assigned.

The Geniza records show that suftajas were much sought after, and sometimes preferred to cash. But they were difficult to come by, since merchant bankers were often reluctant to issue them. The reasons for this reluctance are not stated explicitly but can be inferred from the context. The near absolute convertibility of the suftaja into cash upon presentation and the penalties for any delay in payment meant that any merchant banker issuing it would have to be completely certain of his agent, partner, or colleague at the other end, wherever the suftaja was to be redeemed. Few merchant bankers apparently had such complete confidence. Mercantile and banking activities were based on a network of personal and social relations, and these, in themselves, were not a firm enough foundation upon which to erect economic institutions which could function independently of the social network.

At this point it is important to emphasize the difference between the Near Eastern suftaja and the Western bill of exchange. Scholars have assigned a central role to the bill of exchange in the growth of European banking. The suftaja, while a useful financial instrument, does not seem to have assumed a similar importance in Near Eastern banking. It was not, strictly speaking, a bill of exchange; it did not, in practice, involve any exchange of currencies but simply the payment of a sum of money of a certain type to a merchant banker in one place to be redeemed in the same quantity and type in another. It was more akin to a check or letter of credit whose purpose was to expedite long-distance payment or transfer of funds.

In addition to the ḥawāla and suftaja, there was a broad category of credit papers in use known as *ruqᶜas*, which translates into the rather neutral term "notes." These were employed mostly in local or short-distance trade, and served a variety of functions: as orders for petty payments, as orders for delivery, and also as promissory notes—sometimes for fairly large sums. Their strength as promissory notes derived from the fact that they were issued by well-known merchants. They had the force of cash: they could be used not only in commerce but even to pay government toll collectors. Here again, it was not the ruqᶜa per se but the personal status and reputation of the issuer which imparted its value to it.

In its form and function the ruqᶜa closely approached the modern check. Most of the checks or orders of payment that we encounter in the Geniza documents were for comparatively small sums—one to ten dinars—although we occasionally read of larger sums, as much as one hundred dinars. That mostly small sums were involved indicates, as do other factors, that the function of this aspect of banking was primarily payment of petty debts, very much akin to that of a modern checking account. The check-like ruqᶜas were used to settle a variety of small to medium-size bills, which, given the widespread practice of credit purchases, a merchant inevitably incurred in the course of his activities.

Banking, the Money Market, and Commercial Networks

Beginning with the eleventh century, and probably even earlier, the demand for good coins in the Islamic Mediterranean was constantly greater than the available supply. This held true for virtually all silver and gold coins—especially gold. At certain times and in certain places, the demand for one or another coin type may have slackened; yet, over any extended period, the pressure of demand on the coin supply held steady. The demand for good coins was further increased by expanding international trade. This expansion accompanied a parallel growth in internal, regional commerce around the Mediterranean which extended to continental Europe and across the Indian Ocean. This process increased the demand for reliable and acceptable means of exchange and explains the proliferation of credit and banking techniques in the Near East and their rapid growth and extension to southern Europe.

There was no specialization. Banking activities went hand in hand with regular commercial operations, and were invariably subsidiary to the merchant's endeavors in the more traditional aspects of trade such as buying, selling, exporting, and importing. Indeed, I believe we can assert that a merchant's banking activities were simply an extension of his commercial operations; they were but one more service and skill which any enterprising merchant would be expected to possess. In other words, to one extent or another most merchants actually served as their own bankers. Every aspect of their credit and banking operation—money changing, issuing letters of credit, accepting deposits, acting as a clearinghouse for payments both large and small—can be linked directly or indirectly to their commercial endeavors. We should further keep in mind that even though a wide assortment of credit techniques were known and practiced in the Islamic world from the earliest medieval period—techniques similar to those which began to appear in Europe only in the thirteenth century—their elaboration in economic life was restricted primarily to money changing and related operations, to facilitating payment of debts, and (to a much lesser extent) to the circulation of convertible written instruments of credit.

I would like to return now to the problem posed at the outset. Why in the medieval Near East do we encounter many components of banking activity, but no banks? Why did there not occur any institutional integration of banking functions—of deposits, exchange, money-lending, and other forms of credit? Why, with its considerable chronological headstart and its sophisticated appreciation of the economic role of credit, did the medieval Islamic world not give rise to independent, stable, organized forms of banking?

The special Near Eastern conception of deposit, which severely restricted their use in commerce and credit, may have had an inhibiting effect on the development of banks. Similarly, the loose structure of the Near Eastern money market may have retarded the institutional integration of banking functions. I believe, however, that neither of these factors offers a sufficiently comprehensive explanation for the inertia of banking and credit institutions in the Islamic Middle Ages. That, I think, is to be found in the social context of the region's economic life.

From this point of view, the institutions of credit and banking—one might include many other commercial institutions—reveal the inordinate prominence of status and personal relations in their operations. The most common designation of the credit partnership described above was *sharikat al-wujūh*—"a partnership of those with status and good reputation"—implying that granting of credit presupposed a certain social position or an understood set of relationships and attitudes between the parties. Status and social relationship continue to inform the Geniza data. For example, the infrequent and reluctant use of suftajas (letters of credit), the acceptance of promissory notes in lieu of cash payment, and the occasional overdrafts which merchant bankers allowed their good customers, all were based on the status of the parties concerned and on the intricate, informally structured but nevertheless effective network of social-personal relationships. Rarely if ever do we observe actual, documented credit or merchant banking activities operating outside this network.

Medieval Arabic commercial terminology is quite instructive here and reflects the Near Eastern conception of economic relations. Medieval Arabic has no terms for banks or banking, nor for the abstract notion of money. What we do find are terms for specific activities such as money changing, loans, transfer of debts, and so forth, as well as for specific denominations and types of coins. The terminology, like the reality, was embedded in a network of familiar social-economic relationships, and, like the reality, it was unable to extract itself from its social context in order to give rise to formal impersonal institutions and instruments of commercial life. Informal relationships pervaded and animated the international commerce of the medieval Near East, and banking activities remained closely tied to and dependent on commerce. Consequently, the organization of banking followed the largely informal organization of commerce.[20]

Thus, a somewhat paradoxical conclusion suggests itself. The very factors—status and personal-social relations—which ensured the smooth and successful functioning of credit and merchant banking activities in the Islamic Mediterranean world during most of the medieval period, effectively prevented their growth, elaboration, and development into independent, stable organizational forms. Given the slowness and unpredictability of communications between geographically distant locations, and given the sheer physical and psychological limitations on individual social intercourse, the scale of economic activities was necessarily restricted to numerous small, even intimate, circles. The possibility of expansion into a larger, more cohesive structure was precluded by the comparatively narrow social basis on which economic life was conducted.

20. See Abraham L. Udovitch, "Formalism and Informalism in the Social and Economic Institutions of the Medieval Islamic World," in Amin Banani and Speros Vryonis, eds., *Individualism and Conformity in Classical Islam* (Wiesbaden 1977) 61–81.

10 The Impact of Credit on Sixteenth Century English Industry

HARRY A. MISKIMIN

DURING THE SIXTEENTH CENTURY, England was transformed from an industrial and commercial laggard on the fringes of Europe into one of the more flexible and powerful economies of the early modern world. The factors sustaining these developments are not obvious; indeed, the evidence of monetary history suggests the presence of adverse forces that might well have severely constrained and limited English economic growth. Recent studies have substantially altered older views of the so-called price revolution and provide increasingly sophisticated explanations of price behavior in the period. Structural change within the economy and demographic resurgence now supplement the more traditional analyses predicated almost entirely on bullion flows. Yet many problems remain.

Elsewhere I have noted that the supply of bullion in England at the end of the sixteenth century appears to be roughly comparable to that present three hundred years earlier.[1] Between 1273 and 1372, the London Mint struck 1.9 million Tower pounds of pure silver, almost as much as the 2.2 million Tower pounds coined during the entire sixteenth century.[2] More gold was struck between 1344 and 1374 than was minted during the whole later century. If one defines the money supply in terms of bullion alone, these figures indicate that the money supply of sixteenth century England was no larger than it had been in the hundred year period between 1273 and 1372.

We may explore the further implications of the above figures in terms of the Fisher quantity equation, $MV = PT$—a tautology which states that the money supply times its velocity of circulation equals the price level times the total number of transactions or output. Were we to disregard history and postulate a situation in which the velocity and output terms were fixed in two periods with comparable money supplies, we would then expect similar price levels. Historically, if we compare the fifty year period from 1323 to 1372 with that between 1551 and 1600, and if our assumptions regarding velocity and output were true, we might expect that since the bullion supplies in the two periods were roughly comparable, bullion price levels should also be similar. Price statistics for England have been compiled by Phelps Brown and Hopkins,[3] and when they are converted from money of account to actual bullion value in silver, the suggested comparison is easily made. For the fifty year period 1323–72, the bullion price index level is 106.5; for the last half of the sixteenth century, the index level is 124.5. The sixteenth century figure is slightly higher than that for the earlier period, but it is higher in virtually the same proportion as would be suggested by the minor disparity between the mint output levels

1. Harry A. Miskimin, "Population Growth and the Price Revolution in England," *Journal of European Economic History* 4 (1975) 179–86.

2. Ibid. 182.

3. E. H. Phelps Brown and Sheila V. Hopkins, "Seven Centuries of the Price of Consumables Compared with Builders' Wage-Rates," *Economica* 2nd ser. no. 23 (1956) 296–314.

of the two periods. Given the inherent weakness in such aggregate statistics, however, it is perhaps safer not to attempt too fine distinctions, but to conclude merely that there appears to be substantial parity between the bullion price levels of the two periods. What does this apparent parity imply?

Our theoretical expectation that bullion price levels should be comparable in two periods with equivalent bullion supplies depended on the assumption of constant velocity and output terms. These assumptions, however, are patently false for the historical periods under consideration. There is no doubt whatsoever that England enjoyed a far higher level of production in the latter half of the sixteenth century than in the earlier period. Land was once again fully exploited and agricultural yields seem to have risen well above those attained during the Middle Ages.[4] Industrial output was markedly ahead of that in the earlier period. Now our investigation of the two historical periods 1323–72 and 1551–1600 has so far revealed comparable levels of the bullion supply and comparable bullion price indices, but substantially greater output in the latter span. Under these circumstances, however, if the velocity of circulation had remained constant in the two periods, we would expect to discover a decrease in the bullion price level in the second period rather than the identity or slight increase which actually occurred. If mint output accurately reflects the level of the bullion supply, it would appear that most of the Central European and New World metal that found its way to England during the sixteenth century served merely to replace stocks lost during the bullion drain of the late fourteenth and early fifteenth centuries. Further, it appears that only an upward shift in the velocity of bullion circulation prevented bullion prices from falling in the face of rapidly expanding output in the late

4. See Joan Thirsk, "Farming Techniques," and Joyce Youings, "The Church," in Joan Thirsk, ed., *The Agrarian History of England and Wales* 4 (Cambridge 1967) and A. R. Bridbury, "Sixteenth-Century Farming," *Economic History Review* 2nd ser. 27 (1974) 538–56.

sixteenth century. Put another way, the bullion price level in the second half of the sixteenth century, though numerically roughly equal to that in the mid-fourteenth, was substantially higher than it would have been had fourteenth century levels of velocity prevailed. In this very special sense, it is thus possible to speak of a velocity-induced, concealed inflation at the end of the sixteenth century.

Velocity is a problematical expression. Of the four terms in the quantity equation, it is the most abstract and the least measurable; indeed, it normally is a residual term obtained by dividing the gross national product (PT) by the money supply, however defined. Yet despite its elusive quality, velocity is the link between purely monetary factors and the somewhat broader matters of banking and credit. A number of influences acted upon the velocity of bullion circulation during the sixteenth century, but it may prove useful to group them into two categories: those that proceeded downward from government policy and those which arose independently out of the economy itself. In the former, we may place currency laws, monetary standards, and exchequer policy; in the latter lie such factors as intra-industry and inter-industry credit and all changes in industrial organization and structure that served to economize the bullion balances required for the conduct of business. Population growth should also be included here.

Even though the Tudor monarchs exercised more self-restraint than their continental counterparts, enough English currency debasement went on during the early modern period to have provoked substantial scholarly comment. Unfortunately, this literature rarely endeavors to address the various component effects of currency mutation and thus fails to distinguish among nominal changes in the value of bullion, real effects on the money supply, and the potential role of debasement in altering the velocity of bullion circulation. If we consider as a base with an index level of 100 the period 1351–1411, when 300d. were drawn from the Tower pound, we find that in the years 1552–1601, when 720d. were drawn from the Troy pound of fine silver, the index of fineness falls to 44.4.[5] The pound of account in the latter period contained only 44.4% as much silver as it did during the last half of the fourteenth century. In effect, the same quantity of raw silver would produce two and a quarter times as much nominal money of account in the late sixteenth century as it did in the late fourteenth. Since it has already been established that the amount of bullion struck between 1273 and 1372 was roughly equal to that coined in the sixteenth century, we may safely conclude that the nominal money supply was substantially higher in the later period.

It is important to recall that our investigation of the relationships defined by the quantity equation has been predicated on real rather than nominal values. Both price levels and the money supply were defined in terms of silver bullion, and clearly debasement in itself cannot alter the actual quantity of bullion coined, but only its nominal value. Under certain circumstances, however, debasement can affect the velocity of circulation of the underlying bullion and thus heighten the economic impact of a given quantity of silver. By assigning a higher account value to a given amount of silver, debasement reduces the amount of silver contained in any given specific coin and this subdivision of the bullion supply allows the same quantity of metal to be in more places at once. Less metal lies idle in consumer pockets, and velocity increases.

Such a debasement-induced increase in the velocity of bullion circulation depends on the willingness of the public to accept coin at par. If each vendor in the economy sought individually to preserve the intrinsic value of his selling price,

5. These figures are derived from Sir John Craig, *The Mint: A History of the London Mint from A.D. 287 to 1948* (Cambridge 1953) 412–15. The history of debasement is as follows:

		Index
1351–1411	300d. to the Tower pound	100
1412–1464	360d. to the Tower pound	83.3
1465–1525	450d. to the Tower pound	66.7
1526–1541	540d. to the Troy pound	59.2
1542–1551	576d. to the Troy pound	(55.6) varying fineness
1552–1601	720d. to the Troy pound	44.4

he would raise the price of his product in proportion to debasement, thus demanding the same quantity of bullion as he formerly got and eliminating any velocity effect derivable from debasement. The same amount of bullion would be required for the same job. In the context of our two-period comparison where the bullion supplies were comparable, this stability in the velocity term would entail a decrease in the bullion price index level during the late sixteenth century, when output was rising, if other conditions remained constant. The alternative would have been a decrease in output as economic growth aborted in the face of monetary scarcity. Ironically, in order to allow an increase in the velocity of bullion circulation sufficient to maintain the preexisting bullion price level, the individual seller would initially have to be willing to accept a lower bullion price by taking debased coin at face value.

While it may have been helpful to the English economy in the long run, in the short run such acceptance of royal fiat might represent a considerable sacrifice to the individual. Royal attempts to force the circulation of specie at legislated par values were certainly not unique to the sixteenth century, but earlier efforts appear frequently to have been frustrated by those who weighed the coin and demanded full intrinsic value, thus checking the king's ability to create a fiat currency. In the sixteenth century, however, economic and demographic pressures combined to urge the necessity of a more flexible money supply. Conjoined with these impersonal forces was direct royal power which had grown measurably between the late fifteenth and the early sixteenth century. Henry VIII, in a proclamation of 1538, commanded all mayors, sheriffs, bailiffs, constables, and other faithful officers and subjects "that if any person or persons, of what estate, degree or condition he be, refuse or deny to take the said moneys of gold and silver in manner and form aforesaid, be it for merchandise, victuals, change or rechange, or other cause whatsoever, forthwith to take and arrest the same person or persons making refusal or denial and put him in ward and prison, there to remain, and further to be punished, at the King's pleasure."

One senses here that the royal authority behind the command was more potent than that behind similar earlier documents.[6]

Supplementing and supporting more effective legal tender legislation was the activity of the exchequer itself. If money was the sinews of war, success in gaining it not only enhanced royal power, strengthening the word of the law; it provided a guarantee of the coinage as well. To the degree that each individual was obliged to pay taxes to the government, each found that there was little incentive to accept less than face value for specie which the government would accept at face value for tax payments. The brisk increase in crown receipts over the course of the sixteenth century[7] intensified this fiscal support of the coinage and thus helped to establish a true metal-fiat currency in England. Once this had occurred, debasement could act to accelerate the velocity of bullion circulation.

This subtle alteration in the economic consequences of debasement thrust a new role upon the crown. Variations in the monetary standard had become analogous to shifts in the money supply. Though we have cast our argument and defined the money supply and prices in terms of bullion, it is evident that debasement, by increasing velocity, increases the MV term and produces the same economic impact as that produced by an increase in available bullion. Under these circumstances, monetary mutation acquired some of the attributes of modern fiscal and monetary policies whether consciously exercised by Tudor governments or not. Let us now consider how debasement may have affected the early modern English economy.

Toward the end of the fifteenth century, the population in England began to expand more rapidly, and with increasing numbers came renewed economic activity. The demand for

6. Paul L. Hughes and James F. Larkin, eds., *Tudor Royal Proclamations* 1 (New Haven 1964) Proclamation 178, 27 March 1538.

7. Harry A. Miskimin, *The Economy of Later Renaissance Europe, 1460–1600* (Cambridge 1977) 160–61.

transactions bullion—necessary to turn over the goods and services produced—rose and was, at least in part, satisfied through the diffusion of German and Central European silver across the breadth of Europe. In 1465, debasement supplemented the effects of the incremental bullion supplies by lowering the silver content of the pound of account from 83.3, where it had been for most of the fifteenth century, to 66.7 (1351–1411 = 100). Demographic and economic growth moved briskly ahead during the early sixteenth century, but after 1510, bullion output at the London mint began to decline.[8] In 1526, the silver content of the pound of account was again reduced, this time to 59.2, where it remained until 1541. Between that year and 1544, bullion output was again relatively slight; debasement was accelerated by a reduction in fineness to .833. From 1544 until 1550, when the fineness was restored to sterling quality, the amount of bullion struck rose while debasement worsened. Finally, in 1552, the silver content of the pound stabilized at 44.4 and the amount of silver coined remained at relatively high levels for the last half of the century. Elizabeth's recoinage, while it retained the official standard silver content of 44.4, reduced the aggregate level of debasement by restoring the extant coin to its statutory quality.

Through good luck more than good sense perhaps, Tudor monetary policy appears to have aided economic growth. The early debasements permitted the velocity of bullion to accelerate as economic activity intensified. When growth became more rapid and bullion supplies lagged, the debasement of 1526 again provided monetary stimulus to the economy. In the early 1540s, debasement probably once more alleviated the problems caused by swift economic expansion and comparatively low mint output. Little claim can be made for the hectic years of the late 1540s, since they constituted a period of great turbulence and monetary instability. By 1552, however, a further debasement could be justified by the growing needs of trade, and one might even argue that Elizabeth's

8. Craig (n. 5 above) 412–15.

recoinage in the early 1560s was prudent given the evidence of heightened nominal inflation in the immediately preceding years and the fact that the bullion price index level remained relatively stable for the decade following the recoinage.[9]

Although public borrowing is too broad and well-discussed a subject to reconsider here, it is worth noting that rising levels of public borrowing exercised both positive and negative effects on the MV term of the quantity equation.[10] On the one hand, it mobilized idle bullion balances and thus acted directly to increase the velocity of bullion circulation. On the other, however, to the extent that the receipts were transmitted abroad for political and military purposes, public credit entailed an almost immediate reduction of the domestic bullion stock. Sixteenth century records are too flawed to allow us to strike the balance between these contending forces and measure with confidence the net effect of public credit.

More certain in its effect in increasing the velocity of bullion circulation and in permitting fourteenth century levels of mint bullion production to support the burgeoning economic activity of the late sixteenth century was private credit. The inadequacy of sixteenth century records forbids any realistic estimate of the quantitative significance of commercial credit, but it was undoubtedly a potent and growing element in the prosperity of early modern England. The historical expansion of the use of bills of exchange, for example, was outlined by Chief Justice Terby in 1696, in his summation of the issues relevant to the case of *Bromwitch* v. *Loyd*. There the chief justice notes that at first, bills of exchange were used only by foreign merchants dealing with those of England, and that after that inland bills were used among merchants dealing with one another, then by all sorts of merchants and traders,

9. Phelps Brown and Hopkins (n. 3 above).
10. For a general discussion of public finance and a recent, though somewhat limited, bibliography see: Geoffrey Parker, "The Emergence of Modern Finance in Europe, 1500–1730," in Carlo M. Cipolla, ed., *The Fontana Economic History of Europe* 2 (Glasgow 1974).

and subsequently by all sorts of persons, merchants or not.[11]

The evolution of internal credit is thus portrayed—and I believe accurately—as a continuous process. There is, however, some dispute as to the timing of the introduction of inland bills—de Roover, for example, dates it to the seventeenth century and disputes Tawney's assertion that they were being used for "the making of advances and the raising of loans without goods passing at all" during the sixteenth century.[12] Such polarized views appear to be irreconcilable, yet upon inspection the dispute turns out to be more illusory than real. The literature concerning the development of commercial credit in the early modern period may be divided into that which considers the legal status of commercial instruments and that which considers actual commercial practice among contemporary English merchants. Thus de Roover is perfectly correct in observing that inland bills do not become fully negotiable until the seventeenth century; indeed, full negotiability in the modern sense was only attained in England by statutory law in 1698 and 1704.[13] Tawney, on the other hand, more directly attentive to merchant custom, accurately records the rapid expansion of commercial credit during the sixteenth century and highlights the significance of commercial practice as against formal law. Even within the formalities of law, however, one may find very early evidence of at least partial negotiability. Holden cites the case of *Burton* v. *Davy* in 1437 as clear recognition by the Mayor's Court of London of the

11. *Bromwitch* v. *Loyd*, 2 Lutwyche 1585. Reprinted in *The English Reports*, 125, *Common Pleas III* (London 1912):
Le Ch. Justice Terby dit en ceo Case, que Bills d'Exchange
al primes fueront extend solement al Merchants Strangers
trafficant ove Merchants d'Angleterre, at apres al inland
Bills enter Merchants trafficant l'un ove l'auter icy en
Angliterre, et puis ceo al touts Trafficants et Negotiators,
et de darraine temps al touts persons, Trafficants ou nemy.

12. Raymond de Roover, *Gresham on Foreign Exchange* (Cambridge, Mass. 1949) 105, and Richard H. Tawney, ed., *A Discourse upon Usury . . . by Thomas Wilson* (London and New York 1925) 73.

13. Abbott Payson Usher, *The Early History of Deposit Banking in Mediterranean Europe* 1 (Cambridge, Mass. 1943; rpt. New York 1967) 98.

right of the bearer of a bill of exchange to sue on his own account.[14]

Without a substantial increase in commercial credit it seems unlikely that the velocity effects of debasement would have been sufficient to sustain English economic growth during the sixteenth century. What forces encouraged the expansion of such credit and what forms did it assume? To some extent, though probably minor, the enhanced capacity of the government to enforce the legal tender laws and to command the circulation of specie at par may have eased the difficulties of writing forward contracts in money of account. As intrinsic value became less of a concern, uncertainties over the quality of the currency lent and subsequently returned diminished, since money was simply money.[15] This statement does not deny the operation of Gresham's Law, which depends on the central authority's ability to enforce circulation at face value so as to offer a profit to those who wish to sort coins of differing metal contents circulating at the same account value. This would not be an immediate or primary concern for a merchant engaged in financing a real commercial transaction. One may add that, since commercial credit was generally short-term, the dislocations that might arise from persistent inflation were also minimized.

Of greater import than these minor monetary technicalities in forwarding the broader use of commercial credit was need. Postan long ago noted that the proliferation of the bill of exchange during the fifteenth century resulted from the appearance of fairs with permanent overseas connections, and thus that they developed in response to new institutional demands.[16] By the same token, one might argue that the scarcity

14. James M. Holden, *The History of Negotiable Instruments in English Law* (London 1955) 24–25.

15. Ellis T. Powell (*The Evolution of the Money Market, 1385–1915* [London, *The Financial News*, 1915]), however, still finds evidence of gold coins passing by weight as late as 1588.

16. Michael M. Postan, "Private Financial Instruments in Medieval England," *Vierteljahrschrift für Sozial- und Wirtschaftsgeschichte* 23 (1930) 26–75.

of transactions currency that followed upon the persistent
exportation of bullion during the fourteenth and fifteenth
centuries led to an increasing substitution of bills or writings
obligatory. In their formal version as "covenants under seal,"
these instruments were recognized under the common law since
they implied formal recognition of a preexisting debt.[17] This
safeguard, however, seems to have worked to the detriment of
such obligations as the attitude of the common law to the
assignment of debts hardened during the course of the fifteenth and sixteenth centuries.[18] In consequence, an informal
version of the bill obligatory, resembling a modern promissory
note and not under seal, evolved and found increasing favor
among merchants.[19] Innate utility led to a swift proliferation
of these informal documents, while the potential profitability
of gaining jurisdictional authority over them provoked a con-
test among the various courts. When in 1477 the Fair Courts
were limited by statute to matters arising within the fairs, the
Staple and Admiralty Courts eagerly seized the business; after
1532, however, similar provisions restricted the jurisdiction of
the Staple Courts, and so the Admiralty Courts remained the
only surviving legal body in England that was governed by
the law merchant.[20] At the end of the century, even the
Admiralty Courts found their jurisdiction curtailed, yet the
decline in the legal standing of various forms of commercial
paper does not appear to have resulted in a decrease in the
volume of commercial credit.

The striking shift in the organizational structure of industry
during the sixteenth century may, in large part, account for
the durability of commercial credit in spite of the law's dis-
approval. Division of labor grew more complex during the
period, but it did not follow the pattern of the modern factory
system despite a few experiments along those lines. Instead,
the division occurred in the interstices of the older putting-

17. Ibid. 32.
18. Holden (n. 14 above) 13.
19. Ibid. 10–11.
20. Ibid. 14–20.

out system. Middlemen proliferated and served as intermediaries between growers and spinners, spinners and weavers,
and other members of the textile trades. More sophisticated
forms of marketing were developed, and specialized carters
carried cloths from the drapers to the exporters. Similar innovations followed in the nontextile trades such as tin, leather,
glass, and coal production.[21]

The new arrangements at once encouraged and required
the extension of credit at each of the increasing number of
stages of production. Generally credit was extended in an informal manner, often in the form of a book credit from one
merchant to another without cumbersome documentation.[22]
This avoided altogether the problem of the increasingly
dubious standing of commercial instruments before the law,
while providing a simple but extremely effective method of
maximizing the economic potential of a limited supply of
bullion. One has but to read through the journal of a merchant such as John Smythe of Bristol to observe the rarity of
cash sales and to note the importance of informal commercial
credit arrangements in financing a highly active trading life.[23]
Worth noting, too, is the use of some form of inland bills in
the trade between Bristol and Bruton, some twenty-five miles
to the southeast. On occasion such transactions could become
quite complex, as the following entry indicates:[24]

Itm. the 21 day of Aprell 1544 £34 whereof he [John
Yerbery of Bruton] r. of Stevyn Chick 28s 9d and 6s 8d of
Stevan Rodwey and his son r. of my wif 40s and more he is
content to r. of William Northe £10 and more he r. of me
this present day at Bristowe £20 4s 7d so montith as
aforesseid £34 whereof £27 10s is pd. for the hole & last
payment of a byll dewe the first day of March last past and

21. See Richard D. Richards, *The Early History of Banking in England* (London 1929) 18–22, and Miskimin (n. 7 above) chap. 4.

22. Tawney (n. 12 above) 45–47.

23. Jean Vanes, ed., *The Ledger of John Smythe, 1538–1550,* Bristol
Records Society's Publications 28 (London 1974).

24. Ibid. 237, accounts anno 1543.

£6 10s is putt in the backsyde of a byll dated the 10 of
September 1543.

The entry is far from unique, so there can be no doubt as
to the importance of credit in settling accounts. Despite the
reluctance of the common law to accept the practice, it is
clear that debts were regularly being assigned to others. The
result was a multilateral clearing arrangement for commercial
debt which limited the demands made on the available supply
of bullion-based currency. In effect, the practice increased the
velocity of bullion circulation.

As production processes became more roundabout and as
contacts among middlemen and producers at various stages of
production grew more permanent, informal credit arrangements undoubtedly became easier. The shift in the nature of
production thus encouraged the development of more elaborate lines of credit in England—and this reveals one of the
ironies of English law. While it is probably true that the
predominance of customary law in England delayed the
development and judicial acceptance of formal credit instruments and precluded the creation of fully negotiable paper
until the late seventeenth century, the same law may have
encouraged the type of credit that evolved informally among
merchants. Whereas on the continent, civil law readily recognized a variety of contract forms, it appears as well to have
provided continental monarchs with the means to regulate
industry more closely and thereby to limit the growth of more
roundabout methods of production.[25] In England, custom
constrained royal authority and allowed freedom for new
stages of production to arise between earlier, less specialized
manufacturing processes. With additional stages of production
came easier and more general credit accommodations.

At the beginning of this essay, we suggested that England's
bullion supply was probably not significantly larger in the
late sixteenth century than in the early fourteenth century.

25. Miskimin (n. 7 above) chap. 4.

Since the English gross national product was clearly far higher in the later period and since prices remained comparable in the two eras, we were led to seek out those forces that must have accelerated the velocity of bullion circulation in the later period, since in their absence, growth would have halted or prices fallen as the bullion supply proved inadequate. Two factors, debasement and commercial credit, appear to have increased bullion velocity and thus to have allowed English economic growth to continue despite a limited supply of bullion. In the absence of any semblance of a modern banking system, the English economy developed methods of achieving the same results that we have come to expect from a more financially sophisticated, modern economy. Where a central bank would have promoted growth by expanding the money supply, the Tudors, though not necessarily as deliberate policy, increased the efficiency of imported and domestic bullion by means of debasement. Where modern merchants would have turned to their bankers for additional working capital, sixteenth century merchants turned to each other for credit lines based on mutual trust.[26] In short, English monarchs and merchants of the sixteenth century devised a system of protobanking that met all the challenges which we expect a far more complex and multifaceted system to overcome.

26. One may note that in our day, when the central bankers dictate monetary stringency and high interest rates, modern merchants still turn to each other through the use of trade acceptances and the direct sale of short-term commercial paper.

Index of Dates

CONTAINING ONLY DATES MENTIONED WITHIN THE ESSAYS, this index is *not* a systematic chronological chart. The synchronicities may draw attention to connections that might otherwise be missed; and both the inclusions and the omissions may cast an interesting light on current historiography. More complete references can be found in the general Index.

The dates themselves remain, of course, the responsibility of the individual authors.

Dates	Banking	Trade
Before 1000	8th c. Islam: evidence of credit transactions	8th c. Venice and Amalfi trading with Byzantium and Islam 10th c. Pisa and Genoa engage in overland trade throughout Europe
1000	Mid-11th c. Aragon: money changers in business 1083 Paul *cambiator* lends to St. Peter's at 20% interest	Before 1100 English monarchs control establishment of exchange rates
1100	Early 12th c. Saragossa: money changers in business 12th c. Barcelona: Christian money changers competing with Jewish bankers 1111 Lucca: oath required of money changers inscribed on cathedral walls	
1150	1154 Genoa: earliest notarial minute books, including banking documents	1153 Lucchese merchants at fairs of Champagne

Currencies	Varia	Dates
10th c. Italy: regulation of mint outputs (possibly by 7th c.)		Before 1000
1037 Reactivation of the count of Anjou's mint	1000 Venetians conquer Dalmatia 1049 Council of Reims bans usury 1096 Year of famine in Europe	1000
	1139 Second Lateran Council condemns usury 1140 Gratian's *Decretum,* containing texts condemning usury	1100
	1179 Third Lateran Council excommunicates usurers 1185–87 Pope Urban III's decretal *Consuluit* against usury 1190s Peter the Chanter's *Summa* and *Verbum abbreviatum*	1150

Dates	Banking	Trade
1200	13th c. Lucca: money changers and merchant bankers active 13th c. Valencia: evidence of Christian banking 1200 Genoa: evidence of transfer banking	13th c. Italians involved in English wool trade 13th c. Lucca the center of silk trade 1205–1358 Venetians control Ragusan trade
1210	1217 Catalonia: citizens permitted to lend money at interest	
1220	1222 Vic: municipal exchange bank (Taula de Canvi) open for 40 days, by permission of bishop	
1230	1230s Money changing partnerships thriving in Lucca and Genoa 1235 Catalonia: Christian subjects may lend money at 12% interest, Jews at 20%	
1240	1240 England: Henry III forbids usury 1244–59 Genoa: rise and fall of the Leccacorvo banking partnership	

Currencies	Varia	Dates
	1204 Robert of Courson, *Penitentiale*: treatise *De usura*	
	1206–31 Foulques of Marseille, bishop of Toulouse, stiff antiusury measures	1200
	1215 Thomas of Chobham, *Summa confessorum*	
	1215 Fourth Lateran Council requires annual confession, permits Jews to practice usury	1210
	ca. 1223 Caesarius of Heisterbach, *Dialogus miraculorum*	1220
	ca. 1230 Jacques de Vitry's *Sermones vulgares*, many against usury	
	1234 *Decretales* (commissioned by Pope Gregory IX): include many texts on usury	1230
		1240

Dates	Banking	Trade
1250	1250s Genoa: economic instability 1250s Vic: a Christian moneylender active 1250s Lucca: money changers supplying money to the first merchant bankers	
1260	By 1260s Italians introduce bill of exchange into England	Mid-13th c. Serbia mining and trade in minerals with Europe begin 1261 Genoa and Byzantine Empire sign commercial treaty
1270	1272–94 England: loans to the crown by Ricciardi bank	1275 England: Ancient Custom established
1280	1280s Spain: private money changers must be insured 1280s Lucchese merchants active in Genoa's money market 1280s Credit operations in Dubrovnik	1283 England: first proclamation controlling use of bills of exchange 1284 International banking between Lucca and the fairs of Champagne

Currencies	Varia	Dates
1252 Genoa and Florence reintroduce gold coinage 1259 Perugia considers issuing gold coinage	1250 d. Emperor Frederick II	1250
		1260
1278 England: first ban on export of silver bullion 1279 England: recoinage of silver	1274 Second Council of Lyon: further condemnations of usury; first official recognition of salvation by purgatory	1270
1280s Flemish mints striking crockards and pollards (counterfeits of English coins) 1284 England: *Statutum de Moneta Magnum* bans import of foreign coins		1280

Dates	Banking	Trade
1290	Late 13th c. Spain: high clergy engaged in banking 1206–1310 England: loans to the crown by Fresco-baldi bank	
1300	Early 14th c. Spain: royalty increasingly dependent upon private money changers 1301 Lérida: legislation to control private money changers 1308 *Statute of the Commune of Lucca* limits money changers' involvement in financial affairs of the city	1306 England: Parliament forbids religious houses to use bills of exchange
1310	1311 Failure of Fresco-baldi bank in England 1314 Majorca: death penalty imposed for fraudulent bankruptcy	1318 on Bardi, Peruzzi, and Acciaiuoli banking companies active in Dubrovnik
1320	1320s Dubrovnik: first evidence of use of bills of exchange 1321 Gerona: death penalty imposed for fraudulent bankruptcy 1329 Majorca: economic depression, numerous bankruptcies	

Currencies	Varia	Dates
1290s England: decreased mint output		
1291, 1299 England: two statutes reinforce control over import of foreign coins		1290
1295 France: Philip IV debases the coinage, causing economic instability throughout Europe		
1300–02 England: re-minting of counterfeit coins		
1302–09 England: mint output increases again		1300
1307–44 England: ban on export of gold plate or bullion		
	1311 Council of Vienne reiterates earlier condemnations of usury	1310
1329 Majorca: sale of gold or silver coin for more than its legal value prohibited		1320

Dates	Banking	Trade
1330		1333–35 Buonaccorsi doing business in Dubrovnik
1340	1340s Failure of Bardi and Peruzzi banks in England 1340–60 Barcelona: expansion of private money changing business	1340 England: wool exporters required to supply bullion to the mint
1350		
1360		1363 England: Calais Staple Company formed to control the wool trade
1370	1379 Barcelona: first evidence of loans to purchase mortgages	1379–1487 England: *Employment Acts,* seeking to suppress bills of exchange

Currencies	Varia	Dates
1331 England: slump in mint output creates a money shortage		
1335 England: *Statute of York* bans counterfeiting and export of precious metals	1337 Hundred Years' War begins	1330
1335–51 England: 5 debasements of the penny		
1344 England: gold coinage (the noble) introduced; sterling fineness raised	1340–70 Widespread inflation throughout Europe 1348 Black Death	1340
1352 England: Parliament seeks to prevent king from further coinage debasement *(Statute of Purveyors)* 1353 England: *Statute of the Staple* permits limited export of foreign and domestic coin		1350
1364 England: Calais mint established		
1364–1663 England: total ban on export of gold and silver		1360
		1370

Dates	Banking	Trade
1380	1380s Spain: growing economic instability causes many bankruptcies	
1390	1392 Barcelona: *Lonja* (Exchange) completed, becomes the center of Barcelona's banking activities	
1400	1401 Barcelona: Taula de Canvi, the first municipal bank, created by the city government 1401, 1408 Similar municipal banks established in Majorca and Valencia 1405 Failure of the Gualbes bank in Spain	15th c. Germans become active in overland trade of precious metals from Central Europe
1410	1412 Barcelona: Taula declared independent of the municipal treasury 1416–20 Tarragona: municipal Taula planned but never established 1416 Valencia: failure of the Taula de Canvis	

Currencies	Varia	Dates
1384 Flanders: mint ratio altered to favor silver		
1388–1402 Flanders: extensive counterfeiting of the English noble		1380
		1390
15th–16th c. Bans of bullion export throughout Europe promote use of bills of exchange	15th c. Bernard of Siena revives the church's condemnation of usury	1400
1401 England: recoinage of suspect nobles		
1411 England: debasement of silver coinage	1410 d. Francesco di Marco Datini	1410

Dates	Banking	Trade
1420		1429 England: Calais Staple bullion ordinances require all wool transactions to use cash, not credit 1429–70s Anglo-Burgundian conflict over commerce cripples the wool trade
1430	1438 Barcelona: city council forbids private individuals to engage in banking	1437 England: first recognition of the transferability of bills of exchange (*Burton* v. *Dav*ꞌ decision)
1440	1440s Barcelona: period of economic turbulence 1441–50 Barcelona: laws to protect municipal Taula during periods of economic instability 1443 Gerona: municipal Taula de Canvi planned	
1450		
1460	1464–66 Main branch of Medici bank moves from Geneva to Lyon 1468–76 Barcelona: reorganization of the Taula	1460s Recession in Lyon stimulates shift of trade to Bourges and Troyes for 1(years 1463 England: last enact ment of Calais Staple bullion ordinances

Currencies	Varia	Dates
1425 Flanders: mint ratio altered to favor gold 1425 Burgundian Low Countries begin to counterfeit English nobles		1420
	1436 England: *Libelle of Englyshe Polycye*	1430
		1440
	From 1450 Silver production high in Central Europe	1450
1465 England: debasement of silver coin	1462–72 Civil war in Spain	1460

Dates	Banking	Trade
1470	1479 Antwerp: Ludwig Meuting's bank established	1473 England: reorganization of Calais Staple allows Staplers to make credit transactions 1477 England: limitation of Fair Courts' jurisdiction over credit disputes
1480	1480s Germans and Swiss rise to prominence in commercial banking 1486 Antwerp: Hochstetters' bank established 1487 Germany: Jacob Fugger's company established	1480s Decline of Bruges as a center of trade 1480s England: renewed suppression of credit transactions
1490	1490 Jacob Fugger becomes Maximilian's principal moneylender 1494 Fall of the Medici bank 1498 Antwerp: Anton Welser's bank established 1499 Barcelona: no private money changers may accept deposits	1493–1520 Antwerp replaces Bruges as the major center of trade

Currencies	Varia	Dates
		1470
	late 15th c. England: rapid population growth 1486 Maximilian, first Habsburg emperor	1480
		1490

Dates	Banking	Trade
1500	16th c. England: suppression of bill of exchange causes growth of informal credit based on trust 16th c. Spain: New World silver causes revival of private banking 1504 Basel: municipal bank established 1507 Majorca: new municipal bank, Taula de la Universitat, established	1501 Antwerp begins to control the Portuguese spice trade
1510	1510 Barcelona: laws controlling fraudulent bankruptcy strengthened 1510–12 Gerona: municipal Taula revived despite competition from private bankers 1518 Bruges: Frescobaldi bank fails 1519 Valencia: Nova Taula established	1512 Genoese merchants begin to hold fairs at Montluel, near Lyon
1520	1520s Italian bankers losing control of the money market to Germans 1523 Bruges: Gualterotti bank fails	1520s Large-scale textile production in Dubrovnik 1520–70 Heyday of the Lyon fairs
1530	1530s Genoese bankers compete with Germans in the Franche-Compté region	1532 England: jurisdiction of Staple Courts limited 1535 Genoese move their fairs to Besançon 1538 England: bill of exchange restored to wool merchants

Currencies	Varia	Dates
	16th c. England: rapid economic expansion	1500
1510 England: decline in output of London mint	1516 Spain: Charles Habsburg ascends the throne	1510
1522 England: limited circulation of foreign gold coins permitted 1526 England: debasement of coin		1520
	1530s Clement Armstrong's "A Treatise Concerninge the Staple" and "Howe to Reforme the Realme"	1530

Dates	Banking	Trade
1540		
	1552 Palermo (and Naples soon after): Spaniards help found municipal bank	
1550	1557 Financial collapse throughout Spain	1573–80 End of Lyon as a center of commerce
	1576–77 England: office of the Royal Exchanger created; abandoned next year	
	1609 Barcelona: first Banco de Barcelona established	
1600	1627–28 England: office of Royal Exchanger established and disbanded again	
	1641 Barcelona: reorganization of the Taula	
	1649 Valencia: failure of the Nova Taula	
1650	1698–1704 England: laws establishing full negotiability of inland bills of exchange (first paper money)	1661 England: bills of exchange licensed again
		1696 England: policy for use of bills of exchange outlined (*Bromwich* v. *Loyd* decision)

Currencies	Varia	Dates
1541–44 England: decline in output of London mint	1549 W. Schweicker's manual of bookkeeping	1540
1552 England: silver content of coins stabilized for the rest of the century	Late 16th c. England: severe inflation	1550
		1600
		1650

Contributors

JEAN-FRANÇOIS BERGIER heads the Institute of History at the Swiss Institute of Technology in Zurich; he is currently vice president of the International Economic History Association. His publications include *Genève et l'économie européenne de la Renaissance* (Paris 1963) and *Naissance et croissance de la Suisse industrielle* (Bern 1974).

THOMAS W. BLOMQUIST, associate professor of history at Northern Illinois University, specializes in Italian economic history. He has published articles in *Speculum, Journal of Economic History, Business History Review,* and *Revue internationale d'histoire de la banque.*

BARIŠA KREKIĆ is professor of history at the University of California, Los Angeles, where he was recently appointed director of the Center for Russian and East European Studies. His studies of Dubrovnik have produced two books, *Dubrovnik (Raguse) et le Levant au Moyen Age* (Paris 1961) and *Dubrovnik in the 14th and 15th Centuries: A City between East and West* (Norman, Okla. 1972).

JACQUES LE GOFF, director of studies at the Ecole des Hautes Etudes en Sciences Sociales in Paris, has written widely on medieval social history: *Marchands et banquiers du Moyen Age* (Paris 1956), *Les intellectuels au Moyen Age* (Paris 1957), *La civilisation de l'Occident médiéval* (Paris 1964), and *Pour un autre Moyen Age* (1978). He is coeditor of *Annales: Economies, Sociétés, Civilisations.*

ROBERT S. LOPEZ is Sterling Professor of History at Yale University. His general history of the Middle Ages, first published in French (Paris 1962), appeared in English as *The*

Birth of Europe (New York and London 1967), and has been translated into Portuguese, Italian, Spanish, Slovakian, and Serbo-Croatian. His many studies of medieval commerce and economic history include *The Commercial Revolution of the Middle Ages, 950–1350* (Englewood Cliffs, N.J. 1971).

HARRY A. MISKIMIN is professor of history at Yale University. His study of *The Economy of Later Renaissance Europe, 1460–1600* appeared in 1977 (Cambridge). With David J. Herlihy and Abraham L. Udovitch he edited *The Medieval City* (New Haven 1977), which included his own "The Legacies of London: 1259–1330."

JOHN H. MUNRO is professor of economics in the Department of Political Economy, and associate director of the Centre for Medieval Studies, at the University of Toronto. He has published *Wool, Cloth, and Gold: The Struggle for Bullion in Anglo-Burgundian Trade, c. 1340–1478* (Brussels and Toronto 1973) and numerous articles and book reviews. He serves as consultant on money, coinage, and financial matters for the University of Toronto Press series *The Correspondence of Erasmus.*

MICHAEL PRESTWICH, lecturer in medieval history at the University of St. Andrews, Edinburgh, is the author of *War, Politics and Finance under Edward I* (London and Totowa, N.J. 1972) and articles in such journals as *Economic History Review* and the *Bulletin of the Institute of Historical Research* of London University.

MANUEL RIU is professor of medieval history at the University of Barcelona. His most recent publications are *La Arqueología medieval en España* (Barcelona 1978) and *La feudalització del Camp Català* (Barcelona 1978).

ABRAHAM L. UDOVITCH, professor of Islamic history at Princeton University, is the author of *Partnership and Profit in Medieval Islam* (Princeton 1970) and "Formalism and Informalism in the Social and Economic Institutions of the Medieval Islamic World," in *Individualism and Conformity in Classical Islam*, ed. Amin Banani and Speros Vryonis (Wiesbaden 1977).

Index

Denier. *See* Coinage: silver
Deposit banking: in antiquity and
early Middle Ages, 2, 6–7; with
merchant bankers, 9, 11, 16,
54–55, 95–97, 258–60, 268; and
interest, 11, 66, 142, 143, 258–60,
268; with money changers, 62–
64, 138, 142–43, 148, 153; with
public banks, 127, 150–51, 159–63
Dinar. *See* Coinage: silver
Discounting, 171, 214–15, 265
Domestic bills, 215, 283–88
Dubrovnik, 241–54
Ducat. *See* Coinage: gold
Durandus, William: *Commentarius*,
28

Edward I (king of England), 78–
104 passim, 188–89, 198–99
Edward II (king of England), 79,
82, 84, 87, 88, 91, 98, 101
Edward III (king of England), 79,
80, 84, 86, 89, 190–92, 197,
199–201
Edward IV (king of England), 205
Elizabeth I (queen of England),
173, 210–11, 282–83
Eloi of Limoges, 6
Employment Laws, 197–98, 202–05,
208
England: banking and trade in,
77–104, 169–215, 275–89
Eudes de Sully (bishop of Paris), 43
Exchange: foreign, 7, 9, 15–16, 55,
69–75, 97, 198–214, 258, 261–63,
266–68; contracts of, 15, 16;
"dry," 15, 16, 171, 207; rates of,
71, 73–74, 88, 97, 99, 149, 169–75,
199, 204, 210–11, 252, 266;
letters of, 89, 97–98, 103, 132,
152–53, 155, 246; bills of, 124,
127, 169–75, 195–214, 263,
268–69, 283–85
Exchange, Board of. *See* Banks,
public

Exchequer, 77, 90–91, 278, 281
Exempla, 29–51
Export: of silk from Lucca, 70–71;
of wool from England, 77–78,
82, 94, 97, 102–03, 192–98,
205–06, 208–09; of coin from
England, 97, 174, 188–89, 192; of
bullion from England, 173–76,
179, 184–86, 192–93, 197–205, 208,
210–13; of bullion from the
Balkans, 242–54

Fair Courts, 286
Fairs, commercial: in Champagne,
16, 68–74, 87, 98, 112, 115–16; in
Bruges, 107–08; in Lyon,
107–08, 112, 116–17; in Geneva,
112, 115, 117; in the Franche-
Compté, 115–16; in England, 285
Ferràn, Jaume, 138
Fibla, Ponç, 141
Fieschi family, 14, 16, 19–20, 22
Fisher Identity, 177–78, 276–83
Flanders: banking and trade in,
86–87, 89, 107–08, 111–14, 117,
125, 132, 175, 193, 195–96. *See
also* Antwerp; Bruges
Florence, bankers from, 77–102,
106, 112–14, 124, 172, 246–49; in
England, 77–102 passim, 172;
in Dubrovnik, 246–49
Florin. *See* Coinage: gold
Foulques of Marseille (bishop of
Toulouse), 30, 36
Francis of Assisi (saint), 37
Frescobaldi company, 78–100
passim, 113–14
Fugger, Jacob, 108, 109, 117, 119,
120, 121, 124

Galgani company, 84
Gallerani company, 83, 89, 96, 97,
100, 104
Galley-halfpenny. *See* Counterfeit
coins